Communications in Computer and Information Science 1282

Commenced Publication in 2007
Founding and Former Series Editors:
Simone Diniz Junqueira Barbosa, Phoebe Chen, Alfredo Cuzzocrea,
Xiaoyong Du, Orhun Kara, Ting Liu, Krishna M. Sivalingam,
Dominik Ślęzak, Takashi Washio, Xiaokang Yang, and Junsong Yuan

More information about this series at http://www.springer.com/series/7899

Vladimir Golenkov · Victor Krasnoproshin ·
Vladimir Golovko · Elias Azarov (Eds.)

Open Semantic Technologies for Intelligent System

10th International Conference, OSTIS 2020
Minsk, Belarus, February 19–22, 2020
Revised Selected Papers

 Springer

Editors
Vladimir Golenkov ⓘ
Belarusian State University of Informatics
and Radioelectronics
Minsk, Belarus

Vladimir Golovko ⓘ
Brest State Technical University
Brest, Belarus

Victor Krasnoproshin ⓘ
Department of Information Systems
Management
Belarusian State University
Minsk, Belarus

Elias Azarov ⓘ
Belarusian State University of Informatics
and Radioelectronics
Minsk, Belarus

ISSN 1865-0929   ISSN 1865-0937 (electronic)
Communications in Computer and Information Science
ISBN 978-3-030-60446-2   ISBN 978-3-030-60447-9 (eBook)
https://doi.org/10.1007/978-3-030-60447-9

This Springer imprint is published by the registered company Springer Nature Switzerland AG
The registered company address is: Gewerbestrasse 11, 6330 Cham, Switzerland

Preface

This collection contains articles that were presented at the 10th International Scientific and Technical Conference on Open Semantic Technologies for Intelligent Systems (OSTIS 2020).

The OSTIS conference has been held annually since 2010 in Minsk, Belarus, and is dedicated to the development of flexible and compatible technologies that provide fast and high-quality construction of intelligent systems for various purposes.

At present, the OSTIS conference is well known and recognized, and also has a wide geography of participants: Belarus, Russia, Ukraine, the USA, Latvia, and Kazakhstan.

OSTIS conferences are carried out in collaboration with other commercial and scientific organizations, including the Russian Association of Artificial Intelligence and the Belarusian Public Association of Artificial Intelligence Specialists.

The main topic reported on at the OSTIS 2020 conference was the standardization of intelligent systems. In total, 62 papers were submitted to OSTIS 2020 from five countries. All submitted papers were reviewed by Program Committee members together with referees. As a result, 47 papers were presented in the form of reports at the OSTIS 2020 conference, which was held at the Belarusian State University of Informatics and Radioelectronics, the leading Belarusian University in the field of IT, during February 19–22, 2020.

Throughout all four days of OSTIS 2020, well-known scientists in the field of artificial intelligence made their reports, as well as young scientists, who had the opportunity to present their scientific results and gain important experience in public discussions. In addition, the conference hosted an international meeting on the standardization of intelligent systems, as well as an event dedicated to the 25th anniversary of the Department of Intelligent Information Technologies of the Belarusian State University of Informatics and Radioelectronics.

This year, a collection of selected papers presented at the OSTIS 2020 conference were published in Springer's *Communications in Computer and Information Science* (CCIS) series for the first time. The collection includes 16 of the best papers from the conference, selected by the OSTIS Program Committee. These papers have been extended by their authors and the papers have been reviewed again by the international group of experts.

The collection is intended for researchers working in the field of artificial intelligence, as well as for enterprise specialists in the field of intelligent systems design.

August 2020

Vladimir Golenkov
Victor Krasnoproshin
Vladimir Golovko
Elias Azarov

Organization

General Chair

Vladimir Golenkov   Belarusian State University of Informatics
and Radioelectronics, Belarus

Program Committee Chair

Oleg Kuznetsov   V. A. Trapeznikov Institute of Control Sciences
of the RAS, Russia

Program Committee

Sergey Ablameyko	Belarusian State University, Belarus
Alexey Averkin	Plekhanov Russian University of Economics, Russia
Elias Azarov	Belarusian State University of Informatics and Radioelectronics, Belarus
Alexander Eremeev	National Research University "MPEI", Russia
Tatiana Gavrilova	St. Petersburg University, Russia
Larysa Globa	National Technical University of Ukraine, Ukraine
Vladimir Golenkov	Belarusian State University of Informatics and Radioelectronics, Belarus
Vladimir Golovko	Brest State Technical University, Belarus
Valeriya Gribova	Institute of Automation and Control Processes of the FEBRAS, Russia
Natalia Guliakina	Belarusian State University of Informatics and Radioelectronics, Belarus
Aliaksandr Hardzei	Minsk State Linguistic University, Belarus
Nadezhda Jarushkina	Ulyanovsk State Technical University, Russia
Alexander Kharlamov	Institute of Higher Nervous Activity and Neurophysiology of the RAS, Russia
Vladimir Khoroshevsky	Dorodnicyn Computing Centre of the RAS, Russia
Boris Kobrinskii	Federal Research Center "Computer Science and Control" of the RAS, Russia
Alexander Kolesnikov	Immanuel Kant Baltic Federal University, Russia
Victor Krasnoproshin	Belarusian State University, Belarus
Oleg Kuznetsov	V. A. Trapeznikov Institute of Control Sciences of the RAS, Russia
Boris Lobanov	The United Institute of Informatics Problems of the National Academy of Sciences of Belarus, Belarus
Natalia Loukachevitch	Lomonosov Moscow State University, Russia

Kurosh Madani	Université Paris-Est Créteil Val de Marne, France
Liudmila Massel	Federal State Budget Educational Institution of Higher Education, Irkutsk National Research Technical University, Russia
Gennady Osipov	Federal Research Center "Computer Science and Control" of the RAS, Russia
Boris Palyukh	Tver State Technical University, Russia
Grabusts Pēteris	Rezekne Academy of Technologies, Latvia
Alexey Petrovsky	Federal Research Center "Computer Science and Control" of the RAS, Russia
Galina Rybina	National Research Nuclear University "MEPhI", Russia
Altynbek Sharipbay	L.N. Gumilyov Eurasian National University, Kazakhstan
Sergey Smirnov	Institute for the Control of Complex Systems of the RAS, Russia
Igor Sovpel	IHS Markit, Belarus
Dzhavdet Suleymanov	TAS Institute of Applied Semiotics, Russia
Valery Taranchuk	Belarusian State University, Belarus
Valery Tarassov	Bauman Moscow State Technical University, Russia
Yuriy Telnov	Plekhanov Russian University of Economics, Russia
Alexander Tuzikov	The United Institute of Informatics Problems of the National Academy of Sciences of Belarus, Belarus
Anna Yankovskaya	National Research Tomsk State University, Russia
Alla Zaboleeva-Zotova	Volgograd State Technical University, Russia

Additional Reviewers

Stanley Edlavitch, USA
Tamas Gergely, Hungary
Roberto Gil, Spain
Pēteris Grabusts, Latvia
Sergejs Kodors, Latvia
Ilya Levin, Israel
Kurosh Madani, France
Pēvels Osipovs, Latvia
Anatoliy Sachenko, Ukraine
Volodymyr Turchenko, Canada

In Collaboration With

Belarusian Public Association of Artificial Intelligence Specialists
JSC Savushkin Product
Intelligent Semantic Systems Ltd.

Contents

Artificial Intelligence Standardization Is a Key Challenge for the Technologies of the Future

Vladimir Golenkov[1]([mail]) [iD], Natalia Guliakina[1] [iD], Vladimir Golovko[2] [iD], and Viktor Krasnoproshin[3] [iD]

[1] Belarusian State University of Informatics and Radioelectronics, Minsk, Belarus
{golen,guliakina}@bsuir.by
[2] Brest State Technical University, Brest, Belarus
vladimir.golovko@gmail.com
[3] Belarusian State University, Minsk, Belarus
krasnoproshin@bsu.by

Abstract. Artificial intelligence (AI) is the future of computer technologies and at present it has achieved great progress in different areas. In this paper, we study the general AI problem from a standardization point of view, and introduce a semantic interoperability for intelligent computer systems. We propose a standard for the interior semantic representation of knowledge in the memory of an intelligent computer system, which is called the SC-code (Semantic Code). Integration of various types of knowledge is performed due to hybrid knowledge base models. This model includes a hierarchical set of top-level ontologies that provide semantic compatibility of various types of knowledge and permits to integrate facts, specifications of various objects, logical statements, events, situations, programs and algorithms, processes, problem formulations, domain models, ontologies, and so on. A variant of the presentation of the AI standard based on the semantic representation of knowledge, in the form of a part of the knowledge base of the Intelligent Computer Metasystem (IMS.ostis) is proposed.

Keywords: Artificial intelligence · Standardization · Semantic compatibility · Knowledge based systems · Intelligent computer systems · SC-code

1 Introduction

The intensive evolution of artificial intelligence creates new challenges that require adequate response. AI standards have a great impact on the further development of artificial intelligence systems. Nowadays many international organizations work in the area of Artificial Intelligence technologies standardization, as well as AI related processes [1,13,14,19,37]. Two leading standards organizations, namely ISO and IEEE continue to work concerning artificial

© Springer Nature Switzerland AG 2020
V. Golenkov et al. (Eds.): OSTIS 2020, CCIS 1282, pp. 1–21, 2020.
https://doi.org/10.1007/978-3-030-60447-9_1

intelligence standardization [2–9,11,12]. The important property of the standardization is to accelerate, not slow down the development of artificial intelligence. The current work on AI standards mainly concerns the definition of common terms, quality/reliability and information [49]. Unfortunately, compatibility/interoperability is not the main focus of AI now [49].

Therefore, even existing standards very often are incompatible with each other. For instance, ISO 26262, is not compatible with typical AI methods, namely machine learning [35,49]. As a consequence, the semantic interoperability is of great importance for standardization of AI. In this paper, we study the AI standardization from a semantic compatibility point of view and propose a standard for the interior semantic representation of knowledge in the memory of an intelligent computer system, which is called the SC-code (Semantic Code). Let's consider the related works in this area.

In [14] the problem of **semantic compatibility** of intelligent computer systems and their various components (various types of knowledge and components of a multimodal interface) was investigated.

This paper considers the main factor that can ensure such compatibility—**standardization of intelligent computer systems (ICS)**, as well as methods and tools for their design.

The basis for ensuring *learning* and *semantic compatibility* of systems, as well as the possibility of developing **ICS standard** is the unification of **semantic representation of knowledge** in the memory of systems and the construction of a global **semantic space** knowledge.

Despite scientific advances in *artificial intelligence*, the pace of development of the **market for intelligent computer systems** is not so impressive. The following reasons can be distinguished:

- the big gap between scientific research and industrial technologies for the development of *intelligent computer systems*;
- lack of a formal theory of intelligent systems;
- the complexity of integrating models and methods of artificial intelligence;
- the complexity of designing intelligent systems (compared to technical ones);
- the dependence of the quality of systems development on the mutual understanding of experts and knowledge engineers,
- and etc.

The current state of **artificial intelligence technologies** can be described as follows [1,6,11,13,19,37]:

- there is no general *theory of intelligent systems* and, as a consequence, there is no general *complex ICS design technology*;
- there is no interoperability of private artificial intelligence technologies.

The development of *artificial intelligence technologies* is significantly hampered by the following socio-methodological circumstances:

- The high social interest in the results of work in the field of *artificial intelligence*, the complexity of science itself give rise to superficiality in the development and advertising of various applications. Science is mixed with irresponsible marketing, conceptual and terminological sloppiness and illiteracy.
- The interdisciplinary nature of *artificial intelligence* research makes the research process very difficult. Working at the intersection of scientific disciplines requires high culture and qualifications [41].

To solve the above problems of *artificial intelligence technologies it is necessary to*:

- develop new formal models for solving *intellectual problems* and improve existing ones (logical, neural network, production);
- ensure the **compatibility** of these models.
- move from the eclectic construction of complex ICS to their deep integration, when the same presentation models and knowledge processing models are implemented in different systems and subsystems in the same way.
- close the distance between the modern level of *the theory of intelligent systems* and the practice of their development.

2   Convergence of Activities in the Field of Artificial Intelligence

Further development of artificial intelligence affects all forms and areas of activity in this area. Let's list the main directions of convergence [2,4,5]:

- Convergence of academic disciplines in training specialists in order to form a holistic picture of **problems of artificial intelligence;**
- Convergence of scientific research in order to build a ***general theory of intelligent computer systems***;
- Convergence of development methods and tools in order to create ***integrated technology for the development of intelligent computer systems***;
- Convergence of engineering activities in order to build an ecosystem of semantically compatible and efficiently interacting ICS;
- Convergence of the listed activities aimed at ensuring their consistency.

In fact, convergence will be realized only in the case when each specialist participates and navigates in all types of activities. The idea of the impossibility of such a combination is clearly exaggerated and is the strongest brake on the implementation of convergence processes in the field of artificial intelligence.

3   Semantic Compatibility of Intelligent Computer Systems, Semantic Representation of Knowledge and Standardization

The key problem in the development of the general theory of intelligent computer systems and technology for their development is to ensure *semantic compatibility*

(1) various types of knowledge, (2) models for solving problems (3) and intelligent computer systems in general [3, 8, 9].

To solve this problem, unification (standardization) of the form of knowledge representation in the ICS memory is required. A logical approach for such unification is to focus on the **semantic representation of knowledge** in the memory of intelligent computer systems.

In the development of knowledge-driven computer systems, the way knowledge is internally represented is key. The quality of knowledge representation is determined by how close it is to the semantic (semantic) one. Our approach to formalizing the *meaning* of the knowledge presented is based on the following provisions [7].

The meaning of any information construct is a structure that includes:

- the described objects, which can be entities of any nature (including meta-entities, i.e. fragments of an information structure);
- links between the described objects, where the links themselves can also be considered as such objects (from this it follows that there can be links between links, as well as links between links and objects that are not links);
- a typology of links and objects that are not links. This typology can be reduced to links that link the described objects (including links) with the classes to which the described objects belong. Moreover, these classes are also one of the types of described objects.

Thus, in the final analysis, the meaning of any information structure is the configuration of links between the described objects (entities). In other words, the meaning of the information structure is contained not in the signs of the described entities, but in the configuration of the identified relationships between these entities. At the same time, the links between the signs of the described entities are information models of the links between these entities themselves.

At the same time, we emphasize that the entities are different (material, abstract). The described entities include relationships, classes of entities (concepts), and structures.

Following the principle of Occam's razor, it is necessary to rid the form of the internal representation of information in the memory of an intelligent computer system from details that are not directly related to the *meaning* of the information presented as much as possible.

"It is necessary to bridge the gap between syntactic data structures, on the one hand, and their *meaning*, on the other [12]".

If the characters of the described entities have an internal structure (for example, they are words or phrases), then the configuration of links between the described entities is not explicitly presented, but is "camouflaged" against the background of explicitly and implicitly specified links between fragments of used characters (between letters, words, phrases).

All known languages perform two functions—communicative (as a means of exchanging messages between subjects) and cognitive (as a means of representing the information model of the described World).

The language of the internal representation of knowledge in the memory of a computer system is not obliged to perform a communicative function. The only thing that is required from the language of the internal representation of knowledge is that it provides the storage of knowledge in a form convenient for their processing. The convenience of processing knowledge stored in memory is determined by:

- simplicity of information retrieval procedures for fragments of the stored knowledge base that meet the specified requirements;
- simplicity of procedures for integrating new knowledge added to the knowledge base;
- simplicity of implementation of inference procedures.

Thus, everything that provides only the communicative functions of the language can be excluded from the language of the internal representation of knowledge. The language of the internal representation of knowledge in the memory of a computer system, based on the formalization of the **meaning** of this knowledge, should perform only a cognitive function—to be a means of representing the *internal information model* of some described World (including the external environment of the corresponding computer system).

Signs that are part of the internal representation of knowledge should not have an internal structure, in particular, should not be presented in the form of some name of the corresponding (designated) entity. *Meaning* of each character is determined exclusively by its relationship with other characters that are part of the internal representation of the knowledge base of the computer system.

Within the framework of the internal semantic representation of the knowledge base of a computer system, *synonymy* (duplication) of signs is excluded. Internal signs denoting the same entity must be "glued and identified. As a result, *semantic equivalence* (duplication) of the fragments included in its composition is excluded within each knowledge base, i.e. fragments that carry the same information. At the same time, the possibility of the existence of *logically equivalent* fragments of knowledge bases remains, when one fragment is a logical consequence of the second and vice versa.

Within the framework of the language of the internal semantic representation of knowledge, powerful and simple means of transition from information to meta information are introduced (in particular, from weakly structured data to related data). For this, the texts that make up the knowledge base are also considered as described entities, for the designation of which the corresponding signs are introduced, each of which is interpreted as a sign denoting the set of all signs that make up the designated text, including the signs of all kinds of connections included in it.

The use of a universal language for the internal representation of knowledge with the possibility of its unlimited expansion, if the need arises to represent new types of knowledge, creates conditions for an unlimited expansion of the areas of application of computer systems built on the basis of such an internal language.

Only signs are atomic fragments of the internal semantic representation of the knowledge base. Moreover, each internal sign itself can be a described entity (meaning the sign itself, and not the entity designated by this sign). In addition, each relationship between the described entities is itself also a described entity, which in its internal representation has its own internal sign and which is interpreted as a set, the elements of which are the signs of the entities connected by the described relationship. Thus, from the internal representation of knowledge, everything that is related not to the representation of meaning, but to the form of representation used is excluded. So, for example, in the internal representation of knowledge there are not only letters, words, phrases, but also separators, delimiters, prepositions, conjunctions, pronouns, declensions, conjugations, etc.

The typology of signs that are part of the internal semantic representation of knowledge is completely determined by the typology of entities designated by these signs. At the same time, the basic typology of the described entities is highlighted, which specifies the syntactic typology (alphabet) of internal signs.

The proposed standard for the internal semantic representation of knowledge in the memory of an intelligent computer system is called **SC-code** (Semantic Code) [49]. The characters that are part of the *SC-code* texts are called **sc-elements**. Each *sc-element* can be considered an invariant of the whole variety of forms of representation (in all kinds of languages and sign constructions) of that entity which is denoted by this *sc-element*. Such an invariant is only that the specified sc-element denotes the corresponding entity. Therefore, the *sc-element* has no form. In this sense, he abstracts from the form of his presentation within the framework of one or another sign construction.

It should be emphasized that the unification and maximum possible simplification of **syntax** and **denotational semantics** of the internal language of intelligent computer systems are necessary because the overwhelming amount of **knowledge**, stored in the knowledge base of an intelligent computer system, are **meta-knowledge**, describing the properties of other knowledge. Moreover, for this reason, the constructive (formal) development of the theory of intelligent computer systems is impossible without clarification (unification, standardization) and ensuring the semantic compatibility of various types of knowledge stored in the knowledge base of the intelligent computer system. It is obvious that the variety of forms of representation of semantically equivalent knowledge makes the development of a general theory of intelligent computer systems practically impossible. *Meta-knowledge*, in particular, should include various types of logical statements and all kinds of programs and descriptions of methods (skills), providing solutions to various classes of information problems.

Let's list the basic principles underlying **SC-code**:

- Characters (designations) of all entities described in *sc-texts*, (texts of *SC-code*) are represented as syntactically elementary (atomic) fragments of *sc-texts*.
- The *SC-code* texts (sc-texts) generally have a nonlinear (graph) structure, since (1) the character of each described entity is included in the sc-text once and (2) each such character can be incident to an unlimited the number

of other characters, since each described entity can be associated with an unlimited number of relationships with other described entities.

- The knowledge base, represented by the text *SC-code*, is a graph structure of a special type, the alphabet of elements of which includes a set of nodes, a set of edges, a set of arcs, a set of basic arcs—arcs of a specially selected type that provide the structuring of knowledge bases, and also many special nodes, each of which denotes a file stored in the memory of an intelligent computer system. The structural feature of this graph structure is that its arcs and edges can connect not only a node to a node, but also a node to an edge or arc, an edge or an arc to another edge or arc.

- All elements of the above graph structure are characters included in the text *SC-code*). That is all its nodes, edges and arcs are designations of various entities. In this case, an edge is a designation of a binary undirected connection between two entities, each of which is either represented in the considered graph structure by a corresponding sign, or is this sign itself. An arc is a designation of a binary oriented bundle between two entities. An arc of a special kind (**base arc**) is a sign of a connection between a node denoting a certain set of elements of the considered graph structure, and one of the elements of this graph structure, which belongs to the specified set. In this case, the entities denoted by the elements of the graph structure under consideration can be permanent (always existing) and temporary (entities that correspond to the period of their existence). In addition, the entities denoted by the elements of the graph structure under consideration can be constant (specific) entities and variable (arbitrary) entities.

- In the considered graph structure, which is a representation of the knowledge base in the *SC-code*, different elements of the graph structure, denoting the same entity, can, but should not exist. If a pair of such elements is found, then these elements are glued (identified). Thus, the synonymy of internal designations in the knowledge base of an intelligent computer system built on the basis of *SC-code* is prohibited.

- Any entity that requires a description can be designated as an element of the graph structure under consideration. We emphasize that the elements of the graph structure under consideration are not just designations of various described entities, but designations that are elementary (atomic) fragments of a sign construction, i.e. fragments, the detailed structure of which is not required to "read" and understand this symbolic construction.

- The text of the *SC-code*, like any other graph structure, is an abstract mathematical object that does not require detailing (clarification) of its coding in the memory of a computer system (for example, in the form of an adjacency matrix, incidence matrix, list structure). But such detailing will be required for the technical implementation of the memory in which sc constructs are stored and processed.

- The most important property of the *SC-code* is that it is convenient not only for the internal representation of knowledge in the memory of an intelligent computer system, but also for the internal representation of information in the memory of computers specially designed for the interpretation of semantic models of intelligent computer systems. So, *SC-code* defines syntactic, semantic and functional principles of memory organization of new generation computers, focused on the implementation of intelligent computer systems—the principles of organizing graph-dynamic associative semantic memory.

4   From Standardization of Semantic Representation of Knowledge to Standardization of Intelligent Computer Systems

After we have defined the standard *universal* (!) Internal language for the semantic representation of knowledge in the memory of an intelligent computer system, we can proceed to clarify the standard of intelligent computer systems built on the basis of this language. Since this language is universal, it is possible to describe in it with a sufficient degree of detail and completeness the intelligent computer system itself, in whose memory this description is stored. The integrated body of knowledge stored in the memory of an intelligent computer system and *sufficient* (!) for the functioning of this system is called the **knowledge base** of the specified system. The *Knowledge Base* of an intelligent computer system includes:

- a description of the facts and laws of the external environment in which the intelligent computer system functions ("lives") and, in particular:
  - description of external subjects (for example, users) with whom the system interacts (description of their properties, description of situations and events associated with them, description of protocols of direct interaction with them);
  - a description of the syntax and semantics of languages for communication with external subjects;
  - description of the facts of behavior of an intelligent computer system in the external environment;
  - description of the rules (skills) of the behavior of an intelligent computer system in the external environment;
- description of the rules of behavior of internal subjects of an intelligent computer system performing actions (information processes) in the memory of an intelligent computer system (such subjects will be called internal agents of an intelligent computer system)
- a description of the information processes themselves, planned, currently executed or already terminated in the memory of an intelligent computer system (description of the behavior of an intelligent computer system in the internal environment);
- description of methods (methods, skills) that ensure the solution of the corresponding classes of information problems—a description of the rules of behavior of internal agents of an intelligent computer system in its memory, which is the internal environment of an intelligent computer system.

Thus, the standardization of intelligent computer systems is determined by linguistic means of structuring knowledge bases, means of systematizing various types of knowledge that are part of knowledge bases.

At the same time, the intelligent computer system itself is considered as a system consisting of two main components:

- a knowledge base that is a complete description of this intelligent computer system;
- universal interpreter of knowledge bases of intelligent computer systems, consisting of:
  - the memory into which the processed knowledge base is loaded and stored;
  - a processor that provides direct interpretation of the knowledge base stored in the above memory.

Note that with the hardware implementation of a universal interpreter of knowledge bases that have a semantic representation, the line between memory and the interpreter's processor can be blurred. Those the knowledge base interpreter can be implemented as a processor-memory, in which the processor elements will be connected to the memory elements.

The above *completeness* of the description of an intelligent computer system in the knowledge base of this system itself is determined by the following properties and capabilities of intelligent computer systems.

An intelligent computer system is a **knowledge-based computer system** and is driven by its knowledge. Those an intelligent computer system is based on its knowledge base, which is a systematized information picture (information model) of the world (environment) in which the intelligent computer system functions. The specified environment is understood as the **external environment** of the intelligent computer system, and its **internal environment**, which is the knowledge base itself, stored in the memory of the intelligent computer system.

An intelligent computer system is a computer system that has a high degree of **learnability**, which boils down to expanding the *external environment* of its "habitat" (functioning), to expanding its *internal environment* (your knowledge base) with new declarative knowledge and new skills, to an improved quality of your knowledge base (improving the quality of structuring the knowledge base, following the Occam's razor principle, minimizing contradictions, information holes, information garbage).

The high degree of *learning* of intelligent computer systems is determined by the high speed of practically unlimited expansion of knowledge and skills of the system (and, in particular, the expansion of the variety of types of acquired knowledge and variety of types of acquired skills—types of problem solving models). Such learning ability is provided by:

- semantic compatibility of the knowledge used (including knowledge of different types)—the presence of an automated method for integrating various knowledge;

- semantic compatibility of the skills used—the possibility of associative use of any required knowledge (including the same) when interpreting (performing) any skills (including those recently acquired);
- a high level of flexibility of an intelligent computer system—low laboriousness of modifying intelligent computer systems at all levels while maintaining the integrity of the system (in particular, laboriousness of modifying stored knowledge and skills used);
- high level of stratification;
- high level of reflectivity—the ability for introspection and, in particular, for reasoning.

An intelligent computer system is a social subject capable of exchanging information and coordinating its actions with other intelligent systems (including with people) in the direction of achieving corporate goals, as well as maintaining a sufficient level of semantic compatibility (mutual understanding) with other subjects to prevent syndrome of "Babylonian pandemonium".

An intelligent computer system is a computer system capable of solving a *integral* (!) combination of tasks that ensure the effective functioning of a computer system in a corresponding "habitat" environment. This includes:

- means of *perception* of the current state (situations and events) of the "habitat"
- means of *analysis* of this state,
- means of *goal-setting* (generation of tasks to be solved, specifying their priority),
- means of solving the initiated tasks (corresponding skills and interpreters of these skills),
- means of purposeful impact on the "habitat", that is means of changing the state of this environment.

The approach we propose to ensure the semantic and logical (functional) compatibility of knowledge representation and processing models is based on the following provisions:

- *universal* way of *semantic* representation of knowledge—*SC-code*;
- a hierarchical system of formal ontologies presented in the *SC-code* of compatibility (consistency) of the concepts used;
- general abstract graphodynamic associative memory that integrates all knowledge used by the intellectual system;
- *hierarchical* system of agents over the specified memory;
- programming tools for these agents—means of decomposition (reduction) of agents to agents of a lower level (to interpreting agents).

We emphasize that the development of a standard for an intelligent computer system is a necessary condition not only for ensuring the semantic compatibility of intelligent computer systems, but also for the formation of a developing *industrial* (!) Intelligent computer systems market, i.e. for mass industrial development of intelligent computer systems in various areas [22, 35].

The proposed standardization of intelligent computer systems is the basis for the design technology of semantically compatible intelligent computer systems, focused on the use of specially designed computers of the new generation.

5   ICS Standard as a Knowledge Base of an Intelligent Computer Metasystem

Let us consider a version of the representation of the ICS standard, built on the basis of the semantic representation of knowledge, in the form of a section of the knowledge base *Intellectual computer metasystem* (IMS.ostis). It can have the following structure:

- Subject area and ontology of the internal language of the semantic representation of knowledge in the memory of the ICS (syntax and denotational semantics of the internal language).
- Subject area and ontology of external languages IKS, close to the internal semantic language (syntax and denotational semantics of external languages).
- Subject area and ontology of ICS knowledge base structuring.
- Subject area and ontology of integrated solvers.
- Subject area and ontology of ICS verbal and non-verbal interfaces.

It is important not only to develop ICS, but also to organize a process of permanent and rapid improvement and harmonization of this standard. If the ICS standard is presented in the form of a knowledge base, which is specifically designed to automate the use and improvement of the specified standard and which *itself is built in exact accordance with this standard*, then the process of permanent improvement of the standard of intelligent computer systems becomes a process of permanent collective improvement of the knowledge base of the specified ICS.

This process is based on the following principles:

- any user can carry out free *navigation*, asking ICS a wide range of questions.
- any section of the knowledge base can be represented as a semantically structured source text.
- any user can become a co-author of the next version of the standard. To do this, he needs to register and follow the rules of interaction between the authors of the standard.
- editing of the current *version of the standard* is carried out *automatically* by special internal agents based on the completed review procedure and approval of editorial revisions.
- Any proposal aimed at improving the current version of the standard is subject to review.

– If the proposed fragment of the standard is the result of eliminating a previously identified contradiction, or the result of processing a previously identified dubious fragment, then this should be clearly indicated in the specialization of this fragment.
– the actions of each author are recorded in the knowledge base in the history section of its evolution with automatic indication of the author and the moment of the action.
– the history of the evolution of the standard automatically determines the level of activity of the author and the level of value of his contribution to the development of the standard.
– The activities of the author of the standard include:
  • building a new fragment of the standard;
  • construction of a contradiction specification;
  • building a specification for a fragment to be deleted;
  • construction of a specification requiring revision of a fragment, indicating the directions of revision;
  • construction of an editorial revision specification in the current version of the standard (deletion, replacement);
  • construction of reviews of a proposal made by other authors, indicating their opinion;
  • construction of a repeated review of the revised proposal;
  • building a corrected version of the assumption after eliminating the comments.
– In the process of collectively improving the standard, particular attention should be paid to reaching consensus on issues such as:
  • allocated entities and their formal **specifications**;
  • *basic* terms assigned to selected entities;
  • distinguished subject areas and their structural specifications.

To coordinate the work on the development of the ICS standard and the construction of the corresponding infrastructure, it is necessary to create a Consortium for the standardization of intelligent computer systems, which ensures their semantic compatibility.

6   Standards as a Kind of Knowledge

Standards are essential knowledge for ensuring consistency across mass activities. But in order for standards not to hinder progress, they must be constantly improved.

Standards must be used effectively and competently. Therefore, the design of standards in the form of text documents does not meet modern requirements.

Standards should be framed as intelligent reference systems that can answer a wide variety of questions. Thus, it is advisable to formalize the standards in the form of knowledge bases, corresponding intelligent reference systems. In this case, these intelligent reference systems can coordinate the activities of standards developers aimed at improving them [16, 21, 32].

From a semantic point of view, each standard is a hierarchical ontology that clarifies the structure and systems of concepts of the corresponding subject areas. Which describes the structure and functioning of either a certain class of technical or other artificial systems, or a certain class of organizations, or a certain type of activity.

To build an intelligent reference system according to the standard, its formalization is necessary. This can be done in the form of constructing a corresponding formal ontology.

The convergence of various types of activities, as well as the convergence of the results of these activities, requires deep semantic convergence (semantic compatibility of the relevant standards, for which the formalization of standards is also imperative.

It should also be noted that the most important methodological basis for formalizing standards and ensuring their semantic compatibility and convergence is the construction of a hierarchical system of formal ontologies and observance of the Occam's Razor principle.

7   Integration of Heterogeneous Knowledge and Models Based on Their Standardization

On the basis of the proposed standard for the semantic representation of knowledge, tools have been developed that ensure the coordinated integration of the joint use (when solving problems within the same intellectual system) of various types of knowledge and various models.

Integration of various types of knowledge is provided using the model of hybrid knowledge bases [29]. This model includes a hierarchical family of top-level ontologies that provide semantic compatibility of different types of knowledge. The model allows you to integrate facts, specifications of various objects, logical statements, events, situations, programs and algorithms, processes, problem formulations, domain models, ontologies, and others.

Integration of knowledge processing models is provided within the framework of a hybrid problem solver model. The solver is interpreted as a hierarchical model of agents interacting with each other based on the specification of actions in the common semantic memory. It is supposed to integrate models for solving problems, such as logical ones (including clear, fuzzy, reliable, plausible, etc.), neural network models, genetic algorithms, various strategies for finding ways to solve problems. One of the components of the hybrid problem solver model is a basic programming language focused on processing semantic networks. On the basis of this language, it is planned to develop programming languages of a higher level.

Specific options for integrating various knowledge and models have found application in solving various applied problems [27, 33, 46, 47].

8 From Standardization of Intelligent Computer Systems to Standardization of Their Design Technology and to the Construction of an Intelligent Knowledge Portal

Using the above-described standard IKS meta system, it is easy to move to the standard of integrated design technology. Such technology includes the specified intelligent computer system standard and the standard of methods and means for their development. Moreover, the standard for the specified complex technology can be associated with a metasystem that supports the operation and improvement of the standard of the specified technology. We called this **Metasystem IMS.ostis** (Intelligent MetaSystem for Open Semantic Technology for Intelligent Systems).

Metasystem IMS.ostis it is an intelligent computer metasystem for supporting the design of intelligent computer systems built on the basis of the semantic representation of knowledge. *Metasystem IMS.ostis* can be considered as an intelligent knowledge portal that ensures the effective use and improvement of the ICS standard, systems built on the basis of the semantic representation of knowledge, as well as the standard of methods and design tools for the specified ICS.

The knowledge base of *Metasystem IMS.ostis* has a structure including a description of standards, methods and design tools for ICS, built on the basis of the semantic representation of knowledge.

The reviewed knowledge base will be published as the source text of this knowledge base. Due to the "transparent", formalized structuring of the text and the inclusion of non-formalized information structures (explanations, notes, images) in the knowledge base, it will be understandable for a wide range of specialists [14, 34].

9 Standardization of the Global Semantic Space and the Prospects for the Development of Science, Education, Industry and the Knowledge Market

The structuring of the *semantic space* of knowledge is set by a system of interconnected *subject areas* and the corresponding *ontologies*.

Subject areas and, accordingly, the ontologies that specify them are different.

The subject area and ontology of a certain class of technical systems is one thing, and the subject area and ontology of design actions (including methods) aimed at developing technical systems of the specified class, as well as the subject area and ontology of tools used in the development of these technical systems, is another thing.

In addition, each class of technical systems can be associated with a subject area and an ontology of actions that ensure the effective operation of technical systems of the specified class. Thus, on a set of subject areas and their corresponding ontologies, a whole family of relations connecting them is defined. Here are some of them:

- to be a private subject area or ontology in the set-theoretical sense (for example, the subject area of planar figures and the subject area of polygons and the subject area of triangles are connected);
- to be a private subject area or ontology in a spatial sense, it provides a detailed description of *spatial parts* of objects studied in a given subject area;
- to be a private subject area orontology in the temporal sense, which provides a detailed description of the temporal parts (stages of existence) of objects studied in a given subject area.

The list of types of relationships between subject areas and ontologies can be continued. We also emphasize that

- each scientific and technical or academic discipline and each standard in the semantic space is represented as a hierarchical system of interrelated subject areas and ontologies;
- the convergence of different disciplines ultimately boils down to an increase in the number of connections between subject areas and ontologies belonging to different disciplines.

The experience of convergence of various areas of activity in the field of artificial intelligence can be used to implement a transdisciplinary approach in the development of science in general.

Moreover, the design of knowledge bases of intelligent computer systems should be based on the results of scientific research of the entire complex of scientific and technical disciplines. Knowledge bases of intelligent computer systems should make full use of the results of scientific research, and not distort them by the hands of knowledge base engineers.

Fundamentally important for the development of transdisciplinary research and deepening the convergence of various disciplines is the concept of a formalized (!) **global semantic space**, which is the result of the abstract integration of knowledge bases, formalized in the standard of semantic representation of knowledge and included in the portals of scientific and technical knowledge corresponding to all kinds (!) of scientific and technical disciplines.

If each scientific and technical discipline evolves not only within the framework of its formalized local semantic space, focusing only on its class of research objects and its research subject, but also simultaneously within the formalized *global semantic space*, then obviously interdisciplinary research will develop more intensively, constructively and accurately.

The system of evolving semantically compatible portals of scientific and technical knowledge is the basis of a new level of development of the organization of scientific and technical information and the organization of scientific activity in general. A transition from a system of scientific books and articles to a system of semantically compatible bases of scientific and technical knowledge is necessary, in which duplication of knowledge is fundamentally excluded and in which the meaning (essence) of the contribution of each scientist to the development of the global semantic space of knowledge is clearly defined and localized.

Convergence, integration of the results of various scientific disciplines, trans-disciplinarity of scientific research is the most important trend in the development of modern science:

"... ... the era of analyticism and its inherent differentiation between science and closed scientific theories are already behind us. It became obvious that the real problems facing human society are much more complicated than scientific ones, and science is not able to radically solve them due to the disunity of scientific disciplines and their specialization, poor coordination of research teams and their topics, lack of system monitoring and a common formalized language for representing knowledge" [4].

The most urgent need for the convergence of various disciplines:

- in the field of artificial intelligence to build a general theory of intelligent computer systems;
- in medicine to create intelligent computer systems for complex transdisciplinary diagnostics;
- in education for the formation and learners of a complex picture of the world;
- in complex automation of enterprises and to ensure the semantic compatibility of all levels of enterprise management;
- in the complex informatization of scientific activity.

The problems of human activity solved with the use of artificial intelligence technologies are of a fundamental nature. They largely coincide with the problems of informatization of scientific activity, education (Univercity 3.0), industry (Industry 4.0) and healthcare.

Based on the global semantic space of knowledge, it becomes possible to create a rapidly developing **knowledge market**, within which

- the authorship of each action aimed at the development of the global semantic space is recorded;
- the fact of recognition (consistency) of each proposal is established;
- the significance of the contribution of each author is evaluated;
- the demand for copyright knowledge is assessed by the frequency of its use in solving problems and in the development of various ICS;
- even those points of view are recorded that are correctly formed, but have not received the recognition of the reviewers (over time, such recognition can be obtained).

10   Perspectives for the Development of the Market of Intelligent Computer Systems Based on Their Standardization

The main product of *OSTIS Technologies*, focused on the design of semantically compatible ICS, is not the systems themselves, but the socio-technical ***OSTIS ecosystem***. An ecosystem is a self-organizing system consisting of interacting computer systems built according to *OSTIS Technology* (*ostis-systems*), as well as their users (end users and developers). Systems constantly maintaining compatibility and, as a consequence, a high level of "mutual understanding" between the specified *ostis systems*, as well as between these systems and their users.

Thus, *OSTIS Technologies* is based on constantly evolving standards that ensure the specified interoperability and "mutual understanding".

OSTIS technology is a technology for developing semantically compatible hybrid intelligent systems with a high level of learning. Systems constantly maintaining the specified compatibility with each other and with their users.

We emphasize that the *OSTIS ecosystem* is a hierarchical multi-agent system, since its components (agents) [15] can be not only individual *ostis-systems* and their users, but also their collectives. Moreover, each *ostis-system* or user can be a member of several teams at once.

The transition from individual intelligent computer systems to an ecosystem requires the development of **standards, means to support their evolution and compatibility** (in the course of their evolution and operation), **means of integration and coordination** (within various groups).

11   Conclusion

The creation of *OSTIS Technologies* will solve a number of significant problems. This, in turn, will radically change the capabilities of the ICS developer and expand the range of tasks they solve [24, 30].

To reduce the development time of ICS, it is necessary to organize component design with a powerful and constantly expanding library of reusable components. For this it is necessary to ensure their **semantic compatibility**.

To implement cooperative purposeful and adaptive interaction of ICS within the framework of automatically formed teams, their **semantic compatibility**. This, in turn, requires their unification. Such unification is possible only on the basis of the **general formal theory of intelligent computer systems** and the corresponding **standard**. This requires a deep convergence of different lines of research in the field of artificial intelligence.

The result of the development of artificial intelligence as a scientific discipline is the permanent evolution of the general theory of ICS and the corresponding standard. Therefore, in order to increase the rate of development of artificial intelligence and, accordingly, the technology for developing ICS, it is necessary to create a portal of scientific and technical knowledge on artificial intelligence. This portal should ensure the coordination of the activities of specialists, as well as the coordination and integration of the results of these activities.

For the transition to a new technological structure in the field of artificial intelligence, which is based on the semantic compatibility of ICS and their standardization (unification), certain socio-psychological prerequisites are required: appropriate motivation, a high level of determination, commitment, mathematical and systemic culture.

The key provisions of *OSTIS Technologies* are:

- focus on new generation computers specially designed for the production of semantically compatible ICS;
- adherence to the principle of Occam's Razor at all levels of the ICS. And above all, on the line between their software and hardware. And also the use of *semantic representation of information* in the ICS memory;
- convergence of various types of ICS components, as well as methods and tools for their development;
- focus on solving the problem of semantic compatibility of ICS at all levels of organization of their activities.

A promising object of mathematical research is the concept of a global semantic space presented in the *SC-code*. The composition of the space includes signs of all kinds of entities and, accordingly, connections between these entities and/or their signs. The peculiarity of such a space is that it has a unique combination of properties:

- the property of objectivity (independence from the point of view of a particular subject);
- topological properties, which makes it possible to study it using topological methods (specifying, in particular, the concept of semantic proximity);
- algebraic properties, which allows you to explore it using the theory of algebraic systems and category theory;
- graph-theoretic properties, which allows you to study its structure using methods and tools of graph theory.

References

1. InterNational committee for information technology standards (INCITS): New INCITS Technical Committee on Artificial Intelligence – Notice of January 30–31, 2018 Organizational Meeting and Call for Members. https://standards.incits.org/apps/group_public/download.php/94314/eb-2017-00698-Meeting-Notice-New-INCITS-TC-on-Artificial-Intelligence-January30-31-2018.pdf. Accessed 10 July 2020
2. ISO/IEC AWI TR 24027 Information technology - Artificial Intelligence (AI) -Bias in AI systems and AI aided decision making. https://www.iso.org/standard/77607.html. Accessed 10 July 2020
3. ISO/IEC AWI TR 24368 Information technology - Artificial intelligence - Overview of ethical and societal concerns. https://www.iso.org/standard/78507.html. Accessed 10 July 2020
4. ISO/IEC CD 23053 Framework for Artificial Intelligence (AI) Systems Using Machine Learning (ML). https://www.iso.org/standard/74438.html. Accessed 10 July 2020
5. ISO/IEC CD TR 24029–1 Artificial Intelligence (AI) - Assessment of the robustness of neural networks - Part 1: Overview. https://www.iso.org/standard/77609.html. Accessed 10 July 2020
6. ISO/IEC JTC 1/SC 42/WG 1 Artificial intelligence. Foundational standards. https://www.iso.org/committee/6794475.html. Accessed 10 July 2020

7. ISO/IEC JTC 1/SC 42/WG 4 Artificial intelligence. Use cases and applications. https://www.iso.org/committee/6794475.html. Accessed 10 July 2020
8. ISO/IEC TR 24028:2020 Information technology - Artificial intelligence - Overview of trustworthiness in artificial intelligence. https://www.iso.org/ru/standard/77608.html. Accessed 10 July 2020
9. Iso/iec tr 24028:2020 informatsionnyye tekhnologii. iskusstvennyy intellekt. obzor dostovernosti sistem iskusstvennogo intellekta [Information technology. Artificial intelligence. Review of the validity of artificial intelligence systems]. http://www.standards.ru/document/6528606.aspx. Accessed 10 July 2020
10. IT/APKIT professional standards [Electronic resource]. http://www.apkit.webtm.ru/committees/education/meetings/standarts.php. Accessed 7 May 2012
11. ISO/IEC 2382-31:1997 Information technology - Vocabulary - Part 31: Artificial intelligence - Machine learning (1997). https://www.iso.org/obp/ui/#iso:std:iso-iec:2382:-31:ed-1:v1:en. Accessed 10 July 2020
12. P7009 Project Authorization Request. IEEE-SA, July 2017. https://development.standards.ieee.org/get-file/P7009.pdf?t=93536600003. Accessed 15 Feb 2020
13. Safety and Beneficence of Artificial General Intelligence (AGI) and Artificial Super-intelligence (ASI). The IEEE Global Initiative on Ethics of Autonomous and Intelligent Systems (2017). https://standards.ieee.org/content/dam/ieee-standards/standards/web/documents/other/ead_safety_beneficence_v2.pdf. Accessed 10 July 2020
14. AI Standardization White Paper (CESI) (2018). https://docs.google.com/document/d/1VqzyN2KINmKmY7mGke_KR77o1XQriwKGsuj9dO4MTDo/edit#heading=h.b7nqb0tieikc. Accessed 10 July 2020
15. Batyrshin, I.Z., Nedosekin, A.O., Stetsko, A.A., Tarasov, V.B., Yazenin, A.V., Yarushkina, N.G.: Nechetkie gibridnye sistemy. Teoriya i praktika [Fuzzy hybrid systems. Theory and practice]. FIZMATLIT [M.: PHYSMATLIT] (2007)
16. Bolotova, L.S.: Sistemy iskusstvennogo intelekta: modeli i tekhnologii, osnovannye na znaniyakh [Artificial intelligence systems: knowledge-based models and tech-nologies]. Finansy i statistika [Finance and Statistics], Moscow (2012). (in Russian)
17. Borgest, N.M.: Strategii intellekta i ego ontologii: popytka razobrat'sya [strate-gies of intelligence and its ontology: an attempt to understand]. Ontologija proek-tirovanija. [Ontol. Des.] **9**(9(34)), 407–425 (2019)
18. Davydenko, I.: Semantic models, method and tools of knowledge bases coordinated development based on reusable components. In: Golenkov, V. (ed.) Open Semantic Technologies for Intelligent Systems, vol. 2, pp. 99–118. BSUIR, Minsk (2018)
19. Dutton, T.: An Overview of National AI Strategies. Medium, June 2018. https://medium.com/politics-ai/an-overview-of-national-ai-strategies-2a70ec6edfd. Acce-ssed 10 July 2020
20. Evgenev, G.B.: Ekspertopediya kak sredstvo sozdaniya ontologicheskogo interneta znanii [expetopedia as a means of creating ontological internet of knowledge]. Ontologija proektirovanija. [Ontol. Des.] **9**(3 (33)), 307–319 (2019)
21. Gavrilova, T.A., Kudryavtsev, D.V., Muromtsev, D.I.: Knowledge Engineering. Models and Methods: A Textbook. Lan', Saint Petersburg (2016)
22. Golenkov, V., Guliakina, N., Davydenko, I., Eremeev, A.: Methods and tools for ensuring compatibility of computer systems. In: Golenkov, V. (ed.) Open Semantic Technologies for Intelligent Systems, vol. 4, pp. 25–52. BSUIR, Minsk (2019)
23. Golenkov, V.V., Guliakina, N.A.: Principles of building mass semantic technol-ogy component design of intelligent systems. In: Open Semantic Technologies for Intelligent Systems, pp. 21–58. BSUIR, Minsk (2011)
24. Golenkov, V.V., Guliakina, N.A.: Structurization of sense space. In: Open Semantic Technologies for Intelligent Systems, pp. 65–78. BSUIR, Minsk (2014)

25. Golenkov, V.V., et al.: From training intelligent systems to training their development tools. In: Open Semantic Technologies for Intelligent Systems, pp. 81–98. BSUIR, Minsk (2018)

26. Golovko, V., Kroshchanka, A., Ivashenko, V., Kovalev, M., Taberko, V., Ivaniuk, D.: Principles of decision-making systems building based on the integration of neural networks and semantic models. In: Golenkov, V. (ed.) Otkrytye semanticheskie tekhnologii proektirovaniya intellektual'nykh system [Open Semantic Technologies for Intelligent Systems], pp. 91–102. BSUIR, Minsk (2019)

27. Golovko, V.A., Krasnoproshin, V.V.: Neirosetevye tekhnologii obrabotki dannykh [Neural Network Data Processing Technologies]. Minsk BGU [Minsk BSU], Minsk (2017). (in Russian)

28. Iskra, N., Iskra, V., Lukashevich, M.: Neural network based image understanding with ontological approach. In: Otkrytye semanticheskie tekhnologii proektirovaniya intellektual'nykh system [Open Semantic Technologies for Intelligent Systems], pp. 113–122. BSUIR, Minsk (2019)

29. Kolesnikov, A.V.: Gibridnye intellektual'nye sistemy: Teoriya i tekhnologiya razrabotki [Hybrid Intelligent Systems: Theory and Development Technology]. SPbGTU [SPsSIT], Saint Petersburg (2001). (in Russian)

30. Kolesnikov, A.V., Kirikov, I.A.: Metodologiya i tekhnologiya resheniya slozhnykh zadach metodami funktsional'nykh gibridnykh intellektual'nykh sistem [Methodology and Technology of the Solution of Difficult Tasks by Methods of Functional Hybrid Intellectual Systems]. Moskva IPI RAN [Moscow IIP RAS], Moscow (2007). (in Russian)

31. Manin, Y., Marcolli, M.: Semantic spaces. Math. Comput. Sci. **10**, 459–477 (2016). https://doi.org/10.1007/s11786-016-0278-9

32. Osipov, G.S.: Metody iskusstvennogo intellekta [Artificial Intelligence Methods]. Fizmatlit [Fizmatlit], Moscow (2015). (in Russian)

33. Palagin, A.: Problemy transdisciplinarnosti i rol' informatiki [transdisciplinarity problems and the role of informatics]. Kibernetika i sistemnyj analiz [Cybern. Syst. Anal.] **5**, 3–13 (2013)

34. Rybina, G.V.: Sovremennye arkhitektury dinamicheskikh intellektual'nykh sistem: problemy integratsii i osnovnye tendentsii [modern architectures of dynamic intelligent systems: integration problems and main trends]. Pribory i sistemy. Upravlenie, kontrol', diagnostika [Instrum. Syst. Manag. Control Diagn.] (2), 7–12 (2017)

35. Salay, R., Queiroz, R., Czarnecki, K.: An analysis of ISO 26262: using machine learning safely in automotive software (2017)

36. Serenkov, P., Solomaho, V., Nifagin, V., Minova, A.: Koncepcija infrastruktury standartizacii kak bazy znanij na osnove ontologij [the concept of a standardization infrastructure as an ontology-based knowledge base]. Novosti. Standartizacija i sertifikacija. [News Stand. Certif.] (5), 25–29 (2004)

37. Shoham, Y., et al.: The AI index 2018 annual report. AI Index Steering Committee, Human-Centered AI Initiative (2018). http://cdn.aiindex.org/2018/AI%20Index%202018%20Annual%20Report.pdf

38. Shunkevich, D.: Agent-oriented models, method and tools of compatible problem solvers development for intelligent systems. In: Golenkov, V. (ed.) Open Semantic Technologies for Intelligent Systems, vol. 2, pp. 119–132. BSUIR, Minsk (2018)

39. Spivak, D.I., Kent, R.E.: Ologs: A categorical framework for knowledge representation. PLoS ONE **7**(1), e24274 (2012). https://doi.org/10.1371/journal.pone.0024274

40. Taberko, V., et al.: Design principles of integrated information services for batch manufacturing enterprise employees. In: Golenkov, V. (ed.) Otkrytye semanticheskie tekhnologii proektirovaniya intellektual'nykh system [Open Semantic Technologies for Intelligent Systems], pp. 215–224. BSUIR, Minsk (2019)

41. Taranchuk, V.: Vozmozhnosti i sredstva wolfram mathematica dlya razrabotki intellektual'nykh obuchayushchikh sistem [opportunities and means of wolfram mathematica for developing intelligent tutoring systems]. Nauchnye vedomosti Belgorodskogo gosudarstvennogo universiteta. Seriya: Ekonomika. Informatika [Sci. Statements Belgorod State Univ. Ser. Econ. Comput. Sci.] **33**(1(198)), 102–110 (2015)

42. Tarasov, V.B.: Ot mnogoagentnykh sistem k intellektual'nym organizatsiyam: filosofiya, psikhologiya, informatika [From multi-agent systems to the intellectual organizations: philosophy, psychology, informatics]. Moscow URSS, Moscow (2002). (In Russ)

43. Tsalenko, M.S.: Modelirovanie semantiki v bazakh dannykh [Simulating semantics in databases]. Fizmatlit [Fizmatlit], Moscow (1989). (in Russian)

44. Volkov, A.I., Reingold, L.A., Reingold, E.A.: Professional'nye standarty v oblasti it kak faktor tekhnologicheskogo i sotsial'nogo razvitiya [professional standards in the field of it as a factor of technological and social development]. Prikladnaya informatika [J. Appl. Inform.] **10**(2), 37–48 (2015)

45. Yalovets, A.L.: Predstavlenie i obrabotka znanii s tochki zreniya matematicheskogo modelirovaniya: problemy i resheniya [Presentation and Processing of Knowledge from the Point of View of Mathematical Modeling: Problems and Solutions]. Naukova dumka, Kiev (2011). (in Russian)

46. Yankovskaya, A.E., Shelupanov, A.A., Kornetov, A.N., Ilinskaya, N.N., Obukhovskaya, V.B.: Gibridnaya intellektual'naya sistema ekspress-diagnostiki organizatsionnogo stressa, depressii, deviantnogo povedeniya i trevogi narushitelei na osnove konvergentsii neskol'kikh nauk i nauchnykh napravlenii [hybrid intelligent system of express diagnostics of organizational stress, depression, deviant behavior and anxiety of violators based on convergence of several sciences and scientific directions]. In: Trudy kongressa po intellektual'nym sistemam i informatsionnym tekhnologiyam, IS&IT 2017. Nauchnoe izdanie v 3-kh tomakh. [Works of Congress on Intelligent 17 Scientific Publication in 3 Volumes], pp. 323–329. T. 1, Stupin A. S. publishing House, Taganrog (2017)

47. Yankovskaya, A.: Analiz dannykh i znanii na osnove konvergentsii neskol'kikh nauk i nauchnykh napravlenii [data and knowledge analysis based on the convergence of several sciences and scientific fields]. In: Mezhdunarodnaya konferentsiya "Intellektualizatsiya obrabotki informatsii" (IOI-8) [International Conference "Intellectualization of Information Processing" (IIP-8)], pp. 196–199. Kipr (2010)

48. Zahariev, V.A., Lyahor, T., Hubarevich, N., Azarov, E.S.: Semantic analysis of voice messages based on a formalized context. In: Golenkov, V. (ed.) Open Semantic Technologies for Intelligent Systems, vol. 3, pp. 103–112. BSUIR, Minsk (2019)

49. Zielkes, T.: Is artificial intelligence ready for standardization? May 2020

Tools and Technologies for Artificial Intelligence Systems. What Should They Be?

Valeria Gribova$^{(\boxtimes)}$ (ID)

Institute of Automation and Control Processes, Far Eastern Branch of Russian Academy of Sciences, Radio st., 5, Vladivostok 690041, Russia
gribova@iacp.dvo.ru
http://iacp.dvo.ru/user?id=29

Abstract. This paper provides an overview of the current state in the development of artificial intelligence (AI) systems. It is discussed that an ideal AI system should imitate (support the development) of all the characteristics (cognitive procedures) of natural intelligence. Moreover, not all characteristics of natural intelligence can be automated; some of them can be realized only using human-computer interactions. An important property of AI systems is the integration of cognitive procedures among themselves. Thus, the AI system should support the implementation of a subset (as large as possible) of natural intelligence procedures. Moreover, all procedures should be understandable to a person (described in his or her system of concepts), and the connection between them should be "seamless" way to ensure their integration. The paper identifies and substantiates the requirements for tools for creating AI systems. It is proposed to evaluate the AI system by the number of cognitive procedures that it implements. At the same time, given the complexity of tools, its developers need to develop a set of requirements for compatibility and integration of tools and AI systems of various types.

Keywords: Artificial intelligence · Machine learning · Knowledge base

1 Introduction

Artificial intelligence as a scientific direction was created in the mid-50s, when it became obvious that traditional technologies for creating software systems based on the algorithmic approach are poorly suitable for solving creative or intellectual problems, so specialized technologies are needed to create systems of this class. The main research of scientists in the field of AI was related to models of knowledge representation and methods for solving intellectual problems. During the lifetime of artificial intelligence as a scientific direction, a number of models of knowledge representation and methods for solving intellectual problems

The research is carried out with the partial financial support of the Russian Foundation for Basic Research (projects 19-07-00244 and 20-07-00670).

V. Golenkov et al. (Eds.): OSTIS 2020, CCIS 1282, pp. 22–33, 2020.
https://doi.org/10.1007/978-3-030-60447-9_2

were created. The development of AI systems was supported first by specialized programming languages, then by universal tool, as well as problem-independent and specialized shells. Typically, AI system development tools and shells were intended for knowledge-based AI system design, while AI system development based on other methods were much more poorly supported by specialized tools. However, the situation has changed dramatically in the past few years. Numerous frameworks and libraries have entered the market that support the neural network approach to creating systems of this class. They are convenient, well implemented (they are developed by the leaders of the IT industry), and have a low enough barrier to entry for developers. As a result, AI has often been reduced exclusively to the neural network approach, and the approach based on knowledge is often characterized as outdated, lost its relevance. Is that so? What should AI technologies be, what properties should they have? This article is an extension of the article [1] and contains the author's opinion on all there issues.

2 Current State of Artificial Intelligence System Development Technologies

The first scientific research in the AI field led to the creation of a number of specialized programming languages, such as PROLOG, LISP, SMALLTALK, FRL, Interlisp, Haskell etc. The languages Java, C++ R, Python, and others are also used to develop AI systems. These languages have many advantages, however, their use has shown a high complexity of creation and maintenance of software systems, which, as noted in [1] has led to fact, the development of intelligent systems has become almost inaccessible.

Together with the development of knowledge representation models and methods for solving intellectual problems, universal tools and specialized software shells were actively developed, mainly for creating systems with knowledge bases. Typical representatives of this class of systems are: IACPaaS, OSTIS, Level5, Object, G2, Clips, Loops, AT-TECHNOLOGY, VITAL, KEATS, etc. [2–6]. Significant differences between various tools are related to the level of instrumental support, development technologies, the formalisms used to represent knowledge, the methods for their formation and debugging, the used inference machine, and user interface design tools. Specialized shells designed to solve problems of a certain class are also widely used. The main advantage of this class of tools is significant reduction of development time and maintenance of software. The main disadvantage is limitations of the area of use.

Approximately from the last decade of the 20th century and the first of the current one, active development has received another direction of AI, - machine learning and big data analysis. This is due to the development of new computing platforms, a significant increase in their performance, as well as the creation of new theoretical models and architectures, primarily based on neural networks. To date, we can see a boom in neural networks, that foster a number of tools - frameworks (for example, Deeplearning4j, TensorFlow and Theano, PyTorch), specialized libraries (e.g., Keras, PuzzleLib, Caffe, etc.) allows developers to create, train, test, and deploy a network of any complexity [7–9]. However, it is very important that the use of libraries for machine learning significantly save development time, thereby eliminating the most difficult stages of its development. Many machine learning libraries are free and available, which has led to significant progress in this area in recent years. In addition to tools, developers have access to ready-made, already trained, neural networks for solving various problems.

Unfortunately, the boom in the field of neural networks, as well as a significantly increased interest in AI, has generated not only a huge number of "experts" in this field, who, taking a ready-made model, data and running training, get perhaps even a good solution for simple cases, consider themselves experts in this field and reduce AI exclusively to a neural network approach. Moreover, they actively promote, and not without success, the assertion that the approach based on knowledge bases (while they usually mention only the production model of knowledge representation), hopelessly outdated, in modern AI systems it is used less and less and tends to complete extinction.

Estimating the current state of AI technologies, the following can be stated:

1. AI technologies based on knowledge bases continue to be developed and used. These technologies have evolved significantly. According to a study published in [2], the most popular production model of knowledge representation in the 80–90 years is losing its popularity (according to estimates in [2], the number of systems with this model of knowledge representation has decreased by about 4 times), giving way to systems with other models of knowledge representation. The trend to decrease production can be explained by the expansion of the available tools that support other representation models that are most appropriate to the domain and tasks for which the production representation is not convenient. First of all, it is an ontological approach to the representation of knowledge. The most well-known technology is Protege, which supports the object-oriented representation model [10], as well as the relatively new (compared to Protege), IACPaaS [11] and OSTIS [6] technologies, which support the semantic model of knowledge representation. These three technologies are developed by research teams, which, on the one hand, ensures that the proposed technologies correspond to the current level of scientific research in this area and their continuous improvement, on the other, these technologies, admittedly, lack a "beautiful wrapper", context assistance systems, and other marketing elements, which are important for promoting technologies "to the masses". Research teams have neither the experience of promoting software products, nor the human resources.

2. Machine learning technologies are very popular in many domains. First, there are really huge amounts of data (in digital form) that need to be analyzed. Second, a significant increase in computational power of computers was also a positive factor. Third, leaders of IT-industry have taken up the development of tools, understanding the huge reserves of "unrecognized" knowledge that

store data arrays and the opportunities to monetize them in trade, banking, law, and other areas.

Since the discovery of new knowledge in huge data sets is a task that is still practically inaccessible to natural intelligence, this need has given rise to active research in the field of developing new and improving existing methods of machine learning (neural networks have become the leader here).

Machine learning methods can be divided into 2 types (classes): "conditionally" intelligent ("understanding" information) and "conditionally" non-intelligent.

In "intelligent" methods of data analysis, the development of the method begins with the analysis of the domain and the problems solved in it, and the development of its model in terms of the domain. To do this, a terminological basis (thesaurus) is created for accumulating data sets and representing the discovered knowledge, developing a method and algorithm for solving it.

The advantage of this method of analysis is the potential for generating an explanation of the received knowledge and integrating with systems based on knowledge bases that can form an understandable explanation for their decision. Similarly, methods for solving problems based on knowledge bases are created using the same terminology base. A significant disadvantage of these methods is the complexity of developing a model of the problem, the complexity of the data analysis algorithm, its not-universality, but binding to a specific terminology base, and in many ways, the lack of ready-made algorithms available to a wide range of users.

Creating practically useful systems that support the second type of machine learning begins with searching for methods, algorithms, and libraries that are relevant to the problem being solved, and further adapting the source data to them. The result should be interpreted by experts. The disadvantage of these methods is that it is difficult or impossible to generate an explanation in meaningful terms. New knowledge, as a result of the work of such systems, is "passive" (it is not explicitly represented in a formally, so that it can be used by other software systems to solve different classes of problems). The advantage is a large number of frameworks and specialized libraries that allow you to quickly create, train, test and deploy a neural network of any complexity.

Machine learning technologies, primarily neural networks, are currently leading. It is neural network technologies that are often declared as modern artificial intelligence technologies in contrast to knowledge-based technologies. Yes, in solving some problems primarily related to the analysis of images, text, they demonstrate impressive results, their use is undoubtedly justified for a number of applications and, importantly, world leaders of the IT industry made it easier for developers to use them. However, it is still difficult to agree that the neural network approach is a modern AI that simulates, albeit simplistically, the work of the human brain. Do not forget that a neural network is a fitting of a function implemented by a neural network for training data by selecting the parameters of this function. This is still very little like how the human brain learns.

Accepting and understanding the importance and need of all available technologies today, however, it is worth noting that the two types of technologies work very poorly together, despite some attempts to integrate them and imitate only certain functions of the natural intelligence. Therefore, the scientific community faces an important task of determining the future of artificial intelligence technologies and their development directions.

3   What Is the Perfect Artificial Intelligence System

There are many different definitions of AI that consider it from either general philosophical or technological aspects. One of the most common technological definitions: AI is a field of computer science and information technology, the task of which is to build computer intelligent systems that simulate and enhance the basic abilities of productive natural intelligence [12].

In order to answer the question of what the perfect AI system is, it is necessary to understand what properties, abilities the natural AI has (the author understands that the perfect systems do not exist, in this case, the perfect requirement should be understood as a softer requirement - as close as possible to the perfect one). V.K. Finn listed 13 such abilities [12]. Here's their compressed enumeration: the discovery of the essential in the data; the creation of "goal-plan-action" sequences search for assumptions relevant to the purpose of reasoning; ability to reason: conclusions as consequences from assumptions; conclusions that do not follow directly from assumptions: conclusions by analogy, inductive generalizations of data, conclusions by explaining data (abduction), solving problems through various cognitive procedures; the ability to estimate knowledge and action; the ability to explain - the answer to the question "why?"; argumentation when making a decision; recognition as the answer to the question "what is this?"; the ability to learn and use memory; the ability to integrate knowledge, to form concepts and theories; the ability to refine unclear ideas and transform them into precise concepts; ability to change the knowledge system while learning and changing the situation.

The perfect AI system should have all these properties, and as V.K. Finn notes, that not all natural intelligence functions can be automated, some of them can be implemented only through "man-computer" interaction. Thus, if we really want to create an AI system, it must have at least a subset of these properties. It is important to note: in natural intelligence the result of one (or several) cognitive activities is always (!) integrated (consistent) with other types of cognitive procedures.

The basis of "human" or natural intelligence is the knowledge that he or she acquires during life from various sources: books, textbooks, teachers, parents, etc. An equally important way to obtain new knowledge is to independently generalize the obtained facts and form new knowledge. Using the obtained knowledge, a person can build new theories, justify their actions, search for facts, relevant goals of reasoning, make logical conclusions, evaluate knowledge and actions. Knowledge is a key factor in ensuring the support of the majority of intellectual abilities. In real life, reasoning "by analogy" also plays an important role, when the knowledge system has not yet been formed, but a person is also able to reason, draw conclusions (even if erroneous), and argue their actions on the basis of available facts.

It should be noted that since the birth of artificial intelligence as a scientific field, knowledge has been considered as a key area of research: models of knowledge representation, methods for solving intellectual problems based on knowledge bases have been developed.

For example, if we have knowledge in an area and have an object with a set of attributes, then we, on the basis of our knowledge system, can make some logical inference (depends on the problem being solved). It is possible that the attributes of this object are not consistent with our knowledge system. We have a precedent and need to understand what to do. Next, we make some decisions (possibly wrong). When it is necessary to draw a logical inference about a certain object again, we proceed as follows: draw a conclusion based on our knowledge system, or compare an object with an existing precedent to make a decision (a reasoning by analogy). The accumulation of precedents with a known result (learning) creates a situation where a person needs to correct his or her knowledge system, etc., so it is important that both knowledge (in the computer system is a knowledge base), and precedents (data) are clear to the person. Thus, terminology must be defined, which is understandable and accepted by a certain community, and the connection between cognitive procedures should be "seamless". Such system can claim to be called an AI system. In this case, the knowledge obtained either from a person or as a result of machine learning will be integrated into the knowledge base, which will be continuously improved. Knowledge itself will be available to both the AI system and the person who will be able get new knowledge (using the updated knowledge base) in a way that is not accessible to the computer system. As in real life, a person, using a computer, makes calculations, receives information from external devices, respectively, the AI system must "understand and accept" information from external devices.

Thus, if we are talking about the AI system, it should support a subset of cognitive procedures: the inference of consequences from assumptions - working with the existing system of knowledge, reasoning by analogy (this function is often overlooked and underestimated, although in real life, natural intelligence, it plays a significant role), learning as a way of correction the knowledge system and obtaining new knowledge, the ability to explain and justify their actions. At the same time, all procedures should be understandable to a person (described in his or her system of concepts), and the connection between different types of cognitive procedures should be a natural "seamless" way to carry out their "circle" with the participation of a person.

4   Requirements for Artificial Intelligence System Tools

Here are the basic requirements for AI tools.

Support the Development of Several Intellectual Activities with "Seamless" Integration

This requirement is discussed in the paragraph above. It is undoubtedly fundamental and means that the tools for creating AI systems should be much richer in their functionality than frameworks and tools designed for systems of other classes, because they should allow developers to create knowledge bases, ontologies, solvers, focused on logical inference from the knowledge base. Using them it is possible to describe the algorithms of learning, also oriented to the knowledge bases, reasoning on precedents, generation of explanations and other cognitive activities. Is it hopefully to develop different types of cognitive activity with a set of tools? The answer is yes, you can, but in this case it is difficult to integrate technologies, you need to create additional software modules that provide a link to them into a single whole. And this link is not reduced to a set of formats. It is important that the results obtained are embedded in all other cognitive procedures.

Availability of Means to Support the Viability of the Created Systems and Their Development Tools

This requirement is vast and, in fact, includes many other requirements. Its implementation, like the previous requirement, indicates the maturity of the development. This requirement should be given key attention both when creating tools and AI systems based on them. Unfortunately, it is common practice for most implementations to declare the functionality of a software to demonstrate results. However, developers find it difficult to list the mechanisms providing the viability of the created system. But modern statistics state that the process of evolution, maintenance of the system after implementation of its release in terms of labor costs is many times higher than the stage of actual development.

In general, this requirement should be provided by the following solutions:

- declarative representation of components, shifting the efforts of developers from programming to designing software components;
- automatic generation of software components;
- creation of technology that separates competencies among developers with sequential or parallel work on the formation of models and components, by providing the architectural integrity of the project;
- availability of tools for intellectual support of development of software component, a visual and understandable representation of components to software developers.

In the implementation of these requirements key role belongs to the tools with which the system is created. The longer the life cycle of any system, the more obvious the need for developers to improve their adaptation mechanisms due to changes of user requirements, domain, and operating conditions. It is important that users of the tool can also improve it, so the means for expanding the tool should be as close as possible to the means for developing the AI systems themselves, and the complexity of this process is comparable to the complexity of developing the corresponding components of the AI systems.

Integration with External Software and Components
The AI system should be able to interact with third-party systems based on different interaction models.

Collective Development
The AI system development requires the participation of many specialists, so the tool must have the means to ensure the collective development of system components, including collective development one component (for example, a knowledge base can be developed by several experts). To do this, a hierarchical system should be provided for managing access rights to components, monitoring changes, coordinating between components through user accounts and cloud tools for creating and managing components.

Support for the Creation of Evolving Shells, Knowledge Portals and/or Ecosystems in Various Domains Based on Universal Tools
It is known that there are two approaches to creating tools: universal tool complexes designed to create a wide class of software and specialized tools for development of either a class of tasks or a set of tasks in a particular domain. The evolution of the development of two opposite approaches has shown that these approaches do not conflict with each other, if there are specialized tools, this is preferable for developers due to a significant reduction in the complexity of creating systems of this class, which is supported by specialized tools. It is important that development of such shells or ecosystems is supported by universal tools for permanent modification and evolution of systems based on it.

5 Discussion

The development of AI systems is a complex and time-consuming work that requires the participation of specialists in various fields and domains - programmers, cognitive scientists, interface designers and domain experts.

We have to admit that the scientific community has not yet given a clear and understandable definition of AI systems, which has given rise to many interpretations and definitions of a wide range of "experts".

The situation requires a serious redefining and consolidation, first of all, of the scientific community.

1. It is important to determine what an AI system is. It is justified to give this definition, based on the range of cognitive abilities of the natural intelligence. As a basis I propose to take the list proposed by V.K. Finn (perhaps a little modified). In this case, it is easy to understand the "level" of the intelligence of the AI system. For example, a system based on neural networks implements (imitates) one function of natural intelligence - learning, a system based on

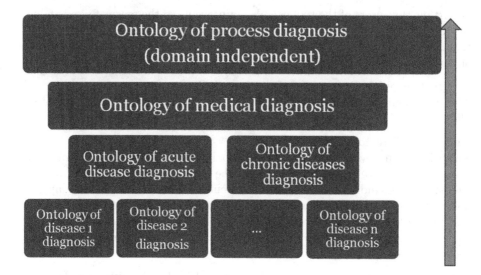

Fig. 1. Evolution of diagnosis process ontologies

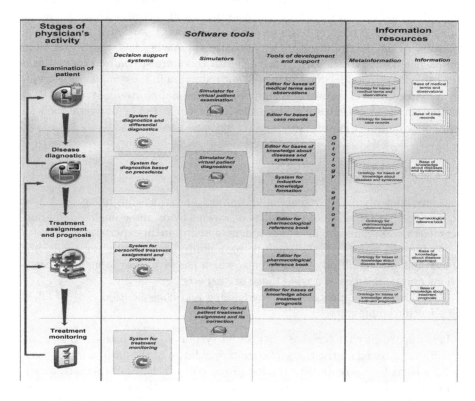

Fig. 2. Cloud infrastructure for creating AI systems in medicine

knowledge base, implementing the search and criticism of hypotheses with the generation of explanations - three functions of natural intelligence, etc. In this case, it is clear what functions the AI system lacks and what needs to be further implemented to increase its intelligence.

2. Technologies for AI system development. It is obvious that they should develop in two directions - the creation of universal tools and specialized, taking into account the specifics of the architecture, methods and models of AI, as well as having a set of tools for automating development. In this case, the scientific community faces a significant challenge in the development of universal and specialized methods of imitation of cognitive abilities providing coherence with other cognitive abilities, and technology developers have to provide instrumental support for their implementation. An important task is the transition from particular models to their generalization (see Fig. 1 Evolution of development of diagnosis process ontologies of Intelligent System Laboratory of Institute of Automation and Control Process FEB RAS).

3. Moving from demonstration prototypes to viable implementations. This requirement is important for all types of software systems, but it is especially important for AI systems. It is obvious that neither the knowledge base, nor the learning process, nor the realization of other intellectual functions can be complete and require permanent revision. Therefore, it is proposed to evaluate the implementation of AI systems not only from the point of view of listing simulated cognitive procedures, but also from the point of view of mechanisms implementing their viability. There is undoubtedly a significant role of tools for the creation of the AI system.

4. Use terminology. Today, there is a wide range of terminology used. The same concepts are called and interpreted differently, and vice versa. It is necessary to bring it (at least within the scientific community) to a common interpretation and designation.

5. Development of tools (universal and specialized). In my opinion, different implementations, different tools and approaches to creating tools for implementing AI is a positive factor in the development of AI. It is unlikely that in the near future we can expect "Babel", if we do not take into account the libraries and frameworks for creating systems based on neural networks, implementing, as discussed in this article, only one of the cognitive abilities. Creating tools is an extremely difficult and, unfortunately, often very thankless job that requires understanding both your own vast experience in this field, and analysis of the literature to generalize methods and models in order to create universal or specialized tools that implement them. Thus, sharing the experience of 30 years of development of the Protege system, M. Musen stated that new scientific results, the availability of alternative/competing systems and tools, feedback and user requests - these are the main drivers of the development of the Protege system [9]. Another issue is that today tool systems, even those created within the same professional community (IACPaaS and OSTIS platforms), although in different countries, supporting a very similar list of basic requirements and key principles of development, do not support compatibility with each other. At the same time, both

platforms have already accumulated a large range of reusable modules, components and implemented systems. For example, the IACPaaS platform has more than 200 active developers, and for example, an ecosystem created on its basis for solving a complex of intellectual problems in practical medicine and education [13], see Fig. 2, contains a terminological base of more than 27 thousand concepts, their properties and values, ontologies for diagnosis, monitoring, treatment of diseases (which is important independent of the section of medicine), knowledge bases only for the diagnosis of diseases containing more than 150 thousand vertices (knowledge bases have a semantic representation), as well as knowledge bases for drug and rehabilitation treatment, problem solvers for decision support systems, computer simulators, and other reusable components. Therefore, it is important to create an interested community of developers of AI tools and applications, which would develop a set of requirements for compatibility and integration of various types of tools and application systems (and, perhaps, a list of the main properties for which you need to compare tools with each other).

6. Intellectual property. This issue is also quite relevant and topical. It is important to preserve the intellectual property of knowledge in knowledge bases, services, and their components.

References

1. Gribova, V.: What technologies should be used to create artificial intelligence systems? Subjective view at the problem. Open Semantic Technology for Intelligent Systems, no. 4, pp. 57–62 (2020). ISSN 2415–7740
2. Rybina, G.V.: Intellektual'nye sistemy: ot A do YA. Seriya monografij v trekh knigah. Kn. 3. Problemno-specializirovannye intellektual'nye sistemy. Instrumental'nye sredstva postroeniya intellektual'nyh system (Intelligent systems: A to Z. A series of monographs in three books. Book 3. Problem-specialized intelligent systems. Tools for building intelligent systems), 180 p. Nauchtekhlitizdat, Moscow (2015). (in Russian)
3. Ogu, E.C., Adekunle, Y.A.: Basic concepts of expert system shells and an efficient model for knowledge acquisition. Int. J. Sci. Res. Int. J. Sci. Res. (IJSR) **2**(4), 554–559 (2013). India Online ISSN 2319–7064
4. Gribova, V., Kleschev, A., Moskalenko, P., Timchenko, V., Fedorischev, L., Shalfeeva, E.: The IACPaaS cloud platform: features and perspectives. In: Second Russia and Pacific Conference on Computer Technology and Applications (RPC), Vladivostok, Russia, 25–29 September 2017, pp. 80–84. IEEE (2017). https://doi.org/10.1109/RPC.2017.8168076
5. Gensym G2: The World's leading software platform for real-time expert system application. http://www.gensym.com/wp-content/uploads/Gensym-l-G2.pdf. Accessed 14 Jan 2020
6. Golenkov, V., Shunkevich, D., Davydenko, I.: Principles of organization and automation of the semantic computer systems development. Open semantic technologies for intelligent systems, no. 3, pp. 53–91 (2019)
7. Markidis, S., Chien, S.W.D., Laure, E., Peng, Vetter, J.S.: NVIDIA tensor core programmability performance and precision. In: IEEE International Parallel and Distributed Processing Symposium Workshops (IPDPSW), pp. 522–531, May 2018

8. Awan, A.A., Hamidouche, K., Hashmi, J.M., Panda, D.K.: S-Caffe: co-designing MPI runtimes and Caffe for scalable deep learning on modern GPU clusters. In: Proceedings of the 22Nd ACM SIGPLAN Symposium on Principles and Practice of Parallel Programming ser, PPoPP 2017, pp. 193–205 (2017)

9. Machine learning. Wikipedia, the free encyclopedia: internet-portal. https://en. wikipedia.org/wiki/Machine_learning. Accessed 14 Jan 2020

10. Musen, M.A.: The Protégé project: a look back and a look forward. AI Matters **1**(4), 4–12 (2015)

11. Gribova, V., Kleschev, A., Moskalenko, P., Timchenko, V., Shalfeeva, E.: The technology for development of decision-making support services with components reuse. In: Hu, Z., Petoukhov, S.V., He, M. (eds.) AIMEE2018 2018. AISC, vol. 902, pp. 3–13. Springer, Cham (2020). https://doi.org/10.1007/978-3-030-12082-5_1

12. Arskiy, Y.M., Finn, V.K.: Principi konstruirovaniya intellektualnih sistem. Informacionnie tehnologii i vichislitelnie sistemi, no. 4., 4–37 (2008). (Principals of intelligent system design. Inf. Tech. Comput. Syst. no. 4, 4–37 (2008)). (in Russian)

13. Gribova, V.V., Petryaeva, M.V., Okun, D.B., Tarasov, A.V.: Software toolkit for creating intelligent systems in practical and educational medicine. IEEE Xplore (2018). https://doi.org/10.1109/RPC.2018.8482130

Convergence of Applied Intelligent Systems with Cognitive Component

Boris A. Kobrinskii[1,2(✉)] and Anna E. Yankovskaya[3]

[1] Federal Research Center "Computer Science and Control" of the Russian Academy of Sciences, Institute of Artificial Intelligence Problems, Vavilova Street 44, kor.2, Moscow 119333, Russian Federation
kba_05@mail.ru

[2] Pirogov Russian National Research Medical University, Ostrovitianov Street 1, Moscow 117997, Russian Federation

[3] National Research Tomsk State University, Institute of Applied Mathematics and Computer Science, 36, Lenin Avenue, Tomsk 634050, Russian Federation
ayyankov@gmail.com

Abstract. This paper considers knowledge convergation problems for different types of intelligence systems with cognitive-based decision-making. The basis is semantic interoperability of knowledge bases, all of which are managed by knowledge metabase of subject domain or several adjacent domains. The concept of using an information system with various intelligent decision support systems provides for the formation of knowledge base rules based on synonyms. To make and to justify decisions in convergent intelligent systems, it is proposed to use two and 3-simplex prisms. 2-simplex prism is more appropriate if analyzed indicators are changing dynamically.

Keywords: Convergence of intelligent systems · Knowledge metabase · Modular structured knowledge bases · Semantic interoperability · Cognitive component

1 Introduction

Intelligent systems can be based on different knowledge acquiring and representation principles and constructed using various mathematical basis. The problem of integrating different intelligent systems is a known challenge both in theory and in practical implementations. In [28], the intelligent systems integration problem was considered from many viewpoints for different applications. One of the examples of such applications is integrating knowledge management and business process management [10]. However, a practice of intelligent system applications indicates the necessity to incorporate various aspects to control the processes and decision-making on intersections of different fields of knowledge.

Unfortunately, it is practically impossible to integrate different intellectual systems. Therefore, it is crucial to represent the hypothesis provided by different intelligence systems (including hybrid ones) using the same program product. Some hybrid systems are already jointly using different technologies. In the

V. Golenkov et al. (Eds.): OSTIS 2020, CCIS 1282, pp. 34–47, 2020.
https://doi.org/10.1007/978-3-030-60447-9_3

present paper, the convergence of different systems using semantic interoperation for knowledge bases [7]. The convergence is proportional to the interpenetration of these fields, and different concepts have to be combined if several requirements should be met.

Such convergence-based knowledge and data analysis was implemented in the self-learning intelligence medical system (IMS) [35]. Such an approach allows the construction of fail-safe diagnostic tests for cognitive systems.

The concept of convergence (from Latin "convergere") is related to the concept of synergy (from Greek "sinergeia" – joint action). However, the synergy-oriented knowledge integration model is proposed to be considered in the team collaboration mode [36]. In this case, collaboration moderator service is in charge of raising awareness of other contributors' priorities and requirements. The partner knowledge management service provides effective mechanisms to manage and utilize all knowledge in synergy system knowledge bases [14].

In the present paper, we expand the intelligent system convergence approach introduced in [13]. Specifically, we consider the knowledge management problem and the distributed knowledge base metasystem. Interaction of the metabase with a system of knowledge bases, including sub-bases, on the one hand, with databases of information systems, on the other hand, is discussed in depth. Cognitive graphics tools in decision making are presented in detail.

2 Knowledge Management and Convergence of Intelligent Systems

In a broad sense, convergence is considered as the interpenetration of different scientific fields. An example of intelligent recognition systems using convergent approaches is described in [7,31,32,35]. Methods used in these systems include logical combinatorial algorithms, soft computing, cognitive graphical tools, test pattern recognition, optimal selection of fault-tolerant diagnostic tests.

In this paper, we consider the problem of convergence and management of distributed knowledge bases, implying their sharing. In particular, bases do exchange knowledge pieces (fragment) while ensuring semantic compatibility. The above should be the basis for managing the formation of diverse information systems (IS). According to [9], critical issues in integrating information systems are the role of the "main" system and the relationship between systems that accumulate different data.

For efficient convergence, the principle of composite application and poor integration can be applied [15]. In this case, the system should be both flexible and redundant at the same time. We assume that the greater the interpenetration, the higher is the degree of convergence. The modular construction of knowledge bases is used to increase information systems management [12]. We note that this approach is applicable only with a certain level of operational knowledge exchange between control systems.

A meta-level in the form of generalized knowledge metabase provides a common knowledge field. Knowledge bases for individual problem areas are forming together a subject area knowledge base. Knowledge modules or sub-bases, characterized by semantic unity, allow displaying various specific information in certain areas. Knowledge exchange based on such modules accelerates the creation of integrated knowledge bases (superbases) controlled by the knowledge metabase. Such a metasystem is shown in Fig. 1. By constructing systems in such a way, new problems can be solved faster. A meta-level in the form of a metabase of generalized knowledge provides a common knowledge field.

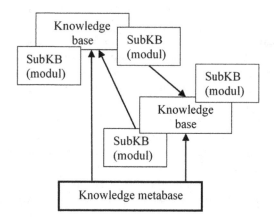

Fig. 1. Knowledge metabase

The managing knowledge metabase makes it possible to activate the corresponding knowledge bases for individual problem areas necessary for solving problems at the intersection of different problem areas. Two levels of convergence can be distinguished: interrelated areas within the same scientific discipline and interdisciplinary cooperation. For example, for the healthcare subject area, the first level includes the interaction of knowledge bases in the clinic fields – pulmonology and cardiology, and second level – knowledge bases in cardiology and molecular biology.

Such systems can be applied to problem-solving in the natural sciences, humanities, and technology areas.

The convergence of intelligent systems implemented on a knowledge bases network through key concepts of subject areas should correspond to an OSTIS system [6]. Thus, the hierarchy of knowledge, structured based on the thesaurus, should provide an effective and efficient exchange of fragments (modules) of knowledge bases.

3   Knowledge Bases Interoperability

The concept of semantic compatibility provides a fundamental basis for knowledge sharing. It can be done during the knowledge exchange on the base of using universal classifiers and knowledge formats.

For the model of the subject area, ontologies can provide a frequent semantic basis. The ontological model of knowledge, which has a modular structure, facilitates integration, exchange, and reuse [21]. An ontological framework can be used in the conceptual design phase [11].

The approaches to the coordination and ensuring the semantically correct interoperability of knowledge resources in the context of the subject area are developed in [3]. It includes the heterogeneity of ontological models and specifications at the conceptual semantics level and the transformation of heterogeneous data. Semantic interoperability validation can be performed by formal comparison with the execution of a reference association. The comparison considers semantic closeness according to an ontology that describes the association and exchanged data [25].

In converged systems, the exchange of modules (subbases of knowledge) is possible with shared control through the knowledge metabase. The real interaction of knowledge bases can only be realized with deep semantic interoperability.

Each of the concepts should be accompanied by synonyms so that synonymous concepts can replace terms entered by users. The semantic core of the domain knowledge metasystem should ensure the interoperability of knowledge bases of the domain's intellectual systems or complementary subject areas, which can be implemented on different principles. In this case, we automatically provide the compatibility of intelligent systems.

Regular correction of synonyms under expert control is a prerequisite for the subject knowledge metasystem (Fig. 2). New concepts can be included in the metabase by experts or rejected. Such an approach will help to increase the life cycle of the system. Simultaneously, the availability of a library of synonyms for users will increase their level of understanding of explanations given by intelligent systems of hypotheses (decisions). The above provides the user with access to the knowledge base rules and the synonyms used in the regulations.

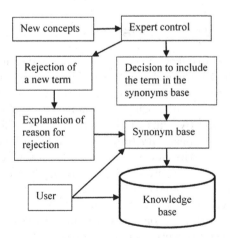

Fig. 2. Synonymic concepts base

In medicine, an example of a unified terminology is the widespread SNOMED CT (Systematized Nomenclature of Medicine – Clinical Terms) [20] or semantic networks and trees, creating hierarchical relationships between multiple terms and supporting multiple parents in one term [26]. An Arden Syntax was developed to exchange knowledge about the health state, which is a widely recognized standard for representing clinical and scientific knowledge in an executable format. Further extensions of the Arden Syntax might eventually help in realizing the vision of a global, interoperable, and shared library of clinical decision support knowledge [22].

4   Formalisms in the Intelligent Systems Construction

Issues of convergence of knowledge in intelligent systems based on various artificial intelligence methods should be considered at different stages of their creation. It includes extraction of knowledge from various sources, knowledge structuring, the formation of knowledge bases (rule bases) and logical inference mechanisms, and fact bases, explanation of proposed hypotheses, and implementation of interfaces. Let us consider some of these issues for medical applications. It should be noted that the signs observed in patients are data. Still, in the process of the physician's mental activity, relevant signs acquire the status of knowledge about diseases and serve as arguments for putting forward diagnostic or prognostic hypotheses and choosing treatment methods.

Ontologies of taxonomic terms in the "Resource Description Framework" (RDF) model can be used as a structurally-formalized representation. It is represented in the form of a triplet "subject - predicate - object." RDF is an abstract data model; that is, it describes the structure, methods of processing, and interpreting data [4]. For example, Metagenome and Microbes Environmental Ontology is based on RDF and presented visually on a Web browser [17,27,29].

5   Interactive Data Exchange

In the paradigm of the five-level medical information system (according to the Gartner classification [8]), the concept of MIS Mentor was introduced, implying a dialogue between the intelligent module and the user to request missing for decision-making data. This approach is especially crucial for the data exchange system between Intelligent Systems and Electronic Medical Records (EMR). The search for the information necessary to confirm the hypothesis in the databases of various EMRs can be carried out under the control of the knowledge metabase. Looking for decisions using a more complete data set improves the efficiency of intelligent systems. It corresponds to the point of view on missing information for decision making with higher accuracy [5].

A modular system diagram for extracting knowledge from various patient EMRs for managing the prevention of chronic diseases is shown in Fig. 3. Risk factors (RF) of chronic diseases accumulate and change over the life of EMR patients. Information about triggers that affect the body for a short period before the disease and risk factors can be given in different EMRs.

Knowledgebase (KB) of risk factors and disease triggers under knowledge metabase management allows identifying patients under disease threat. They are formed as bases or subbases (modules) of knowledge for various classes and pathology groups. KB convergence should provide the ability to monitor RFs and triggers during the life of patients.

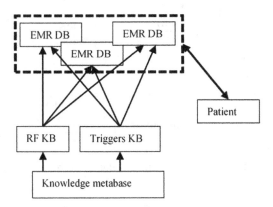

Fig. 3. Diagram of converged knowledge bases of risk factors and triggers of chronic diseases

Some intelligent systems can be immersed in the information system that provides solutions to various problems. In this case, the issue of their incompatibility arises. Therefore, we feel necessary to emphasize the need to solve the problem of exchanging data and messages. The structure of the terminological representation of domain knowledge should be uniform and replenished; otherwise, no convergence is possible.

The modular structure of knowledge bases will simplify and accelerate restructuring when new or adjusted knowledge is included. However, the modularity of knowledge bases, ensuring the speed of correction of rules in knowledge bases, has not yet been adequately reflected in intelligent systems' construction. At the same time, full user support should include various aspects of the technological process online and offline management, for which individual knowledge subbases can be used.

6   Intelligent Decision Support in Information Systems

When the user is working with an information system (IS), it is necessary to support different decisions, and more than one intelligent system or knowledge-based can be used. The efficiency of knowledge-driven information systems is improved by ensuring modular knowledge bases [12]. The general structure presented in Fig. 4.

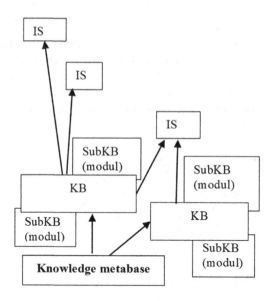

Fig. 4. IS, driven by intelligent systems

7 Specialized Modules for Decision Managing and Supporting

The medical informatics manual [8] emphasizes the need to make greater use of artificial intelligence systems as a cognitive assistant for a physician. For example, it is useful to search for specific clinical data patterns, indicating essential changes in the patient's health state. Computerized clinical decision support systems have seen rapid evolution and now commonly administered through electronic medical records with advanced capabilities and other digital clinical workflows [24].

The task is to implement the necessary functional properties and characteristics in the decision support modules that satisfy user requirements. Let us consider an example of the Russian healthcare system. A specialized module for assessing central hemodynamics with a graphical representation of information about cancer patients was created to support decisions in the intensive care unit [2]. In the form of visual representation, a six-axis polar diagram is used on each beam of which a specific hemodynamic parameter's value is shown.

Monitoring the human body's physiological parameters using intelligent systems for health protection or critical state patients should be based on the method of situation-driven control [16,18]. This method is advisable to use in any systems that undergo periodic or constant changes.

8   Cognitive Decision-Making Component

To study cognitive tasks that require the transformation of information presented in mind and the external environment, a theoretical structure of distributed representations, and a methodology of representative analysis are proposed. The basic principle of distributed representations is that a cognitive task is a set of internal and external images that can be characterized as an abstract structure of a problem. The underlying representation analysis strategy is to decompose the representation of a hierarchical task into its component levels so that the representational properties at each level can be independently examined [38]. The clustering of a certain kind of causation by internal workings functions for representation with robustness, and stabilization underpins the purchase of representational explanation [23].

The problem of convergence of intelligent systems is directly related to improving the efficiency of information systems. Of particular interest are cognitive graphic tools developed as part of artificial intelligence research in the 70s of the 20th century in [1,19,37]. Visual information began to be interpreted from the position of the knowledge contained in it. Cognitive Graphics tools (CGT) visually display a complex object, phenomenon, or process on a computer screen, allowing users to formulate a new solution, idea, or hypothesis based on visual elements. The CGT n-simplex was first proposed in [30] and was further developed in [32–34].

Initially, 2, 3 simplexes were used to create dynamic, intelligent systems. Later it was proposed to use 2-simplex prism (a triangular prism, at the base of which identical equilateral triangles are located - 2-simplexes), for various problem areas.

In dynamic, intelligent systems, the 2-simplex prism height corresponds to the considered time interval of the dynamic process [33]. It is divided into several time intervals. The number of intervals corresponds to the number of prognostic decisions. The distance between two adjacent 2-simplexes is proportional to the time interval (Fig. 5).

The cognitive tool "2-simplex prism" can be considered a converged dynamic, intelligent system (by dynamic we consider the human-based time scale - hours, days, weeks).

The distance from the base of the 2-simplex prism to the i-th 2-simplex h_i', representing the object under study at a given point in time, is calculated by the following formula:

$$h' = H' \cdot \frac{T_i - T_{min}}{T_{max} - T_{min}} \qquad (1)$$

where H' is the height of the 2-simplex prism, set by the user corresponding to the study duration, T_i – is the moment of the i-th fixation of the object's parameters under study, T_{min} and T_{max} are the moments of first and last fixations.

User-oriented graphical tools, including cognitive ones, are developed under the guidance of A.E. Yankovskaya [32–34]. They are designed to visualize information structures, identify patterns, substantiate decisions both for specific

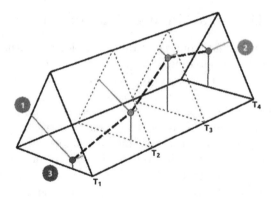

Fig. 5. Example of a 2-simplex prism used to visualize a dynamic process

problem areas that have a mapping in ordinary (natural) reality and for those that are invariant to problem areas, that is, that do directly correspond to the reality [33,35]. For example, the n-simplex cognitive tool (n = 2, n = 3) allows you to save the sum of the distances to the faces and the relationship between the distances [32]. This tool has no display in ordinary reality and, since it is invariant to problem areas, can be efficiently used for the convergence of intelligent systems. Display in ordinary reality is based on real objects images [31,34,35] by cognitive means.

Classification of CGT is given in [34]:

1. Naturalistic CGT, familiar graphic images of real objects are used as CGT. For example, visualization of the tree data structure of pathological processes in bronchus (bronchial asthma, Fig. 6).
2. CGT n-simplexes do not map in ordinary reality; CGT 2, 3-simplexes, not having a mapping in the ordinary reality.

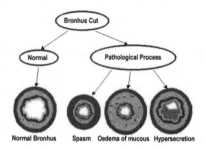

Fig. 6. Example of naturalistic based CGT

For synergetic intelligent systems, a cognitive tool 2-simplex prism is proposed that is invariant to problem areas. It was implemented for medical and other problem areas characterized by dynamic time changes (in differential diagnosis and the dynamics of the pathological process), as well as for geographic information systems taking into account changes in space (such as map distance) [33, 35].

For differential diagnosis of various diseases, the 3-simplex cognitive tool was used [32], which visualizes the degree of disease manifestation [33] and the presence of one or several out of 4 diseases, indicating the accuracy of each decision.

Diagnosis and intervention of organization stress using a 2-simplex prism is another exciting example of usage CGT. The idea of diagnosis is based on a three-step diagnosis for each stage of organization stress (1 – intenseness, 2 – adaptation, 3 – exhaustion) based on G. Selye's conception. This scenario is interesting because there are used four patterns (0 – for the absence of organization stress), which is more than can be visualized and justified in 2-simplex-prism. So there can be used two 2-simplex prisms: the one for the beginning of intervention (Fig. 7a) and another one for the ending of response (Fig. 7b). There is reasonable to use only one 2-simplex prism for cases. Then intervention begins from the intenseness or adaptation stage. This CGT is efficient for visualization of depression intervention process and justification of each intervention step's decision-making.

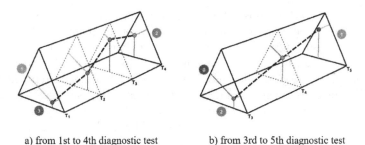

a) from 1st to 4th diagnostic test   b) from 3rd to 5th diagnostic test

Fig. 7. Results of diagnostic tests for organizational stress revealing using 2-simplex prism

Another exciting scenario of usage is an investigation of dependency of some objects parameters on the base of distance from some point. There is also reasonable to use a 2-simplex prism. The height corresponds to the distance from the initial point to the final destination. The distance between two adjacent 2-simplices corresponds to the distance between two points on a map. An example of a health problem diagnosis on the base of length is given in Fig. 8.

Since the 2-simplex prism is based on the use of 2-simplexes, all the properties of representing objects on the 2-simplex are also valid for the 2-simplex prism. 2-simplex prism can be used to simulate and display dynamic processes.

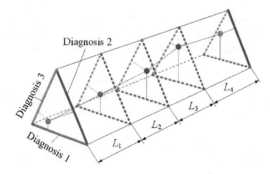

Fig. 8. Results of diagnostic tests for intelligent geoinformation systems

9   Conclusion

The convergence of intelligent systems with knowledge bases built on a modular principle provides new possibilities for managing the decision process in distributed information systems. We need technological solutions to combine software components from various developers, perform semantic integration, and implement standards for uniform knowledgebase modules that can be used for a low-level connection.

The cognitive tools proposed for use in converged intelligent systems can be divided by those that have and do not reflect ordinary reality. These tools are applicable for modeling various processes in problematic and interdisciplinary areas, such as medicine, genetics, psychology, sociology, ecology, geology, and others. For the decision-making and justification of it in concurrent intelligent systems, means of cognitive graphics in the form of 2, 3-simplexes have been developed. In the case of dynamic systems, 2-simplex prisms should be used. It was shown that cognitive tools usage allows making and justifying decisions for both static and dynamic intelligent systems.

The convergence of intelligent systems as part of Open Semantic Technology in cloud computing is one prerequisite for significant expansion of decision support capabilities in large information systems.

References

1. Axelrod, R.: Structure of Decision: The Cognitive Maps of Political Elites. Princeton University Press, Princeton (1976). https://doi.org/10.1515/9781400871957
2. Belyaev, E.G., Petrova, M.V., Shvyrev, S.L., Zarubina, T.V.: Ispol'zovanie informacionnoj sistemy "INTERIS" dlja sindromal'noj ocenki narushenij central'noj gemodinamiki u onkologicheskih bol'nyh v rannem posleoperacionnom periode [Using the INTERIS information system for the syndromic assessment of central hemodynamic disturbances in cancer patients in the early postoperative period]. Inf. Measur. Control Syst. **9**(12), 63–67 (2011). (in Russian)

3. Bova, V.V.: Ontologicheskaya model' integracii dannyh i znanij v intellektual'nyh informacionnyh sistemah [Ontological model of data and knowledge integration in intelligent information systems]. News SFU. Tech. Sci. **4**, 225–237 (2015). (in Russian)

4. Buraga, S.C.: A model for accessing resources of the distributed file systems. In: Grigoras, D., Nicolau, A., Toursel, B., Folliot, B. (eds.) IWCC 2001. LNCS, vol. 2326, pp. 224–230. Springer, Heidelberg (2002). https://doi.org/10.1007/3-540-47840-X_23

5. Coiera, E.: Guide to Health Informatics. CRC Press, Boca Raton (2015)

6. Golenkov, V.V., Gulyakina, N.A.: Semanticheskaya tekhnologiya komponentnogo proektirovaniya cistem, upravlyaemyh znaniyami [Semantic technology of component design of knowledge-driven systems]. In: Golenkov, V.V. (ed.) Open Semantic Technologies for Intelligent Systems (OSTIS-2015): Proceedings of the V International Scientific and Technical Conference, Minsk, 19–21 February 2015, pp. 57–78. BSUIR, Minsk (2015). (in Russian)

7. Hamilton, S.L., Gunther, E., Drummond, R.V., Widergren, S.E.: Interoperability - a key element for the grid and DER of the future. In: 2005/2006 IEEE/PES Transmission and Distribution Conference and Exhibition, Dallas, TX, USA, pp. 927–931 (2006). https://doi.org/10.1109/TDC.2006.1668622

8. Hieb, B.R., Handler, T.J.: 2007 CPR Generation Criteria Update: Clinical Decision Support. Gartner Research (2007). https://www.gartner.com/en/documents/502597/2007-cpr-generation-criteria-update-clinical-decision-sup

9. Jacklin, J.: Meeting new national requirements with existing local information systems: integration, integration, integration. Br. J. Healthcare Comput. Inf. Manag. **23**(4), 18–20 (2006)

10. Jung, J., Choi, I., Song, M.: An integration architecture for knowledge management systems and business process management systems. Comput. Ind. **58**, 21–34 (2007). https://doi.org/10.1016/j.compind.2006.03.001

11. Kitamura, Y., Kashiwase, M., Fuse, M., Mizoguchi, R.: Deployment of an ontological framework of functional design knowledge. Adv. Eng. Inf. **18**, 115–127 (2004). https://doi.org/10.1016/j.aei.2004.09.002

12. Kobrinskii, B.A.: Formirovanie medicinskih informacionnyh sistem, upravlyaemyh znaniyami [forming of medical information systems, knowledge management]. In: Golenkov, V.V. (ed.) Open semantic Technologies for Intelligent Systems (OSTIS-2016): Proceedings of the VI International Scientific and Technical Conference, Minsk, February 18–20 2016. pp. 89–92. BSUIR, Minsk (2016). (in Russian)

13. Kobrinskii, B.A., Yankovskaya, A.E.: The problem of convergence of intelligent systems and their submergence in information systems with a cognitive decision-making component. In: Golenkov, V.V. (ed.) Open Semantic Technologies for Intelligent Systems, pp. 117–122. Belarusian State University of Informatics and Radioelectronics, Minsk (2020)

14. Lorre, J.P., Verginadis, Y., Papageorgiou, N., Salatge, N.: Ad-hoc execution of collaboration patterns using dynamic orchestration. In: Popplewell, K., Harding, J., Poler, R., Chalmeta, R. (eds.) Enterprise Interoperability IV, pp. 3–12. Springer, London (2010). https://doi.org/10.1007/978-1-84996-257-5_1

15. Mocanu, M., Muste, M., Radu Drobot, V.L.: Composite application for water resource management. In: Dumitrache, L. (ed.) Advances in Intelligent Control Systems and Computer Science. Advances in Intelligent Systems and Computing, vol. 187, pp. 295–306. Springer, Heidelberg (2013). https://doi.org/10.1007/978-3-642-32548-9_21

16. Ocelíková, E., Madarász, L.: Multicriterial classification at situational control of complex systems. Micro CAD. In: International Scientific Conference, 7–8 March 2002, pp. 13–18. University of Miskolc, Hungary (2002)
17. Ondov, B.D., Bergman, N.H., Phillippy, A.M.: Interactive metagenomic visualization in a web browser. BMC Bioinform. **12**(1), 385 (2011). https://doi.org/10.1186/1471-2105-12-385
18. Pospelov, D.A.: Situation control presentation. In: Cybernetics and Situational Control Workshop, Columbus, Ohio, 20–24 March 1995, p. 11. Ohio State University, Ohio (1995)
19. Pospelov, D.A.: Desyat' "goryachih tochek" v issledovaniyah po iskusstvennomu intellektu [Ten "hot spots" in artificial intelligence research]. Intell. Syst. (MSU) **1**, 47–56 (1996). (in Russian)
20. Price, C., Spackman, K.: SNOMED clinical terms. Br. J. Healthcare Comput. Inf. Manag. **17**, 27–31 (2000)
21. Roda, F., Musulin, E.: An ontology-based framework to support intelligent data analysis of sensor measurements. Expert Syst. Appl. **41**, 7914–7926 (2014). https://doi.org/10.1016/j.eswa.2014.06.033
22. Samwald, M., Fehre, K., de Bruin, J.S., Adlassnig, K.P.: The Arden syntax standard for clinical decision support: experiences and directions. J. Biomed. Inf. **45**(4), 711–718 (2012). https://doi.org/10.1016/j.jbi.2012.02.001
23. Shea, N.: Representation in Cognitive Science. Oxford University Press, Oxford (2018)
24. Sutton, R.T., Pincock, D., Baumgart, D.C., Sadowski, D.C., Fedorak, R.N., Kroeker, K.I.: An overview of clinical decision support systems: benefits, risks, and strategies for success. NPJ Digit. Med. **3**(1), 17 (2020). https://doi.org/10.1038/s41746-020-0221-y
25. Szabo, C., Diallo, S.Y.: Defining and validating semantic machine to machine interoperability. In: Tolk, A., Jain, L.C. (eds.) Intelligence-Based Systems Engineering. Intelligent Systems Reference Library, vol. 10, pp. 49–74. Springer, Heidelberg (2011). https://doi.org/10.1007/978-3-642-17931-0_3
26. Tao, Y., Mendonca, E., Lussier, Y.: A "Systematics" tool for medical terminologies. In: AMIA Annual Symposium Proceedings 2003, pp. 1028–1030 (2003)
27. The National Center for Biomedical Ontology: Metagenome and microbes environmental ontology (2017). https://bioportal.bioontology.org/ontologies/MEO
28. Thórisson, K.R.: Integrated AI systems. Minds Mach. **17**, 11–25 (2007). https://doi.org/10.1007/s11023-007-9055-5
29. Wooley, J.C., Field, D., Glöckner, F.O.: Extending standards for genomics and metagenomics data: a research coordination network for the genomic standards consortium (RCN4GSC). Stand. Genomic Sci. **1**, 87–90 (2009). https://doi.org/10.4056/sigs.26218
30. Yankovskaya, A.E.: Preobrazovanie prostranstva priznakov v prostranstvo obrazov na baze logiko-kombinatornyh metodov i svojstv nekotoryh geometricheskih figure [The transformation of the feature space into the pattern space based on logical combinatorial methods and properties of some geometric figures]. In: Pattern Recognition and Image Analysis: New Information Technologies. In: Proceedings of the I All-Union Conference, Part II, pp. 178–181. Minsk (1991). (in Russian)
31. Yankovskaya, A.E.: Analiz dannyh i znanij na osnove konvergencii neskol'kih nauk i nauchnyh napravlenij [Analysis of data and knowledge on the basis on the sinergy of several sciences and scientific directions]. In: Intellectualization of Information Processing: 8th International Conference, pp. 196–199. MAKS Press, Moscow (2010). (in Russian)

32. Yankovskaya, A.: Logicheskie testy i sredstva kognitivnoj grafiki [Logical Tests and Means of Cognitive Graphics]. LAP LAMBERT Academic Publishing, Saarbrigge (2011). (in Russian)

33. Yankovskaya, A.: 2-simplex prism as a cognitive graphics tool for decision-making. In: Lee, N. (ed.) Encyclopedia of Computer Graphics and Games, pp. 1–13. Springer, Cham (2019). https://doi.org/10.1007/978-3-319-08234-9_285-1

34. Yankovskaya, A.E., Galkin, D.V., Chernogoryuk, G.: Computer visualization and cognitive graphics tools for applied intelligent systems. In: Proceedings of the IASTED International Conferences on Automation, Control and Information Technology, vol. 1, pp. 249–253 (2010). https://doi.org/10.2316/P.2010.691-081

35. Yankovskaya, A.E., Gorbunov, I.V., Hodashinsky, I.A., Chrnogoryuk, G.: On a question of the information technology construction based on self-learning medicine intelligent system. In: Proceedings of the 2016 Conference on Information Technologies in Science, Management, Social Sphere and Medicine (ITSMSSM), vol. 51, pp. 22–28. Atlantis Press (2016). https://doi.org/10.2991/itsmssm-16.2016.14

36. Yi, S., Su, L., Wen, P.: A study on R&D team synergy-oriented knowledge integration. In: Rebelo, F., Soares, M.M. (eds.) Advances in Usability Evaluation Part II, Chap. 17, pp. 154–163. CRC Press, Boca Raton (2012). https://doi.org/10.1201/b12324

37. Zenkin, A.A.: Kognitivnaya komp'yuterna grafika [Cognitive Computer Graphics]. Nauka, Moscow (1991). (in Russian)

38. Zhang, J., Norman, D.A.: Representations in distributed cognitive tasks. Cogn. Sci. **18**, 87–122 (1994)

Cognitive Knowledge Discovery in Social Sciences

Maria A. Mikheyenkova[1,2(✉)]

[1] Federal Research Center "Computer Science and Control",
Russian Academy of Sciences, 119333 Moscow, Russia
m.mikheyenkova@yandex.ru

[2] Russian State University for the Humanities, 125993 Moscow, Russia

Abstract. The paper deals with the knowledge discovery problem in subject areas with open empirical data, where formal means are absent and the procedures for the theories' formation are heuristic. The inherent challenges of the exact epistemology in such sciences are represented. Approaches to solving these problems by means of the JSM Method of automated support for research are described. We present the intelligent system JSM Socio implementing the JSM Method. JSM Socio automatically reproduces an imitation of the natural (rational) intelligence' abilities to solve various problems of sociological data analysis. We have studied various forms of constructive social activities by the JSM Socio, the results obtained are presented. The JSM Method of automated support for research proved to be the knowledge discovery tool.

Keywords: Knowledge discovery · Cognitive reasoning · JSM Method · Plausible reasoning · Formalized qualitative analysis · Social data analysis

1 Introduction

According to the main ideas that have defined the development of Artificial Intelligence, research in this area can be divided into two important parts – an epistemological part and a heuristic part. The first one means formalization and automatization (in computer systems) the cognition process as such. Modern researchers consider this to be critically essential for artificial cognitive systems creating [3]. The heuristic problem of how to create constructive tools for knowledge acquisition has a variety of approaches [19]. Computer intelligent systems – the ultimate product of AI – combine technological headway with formal means of cognitive activity modelling and imitation, being a tool for supporting and organizing scientific research. The most important result of practical realization of theoretical principles and procedures in intelligent systems (AI-systems) is

The work was partially supported by the Russian Foundation for Basic Research (project 18-29-03063mk).

© Springer Nature Switzerland AG 2020
V. Golenkov et al. (Eds.): OSTIS 2020, CCIS 1282, pp. 48–63, 2020.
https://doi.org/10.1007/978-3-030-60447-9_4

the possibility of new knowledge generation as a result of intelligent analysis of empirical data.

It is important to distinguish data analysis as pattern extraction from data (data mining) from intelligent data analysis (IDA) as new knowledge generation (knowledge discovery). The final product of the empirical data analysis should be a new knowledge, which is provided by the full process of Knowledge Discovery (KD) [7,29]. Data Mining represents one of the stages of this process—application of specific algorithms for extracting models (patterns) from data. The most important principle of intelligent data analysis is the tools' adequacy to the subject domain and the nature of the problem in hand (importance of this principle for social phenomena analysis is discussed in detail in [36])—in contrast to the dominant role of the tools in data analysis. Knowledge discovery includes the specification and simulation of the subject area and involves the use of a synthesis of cognitive procedures. In addition, the openness of available data and knowledge should be taken into account. One should also monitor the reproducibility of the analysis results (detection of regularities in the data) when expanding the databases of empirical facts.

Intelligent data analysis (knowledge discovery) is highly demandable for empirical research in areas where there are no developed formal tools and, accordingly, the procedures for theories formation are heuristic in nature. Machine learning methods are increasingly being used to extract information and knowledge from data in such areas as economics, political science, sociology [27]. Approaches that formalize the relevant research heuristics with implementation in computer systems are considered to be fruitful for the purpose of discovering new (with respect to the existing fact bases, FB, and knowledge bases, KB) knowledge. Heuristics, according to [30], refers to the organization of rules and methods for hypothesizing and obtaining new knowledge through cognitive reasoning [3] that includes plausible reasoning (primarily, induction and analogy). Such systems using artificial intelligence (AI) methods can be a tool for automated research support in sociology.

2   Problems of Epistemology and Heuristics of Social Sciences

Nowadays sociological research inherits the characteristic problems of epistemology of the Humanities. On the one hand, there is a tradition of critical perception of methodological monism (the uniformity of the scientific method, regardless of the difference in the areas of research [28,32,37]—up to the assertion of the fundamental dissimilarity of knowledge in the "nature sciences and cultural sciences" [33]. On the other hand, a movement towards objectification of the results of the empirical data analysis requires the use of sufficiently developed formal methods.

The mass nature of many social phenomena and the obvious difficulties of taking into account the many factors influencing them led to the dominance of quantitative (statistical) methods of studying social reality. Statistical methods of analysis deal with an impersonal subject and mainly quantitative data. This considerably complicates the task of studying interactions between individuals. These methods are quite effective in the analysis of global and mass phenomena, but are of little use at the microsociological level, where mechanisms, motivation, and incentives of social behavior "individual and group" are considered. Insufficiency of Quantitative approach in AI design for social sciences is the main idea in contemporary research [35].

Great expectations were initially connected with the use of the data mining (DM) method in the social sciences [4]. Data mining (DM) offers an approach to data analysis that differs in important ways from the conventional statistical methods. These methods can be characterized as variable-oriented and verification-driven, whereas DM is evidence-oriented and discovery-driven. DM are a variety of computer-intensive techniques for discovering structure and for analyzing patterns in data. These methods permit one to concurrently analyze heterogeneous and incomplete data (statistically unrepresentative data), including non-numerical data, consider nonlinear relationships, and visualize the results in a convenient and descriptive manner. Sociologists mastered artificial neural nets, recursive partitioning or decision trees, including CART (classification and regression trees), and, at last, systems of expert knowledge processing. Using generated patterns, DM can create predictive models, or classify things, or identify different groups or clusters of cases within data.

The accumulated experience on DM use generated a less optimistic view on these methods' possibilities. As a rule, it is very problematic to interpret (in terms of subject domain) and to explain the results obtained. Solving problems of classification, clustering, forecasting, etc. is far from solving the problem of formalizing the logic of reasoning and generating empirical regularities, i.e. obtaining new knowledge.

Studying the actions of human individuals (notably in their social relations with each other), analysis of the problems of local communities and individuals is based on qualitative methods (devoid of methodological unity) that transform subjective personal experience into typical models by informal means [14]. This leads to a significant dependence of the results on the attitudes, professional level and theoretical basis of the researcher.

Qualitative Comparative Analysis (QCA) [18], which is rather popular in sociological practice, can be considered as the certain approximation to the formalization of the typical qualitative methodology of case-study. The method is based on minimization of Boolean functions describing the dependence of the studied effect (presence or absence of phenomena, processes, structures) on presence or absence of some independent variables (possible causal conditions) and their combinations. The use of both nominal and interval scales for describing variables is allowed. In the second case, the interval values are converted into a fuzzy scale, which serves as the basis for a special table. This table is further transformed to the two-valued logic truth table to obtain conjunctive-disjunctive descriptions. Thus, only the analytical component of the research process is represented by formal means. Of course, formalism of this level seems obviously insufficient to study complex social phenomena [23].

The need for objectification of the results of qualitative analysis is to some extent satisfied due to the development of CAQDAS (Computer Assisted Qualitative Data AnalysiS systems) [34]. Second edition of the book (named earlier "the new bible for qualitative researchers using software') offers information and a productive review of some of the most commonly used software programs such as the latest versions of ATLAS.ti, HyperRESEARCH, MAXQDA, NVivo, QDA Miner and so on. These software programs have an impressive set of features. They create and visualize a hierarchy of codes, integrate categories by creating structured representations, generate a hierarchy of texts according to a sequence of coding steps and also provide hyperlinked navigation across the source text base and comparison of interpretations from different researchers working with the same material. Some of them allow one to export results to statistical packages and also have certain proper capabilities for quantified analysis.

However, CAQDAS programs does not replace the analyst but rather intensifies a researcher's capabilities. They do not perform qualitative analysis in the sense that SPSS (Statistical Package for the Social Sciences, the most popular international tool for sociological analysis) performs variables analysis; they merely make qualitative analysis easier by simplifying technical problem solving, mostly according to the qualitative methodology of grounded theory [6], which is referred to as "code analysis" by sociologists. The use of these tools provides systematic nature, efficiency and reliability of standard procedures for processing qualitative data (but not theory building), thereby increasing the validity of conclusions.

However, this is far from solving the actual problem of formal imitation and computer realization [8] of the inductive strategy of qualitative analysis. In general, research heuristics of sociologists aimed at building theories based on revealing dependencies from an analysis of empirical facts can be represented by a universal cognitive cycle "data analysis—prediction—explanation". The formalization of this process—KD (IDA)—provides a transition from phenomenology to a knowledge system in the sciences with a poorly developed formal apparatus.

The irreducibility of human reasoning to axiom-based proof schemes has determined both the "cognitive turn" of modern logic—a departure from "antipsychologism" [5], and the emergence of ideas of "humanization" of AI systems among AI founders [20,21]. At the current stage of AI development, the main goal of research in this area is believed to be a constructive imitation (only to some extent) and the strengthening of human cognitive abilities in intelligent systems (IS) [9].

The practical implementation in intelligent systems of the developed theoretical principles of epistemology and the means of constructive heuristics created on their basis means the automatization of the process of obtaining new knowledge as a result of knowledge discovery in empirical data.

3   JSM Method as a Tool for the Sociological Research

Examples of such systems are intelligent JSM-IS systems that implement the JSM Method of automated support for research [11] (JSM ASR). The JSM Method is a means of formalization, imitation and intensification of intelligent processes and a methodology for creating intelligent systems based on these tools. The method reproduces research heuristics of mentioned type, using cognitive plausible reasoning with ampliative conclusions (the consequences of which are not contained directly in the premises) in the open world in the form of synthesis of non-elementary cognitive procedures: empirical induction (analysis), structural analogy (prediction), abductive acceptance of hypotheses. A formal language with a descriptive and argumentative functions has been created for this purpose. Descriptive function provides initial data and knowledge structurization (with possibility of similarity determination) and formation of relation system. Argumentative function enables to formalize reasoning—analytic and prognostic procedures as well as procedures of explanation, falsification and possible verification of the results obtained [13, 31]. The induction is represented by formal elaborations and extensions of J.S. Mill's (after whom the method is named) inductive methods [26], abductive acceptance of hypotheses is based on the initial data explanation [15]. This kind of abduction solves the problem of forming a criterion for sufficient reason for inductive hypotheses acceptance and has a fundamental importance for open areas with poorly developed (or completely absent) formal apparatus.

The JSM ASR Method has seven components: applicability conditions (which can be formalized); JSM reasoning (the synthesis of cognitive procedures: induction, analogy, abduction); open quasi-axiomatic theories (QAT), which are means of knowledge representation; ordered strategies of JSM reasoning (distributive lattices of inductive procedures); metalogical tools for the subject area research; heuristics for empirical regularities revealing; Intelligent Systems implementing the JSM Method (IS-JSM). IS-JSM is a partner man-machine system, which automatically reproduces such abilities of natural intelligence as reasoning, argumentation, learning, and explanation. Such abilities as adaptation and correction of knowledge and the choice of reasoning strategy are implemented in an interactive mode.

Compliance with the conditions of applicability—essential ontological assumptions about the nature of the phenomenon under study—serves as the basis for effective use of the JSM Method as an KD tool. These conditions include the possibility of formalizing the structural (non-metric and non-statistical) similarity of facts and the presence in the Fact Database (FB) of positive $(+)$- and negative $(-)$-examples of the effects studied, including, respectively, $(+)$- and $(-)$-causes (real influences) of the effects. This allows you to automatically generate falsifiers of inductive hypotheses and can be considered as the basis for their abductive acceptance.

The realization of JSM-procedures and their combinations—strategies—in IS-JSM for the analysis of sociological data JSM Socio [25] is aimed at building a theory based on empirical facts which correlates with the methodological approach of qualitative analysis (using informal inductive inference). The system contains the means for knowledge extraction from fact bases (FB), for automated generation of hypotheses, as well as for explanation of existing facts on the basis of generated hypotheses. JSM Socio is considered to be a tool for formalized qualitative analysis of sociological data (FQASD): the study of individual behavior, generation of determinants of behavior and (empirical) typologization of society on their basis, as well as analysis and forecasting of respondents' opinions (a specific form of behavior). Expert-sociologist requirements reflected in the principles of formation of the information environment (fact base FB and the knowledge base KB) and the features of the user interface. Knowledge base includes both a priori (conventional) and obtained new knowledge as a result of the application of procedures.

According to the micro-sociological paradigm, the social interaction of individuals is forced by internal motivation and possible external influences, which necessarily requires a multi-parametric description [17]. This circumstance, coupled with the discrete nature of qualitative variables and the need to form a relational system that displays the semantics of the subject area, is taken into account by the descriptive function of the JSM-language intended for the FQASD.

The procedural semantics of the JSM Method can be formulated for various data structures that preserve the algebraic expressibility of similarity. The basic representation is the Boolean data structure. Accordingly, finite sets $\mathbf{U}^{(i)}$ and Boolean algebras defined on them $B_i = \langle 2^{\mathbf{U}^{(i)}}, \varnothing, \mathbf{U}^{(i)}, -, \cap, \cup \rangle, i = 1, 2, 3$, are considered. Thus, subjects of behavior are characterized by a set of differential indicators $\mathbf{U}^{(1)} = \{d_1, \ldots d_{r_1}\}$ that include elements of a social character (including value-normative attitudes), individual personality characteristics and biographical data. $\mathbf{U}^{(2)} = \{a_1, \ldots a_{r_2}\}$ is a set of behavioral effects (actions and attitudes), $\mathbf{U}^{(3)} = \{s_1, \ldots s_{r_3}\}$ is a set of situational parameters.

The individual variables $X, Z, V, \ldots$ of the 1-st kind (perhaps with subindices) and constants $C, C_1, C_2, \ldots$, being the values of the variables for objects and subobjects X, Z, V, etc., are introduced to represent persons (subject of behaviour) in the language, $X \in 2^{\mathbf{U}^{(1)}}$ The objects properties (for example, subjects' behavioural effects) are represented with the individual variables of the 2-nd kind $Y, U, W, \ldots$ (perhaps with lower indices) and constants $Q, Q_1, Q_2, \ldots$, $Y \in 2^{\mathbf{U}^{(2)}}$. The variables $S, S_1, \ldots$, and the constants $\bar{S}, \bar{S}_1, \ldots$, $S \in 2^{\mathbf{U}^{(3)}}$, of the 3-rd kind are introduced for the context (situational) parameters.

Social phenomena reflect the interaction of motivated, purposefully acting individuals taking into account important factors for them. Accordingly, the most important component of the JSM-language for FQASD is the representation of the opinion φ—the individual's personal perception of various aspects of social reality. Opinion is formed on the basis of the respondent's evaluation of the statements $p_1 \ldots p_n$, characterizing the situation of interaction and argue the attitude towards it [12]. Statement $J_\nu p_i$ is the answer to the question "what is the value v of the statement p?" $(i = 1, \ldots, n)$; $J_\nu p_i = t$ if $v[p_i] = \nu$; otherwise, $J_\nu p_i = f$; t and f are truth values of two-valued logic "true" and "false", respectively. In the general case of an m-valued poll (if there are m variants of sociologically interpreted estimates of statements $p_1 \ldots p_n$) the evaluation function $v[p_i]$, $(i = 1, \ldots, n)$ takes values $\nu \in \left\{0, \frac{1}{m-1}, \frac{m-2}{m-1}, 1\right\}$, $v[p_i] = \nu$. The j-th individual's opinion is the maximal conjunction $\varphi_j = J_{\nu_1^{(j)}} p_1 \& \ldots \& J_{\nu_n^{(j)}} p_n$, where $\nu_i^{(j)}$ is corresponding evaluation of statements p_i $(i = 1, \ldots, n)$, $\nu_i^{(j)} \in \left\{0, \frac{1}{m-1}, \frac{m-2}{m-1}, 1\right\}$, $j = 1, \ldots, m^n$. Let's $[\varphi_j] = \left\{J_{\nu_1^{(j)}} p_1, \ldots, J_{\nu_n^{(j)}} p_n\right\}$ be the set of corresponding conjunction's atoms.

Thus, the subject of social interaction is defined by the term $\bar{X}$ (complete object), $\bar{X} = \langle X, S, [\varphi]\rangle$. The complex multi-parameter structure of social systems and the various mechanisms of social interactions require an epistemologically adequate language for data representation (in particular, their parametrization), the choice of effective analysis procedures and strategies, and the conscious formation and enlargement of empirical facts set. In general case initial data are represented by (+)-facts $FB^+ = \left\{\langle \bar{X}, Y\rangle \mid J_{\langle 1,0\rangle}(\bar{X} \Rightarrow_1 Y)\right\}$ ("object (person, for example) $\bar{X}$ possesses the set of properties (effect of behavior) Y"), (−)-facts $FB^- = \left\{\langle \bar{X}, Y\rangle \mid J_{\langle -1,0\rangle}(\bar{X} \Rightarrow_1 Y)\right\}$ and facts that describe objects with previously undefined properties, $FB^\tau = \left\{\langle \bar{X}, Y\rangle \mid J_{\langle \tau,0\rangle}(\bar{X} \Rightarrow_1 Y)\right\}$, $FB = FB^+ \cup FB^- \cup FB^\tau$. This allows us to vary the relational structure depending on the sociological model [16, 25]. Types of "internal" truth values in JSM Method are $1, -1, 0, \tau$ (factual truth, factual falsity, factual contradiction ("conflict"), uncertainty) correspond to the semantics of the four-valued logic of argumentation [10].

The JSM-language use logical connectives of two-valued logic $\neg$, $\&$, $\vee$, $\rightarrow$, J-operators described above and quantifiers $\forall$, $\exists$. The basic predicates are $\Rightarrow_1$ and causal predicate $\Rightarrow_2$ (see below). Truth values $\langle \nu, n\rangle$, where $\nu \in \{1, -1, 0\}$, and (τ, n), are valuations of empirical facts and generated hypotheses (if $n = 0$ or $n > 0$, respectively). Truth values t, f are "external" truth values for representation of facts with valuation and plausible inference rules. J-operators take into account the difference between "internal" and "external" valuations.

The conditions that force the presence or absence of effects in the objects under consideration are interpreted as the causes of these effects. The source of determination in this case is the structural similarity of objects represented by qualitative (non-quantitative) characteristics. The JSM-research strategies are formed in accordance with the empirical situation of the study. The key procedures for inductive generation of causal hypotheses are formalization of Mill's inductive methods, as well as their extensions and elaborations. We give here the predicates description that is minimally necessary for our purposes; a more complete representation of the JSM Method formal means one can found in [11]. The minimal predicates representing the inductive similarity method are the predicates $M_{a,n}^+(V, W)$ and $M_{a,n}^-(V, W)$ for generating possible hypotheses on the causes of (+)- and (−)- facts, respectively (parameter n shows the number of applications of the plausible inference rules to the FB, a – agreement – is the "name" of the Mill's inductive similarity method).

Here $J_{(v,n)}\psi \rightleftharpoons \bigvee\limits_{s=1}^{n} J_{(1,s)}\psi$, $\nu \in 1, -1, 0$, ψ is a formula of JSM-language.

i. The predicate of "simple direct positive similarity" $\widetilde{M}_{a,n}^{+}(V, W, k)$ recognizes the local similarity $(\bigcap\limits_{i=1}^{k} C_i = V)\&(V \neq \varnothing)$ on the set of $(+)$-examples $J_{(1,n)}(C_i \Rightarrow_1 Q_i)$, $i = 1,\ldots,k$, $(k \geq 2)$, which is the basis for generating causal hypotheses. When identifying the similarities, the so-called "exhaustibility condition"—the requirement to consider all the $(+)$-examples in the FB that are similar by V—should be satisfied.

ii. The predicate describes the empirical dependency (ED)

$$\forall X \forall Y ((J_{(1,n)}(X \Rightarrow_1 Y)\&\forall U (J_{(1,n)}(X \Rightarrow_1 U) \to U \subseteq Y)\&V \subseteq X) \to (W \subseteq Y \& W \neq \varnothing))$$

of the type "similarity of objects in $(+)$-examples involves the similarity of effects". ED becomes a causal hypothesis after verification the corresponding rules.

$M_{a,n}^{\sigma}(V, W) \rightleftharpoons \exists k \widetilde{M}_{a,n}^{\sigma}(V, W, k)$, $\sigma \in \{+, -, 0, \tau\}$.

The predicates $\widetilde{M}_{a,n}^{\sigma}(\bar{V}, W, k)$, $M_{a,n}^{\sigma}(\bar{V}, W)$ for complete objects are formulated similarly with the substitution X by $\bar{X}$, V by $\bar{V}$. The similarity of objects is defined as $\bar{X}_i \cap \bar{X}_j = \langle C_i \cap C_j, S_i \cap S_j, [\varphi_i] \cap [\varphi_j]\rangle$, where $C_i \cap C_j$, $S_i \cap S_j$ and $[\varphi_i] \cap [\varphi_j]$ mean the intersection of corresponding sets.

The similarity predicates can be strengthened by additional conditions, including those allowing formalizing other Mill's inductive Methods (Method of difference, Joint method of agreement and difference), as well as condition of counterexamples prohibition). Let I^+ be the set of $M_{a,n}^{+}(\bar{V}, W)$ strengthening (indices), I^- be the set of $M_{a,n}^{-}(\bar{V}, W)$ strengthening. Then the JSM strategies $Str_{x,y}$ will be the sets of inductive inference rules $(I)_{x,y}^{\sigma}$, $\sigma \in \{+, -, 0, \tau\}$, such that they are formed by possible Boolean combinations of $M_{x,n}^{+}(\bar{V}, W)$ and $M_{y,n}^{-}(\bar{V}, W)$ predicates (for example, $M_{x,n}^{+}(\bar{V}, W) \& \neg M_{y,n}^{-}(\bar{V}, W)$ for $(I)_{x,y}^{+}$). Thus, induction in the JSM Method includes an argumentation condition that ensures mutual falsifiability of conclusions and constructiveness of their truth values generating. Here $M_{x,n}^{+}(\bar{V}, W) \rightleftharpoons M_{a,n}^{+}(\bar{V}, W)\&(x)$, $x \in I^+$, $M_{y,n}^{-}(\bar{V}, W) \rightleftharpoons M_{a,n}^{-}(\bar{V}, W)\&(y)$, $y \in I^-$. As a result of the rules $(I)_{x,y}^{+}$, $(I)_{x,y}^{-}$, $(I)_{x,y}^{0}$ and $(I)_{x,y}^{\tau}$, causal hypotheses $J_{(1,n+1)}(\bar{V} \Rightarrow_2 W)$, $J_{(-1,n+1)}(\bar{V} \Rightarrow_2 W)$, $J_{(0,n+1)}(\bar{V} \Rightarrow_2 W)$ and $J_{(\tau,n+1)}(\bar{V} \Rightarrow_2 W)$, are generated, respectively ($\Rightarrow_2$ is the causal predicate, $(\bar{V} \Rightarrow_2 W)$ means "$\bar{V}$ is supposed to be the cause of the properties W").

The partial order relations based on the relation of logical deducibility are generated on the sets of predicates $M_{x,n}^{+}(\bar{V}, W)$ and $M_{y,n}^{-}(\bar{V}, W)$. The partially ordered sets of predicates $M_{x,n}^{+}(\bar{V}, W)$ and $M_{y,n}^{-}(\bar{V}, W)$, as well as the rules of plausible inference including them, form distributive lattices, and the direct products of these lattices form possible strategies $Str_{x,y}$ of JSM reasoning [10]. Thus, the strategies of the JSM Method have an algebraically definable structure, and the difference in the plausibility degrees of the hypotheses generated as a result of application of various strategies is given constructively. The use of various strategies characterizes the mechanism of causal forcing of the studied effects, which means the realization of the idea of syntax adequacy to the semantics of the subject area and the method's adaptability to the class of problems being solved.

A characteristic feature of empirical sociological research is the incompleteness (openness) of knowledge about the world, facts available to the researcher and data describing them. Developed logical means of the method provide the research possibility: empirical regularities (ER) (nomological statements) discovery. ER are inductive operationally definable (non-statistical) generalizations of the results of formalized JSM heuristics when enlarging (changing) data. ER are defined as regularities in sequences of nested $FB(p)$, $p = 1, \ldots, s$, using various JSM strategies from the set $\overline{Str} = \{Str_{x,y} \mid x \in I^+, y \in I^-\}$ [11].

Let $V \Rightarrow_2^{(p)} Y$ and $X \Rightarrow_1^{(p)} Y$ designate basic JSM-predicates for $FB(p)$. Consider $\widetilde{FB}^{\sigma}(p) \subseteq FB^{\sigma}(p)$ $(p = 1, \ldots s)$ such that for every (σ)-fact from this subset there are (σ)-hypotheses that explain it, $\sigma \in +, -$.

$$\widetilde{FB}^{\sigma}(p) = \{\langle X, Y \rangle | \exists n \exists V \left(J_{\langle \nu, 0 \rangle}(X \Rightarrow_1^{(p)} Y) \& J_{\langle \nu, n \rangle}(V \Rightarrow_2^{(p)} Y) \& (V \subset X) \right) \}$$

$(\nu = 1$, if $\sigma = +$; $\nu = -1$, if $\sigma = -$).

It means that so called causal completeness axioms CCA^{σ} are hold for $\widetilde{FB}^{\sigma}(p)$. The degree causal (abductive) completeness $\rho^{\sigma}(p) = \frac{|\widetilde{FB}^{\sigma}(p)|}{|FB^{\sigma}(p)|}$ is considered to be the criterion of the limitation of FB enlarging process. If there is s for set value $\tilde{\rho}^{\sigma}$ of abductive acceptance of hypotheses such that $\rho^{\sigma}(1) \leq \ldots \leq \rho^{\sigma}(s) \geq \tilde{\rho}^{\sigma}$, $\sigma \in \{+, -\}$, JSM Method's abductive convergence occurs, and final $FB(s)$ has an acceptable abductive explanation.

Semantically, this means recognition of the conservation of the cause – effect relation, i.e. the constancy of the truth values type in inductive hypotheses about $\pm$-causes and hypotheses-predictions obtained using causal hypotheses in the conclusion by analogy. Acceptance of the results of the JSM study on the basis of a non-singular assessment of the quality of reasoning and hypotheses allows correction of open (quasi-axiomatic) empirical theories. In combination with falsification tools built into the JSM procedures, this forms a enhancement of the K.R. Popper demarcation criterion [31], which separates the completed scientific research from the pre-research and provides sufficient reason for grounded decision-making.

4   Application Experience

4.1   Typologization Problem

The most complete analysis of the social behavior of individuals is realized when considering the relational structure $\bar{X} \Rightarrow_1 Y$. The representation of the initial fact base by the predicates $\langle X, S, [\varphi] \rangle \Rightarrow_1 Y$ was used in the analysis of the constructive social activity, performed in collaboration with the Institute of Sociology, RAS. The chosen representation is related to the complex and multiple influence of the society characteristics on social activity. The focus of the study was the problem of society typology, based on the generation of determinants of political or civil forms of social activity.

The typologization of society, i.e the differentiation of social formations characterized by integrative properties, is one of the main tasks, and sometimes the goals of sociological research. Empirical typologization is the basis for constructing a theory and is the source of a scientific prediction.

Social types are formed on the basis of stable (reproducible) behaviour determinants generated on the final stage of JSM reasoning, which is the synthesis of cognitive procedures. Let $\bar{C}$ be the constant for the similarity $\bar{V}$. Consider the sets formed by objects including common causal dependencies.

$$\Gamma_i^+ \rightleftharpoons \{X \,|\, \exists n \exists Y (J_{\langle 1,0 \rangle} \left(\bar{X} \Rightarrow_1 Y\right) \& J_{(1,n)} \left(\bar{C}_i \Rightarrow_2 Y\right) \& \left(\bar{C}_i \subset \bar{X}\right))\},$$

$$i = 1, \ldots, l_1$$

$$\Gamma_j^- \rightleftharpoons \{X \,|\, \exists n \exists Y (J_{\langle -1,0 \rangle} \left(\bar{X} \Rightarrow_1 Y\right) \& J_{(-1,n)} \left(\bar{C}_j \Rightarrow_2 Y\right) \& \left(\bar{C}_j \subset \bar{X}\right))\},$$

$$j = l_1 + 1, \ldots, l_2$$

Remind that in accordance with the conditions of mutual falsification in the JSM Method's inductive inference rules $\forall i \forall j (\bar{C}_i \neq \bar{C}_j)$; $|\Gamma_i^+| \geq 2$, $|\Gamma_j^-| \geq 2$, in accordance with induction parameter k, $i = 1, \ldots, l_1$, $j = l_1 + 1, \ldots, l_2$.

Consider the partial order relation $\Gamma_{i_p}^+ \prec \Gamma_{i_q}^+$, if $\bar{C}_{i_q} \subset \bar{C}_{i_p}$. The number of vertices of this order's diagram $l_1 \leq 2^{r_1} - r_1 - 1$, $r_1 = |FB^+|$. The typology is based on the maximal vertices of the diagram, to which the following social groups correspond

$$\Gamma_i^+ \rightleftharpoons \{X \,|\, \exists n \exists Y \left(J_{\langle 1,0 \rangle} \left(\bar{X} \Rightarrow_1 Y\right) \& J_{(1,n)} \left(\bar{C}'_i \Rightarrow_2 Y\right) \& \left(\bar{C}'_i \subset \bar{X}\right)\right) \&$$
$$\neg \exists \bar{V} J_{(1,n)} \left(\bar{V} \Rightarrow_2 Y\right) \& \left(\bar{V} \subset \bar{X}\right) \&(\bar{C}'_i \subset \bar{V})\}, \; i = 1, \ldots, l'_1, \, l'_1 \leq l_1$$

The partial order relation for Γ_j^- is defined similarly, the maximal vertices of this order's diagram Γ_j^-, $j = l_1 + 1, \ldots, l'_2$, $l'_2 \leq l_2$, form the basic typology.

4.2 Constructive Social Activities

A concept and model for the study of the determinants of social behavior (political/civic participation/non-participation) was formed, parameterization of the initial data with the inclusion of situational parameters—a set of socio-economic and functional characteristics of the respondent's area of residence (administrative status of the city, population income, cultural status, etc.), representing the territorial context of actions was proposed. The set of potential determinants included individual characteristics of the respondents' status; opinions, assessments that characterize the civil position. Different levels of determinations (situational, value, normative) were taken into account. Political activists—participants in political actions, (+)-examples in the JSM Method language—opposed (was considered as (−)-examples) civil activists (members of public organizations, do not participate in political activities), as well as helping individuals and nowhere involved passive citizens.

Visualization of the results of a computer experiment in the form of a "hypothesis tree" provides the sociologist with the opportunity to interpret the results and build a typology based on the revealed determinants. The basis of typologization—"the core"—is formed by the maximal intersections of respondents' descriptions, i.e. by maximal vertices Γ_i^+, Γ_j^- of the corresponding diagrams. Similarities of subsets of respondents included in the maximum intersection allow to identify additional "peripheral" features. Peripheral features in different combinations form subtypes, which makes it possible to characterize the nuances of the position of subjects belonging to the same type of behavior, i.e. to suggest typology clarification.

As a result, the characteristic features of social types that implement various forms of social activity—political, civil, individual and passive (lack of social activity)—were described, and the features of interaction between these types were revealed. A non-trivial meaningful conclusion concerns the self-reference of "political activists" and "active citizens". Political activists consistently attribute the status of the subject of social action to themselves, denying this status to others. In other words, a feature of all political activists (who are representatives of systemic political parties in Russia regions) is the "leader" ideology, which is transmitted from political authorities to political activists. This seems to be due to the fact that the recognition of civic partners as social actors is uncomfortable for political activists, since it implicitly calls into question their social role. However, the rejection of partnerships with active citizens, attributing them the role of followers destroys the civil dialogue. On the contrary, active citizens ascribe to citizens the status of subjects of social action and declare their own readiness to participate in solving social problems and to unite.

A significant contribution of the regional context to the difference in forms and degrees of civic engagement was identified. This allows us to talk about the influence of the social system on the formation of individual behavioral strategy and the danger of transferring contextual features to the individual level.

The similarity of socio-demographic characteristics and the similarity of basic signs of social behavior of corporate, independent and combining both types of civil activity of volunteers, in particular, a high level of interpersonal trust, was found. The phenomenon of "open social borders" between "systemic" and "non-systemic" civil activists, discovered by means of the JSM Method, turned out to be interesting. A rather intense mobility between these groups was revealed, which indicates that there is no value confrontation among representatives of different socially active communities. This effect is difficult to detect by statistical methods.

4.3   Civic Activity: Volunteer Movement

The obtained results aroused interest in the study of various forms of non-political (civic) activity. The material was a study of helping (pro-social) behavior, including semantic opposition "private helping behavior—volunteering". The first is situational, sporadic, i.e. is an act of social action. The second is a reflective, prolonged social activity. The work is also carried out in collaboration with researchers from the Institute of Sociology of Russian Academy of Sciences on the empirical data provided by them.

Based on the proposed conceptual model of the research object, a structure of empirical data (a set of variables and indicators) was formed on the basis of a sociological study in different organizations and different regions of the country. Respondents are described by socio-demographic and status characteristics, situational characteristics represent the development of the locality and other parameters of the regional context, opinions and assessments characterize the value aspects of relations between people, their attitude to volunteering and to the organization of this activity where respondents work.

As a result of the method operation, typological groups were formed for both independent volunteering and corporate volunteering, which is included in the corporate social responsibility program implemented by the organization. The results of the analysis of a group of "involved" volunteers (combining both types of helping behavior) using the JSM Method indicate the significance of value-motivational factors for this type of social activity.

Applied conclusions for companies' social policy in relation to volunteering can consist in the specification of a policy for using volunteers with different types of motivation for different corporate programs. In particular, the "involved" are able to participate in building a long-term social responsibility policy of their company. "Corporate", in accordance with their rather strict loyalty principles, are able to implement existing projects in a disciplined manner. Independent volunteers can hardly be counted on for more than one-time charity events (such as buying gifts for recipients).

Volunteering is a complex social phenomenon that requires serious study. It represents a valuable collective behavior that creates the phenomena of practical solidarity. These phenomena are socially significant both in everyday life (for vulnerable groups) and in emergency situations when large groups of people need emergency assistance (natural and social disasters).

5   Conclusion

The proposed approach to empirical typologization provides a formal reproduction and implementation in intelligent systems of inductive research heuristics of sociologists. The synthesis of cognitive procedures – induction, analogy, and abduction – allows to study the individual behavior and to discover its determinants, the latter being followed by the typologization of society.

Note that the constructed social types are determined by the initial information (the base of facts, including positive and negative examples of the phenomenon under consideration), and by particular JSM-strategy—the predicates of inductive inference $M_{x,n}^+(\bar{V}, W)$ and $M_{y,n}^-(\bar{V}, W)$ used. The stability of the generated typology is achieved as a result of the complete JSM research [11], which reveals invariants in a set of hypotheses under enlargement of the BF in different ways.

Knowledge discovery is performed by computer systems that implement an intellectual process represented by the interaction of the mental process and the cognitive process (controlled by the mental one) [22]. The formal representation of the universal cognitive cycle "data analysis – prediction – explanation" provides imitation of natural (rational) intelligence abilities (reasoning, argumentation, learning, explanation of the results obtained) and allows reproduction in intelligent computer systems in automatic mode. However, a poorly formalized mental process, including attitudes, imperatives, goal-setting, the formation of open empirical theories and their adaptation in the context of data and knowledge correction, requires human participation and can be implemented in such systems only in an interactive mode.

For the effective implementation of knowledge discovery, which does not replace human intelligence, but rather intensify it, a transition from the "man-machine" opposition to partner man-machine systems is necessary ([1], p. 64). Even the successful implementation of the descriptive function of a formal language depends (to a large extent) on the meaningful interpretation of the cognizing subject (expert). Interactive pre-processing of open empirical data, control of the use of formalized heuristics, expert evaluation of generated empirical regularities ensure meaningfulness of the results obtained and determine the effectiveness in a specific study of the argumentative function of the language. The interpretability and explainability of the results generated by the IS tools play a fundamental role in the acceptance of KD results, since the responsibility for final decisions is the human prerogative. We can say that it was the widespread use of AI methods, the results of which are uninterpretable, that showed their limitations in solving many problems and aroused interest in research in Explainable Artificial Intelligence [2].

Intelligent systems that implement the JSM Method are a technological means of exact epistemology and are partner human-machine systems. They effectively implement the generation of new knowledge, but at the same time do not replace, but support and strengthen the meaningful work of the researcher in various subject areas, including social sciences.

This work is an extended version [24], it includes a more detailed review and formal apparatus, as well as some new results.

Acknowledgments. The authors would like to thank Dr. Svetlana G. Klimova, Leading Researcher from Federal Scientific and Research Sociological Centre of Russian Academy of Sciences for many years of cooperation.

References

1. The AI Index 2018 Annual Report. Technical report, AI Index Steering Committee, Human-Centered AI Initiative, Stanford University, Stanford, CA, December 2018. https://hai.stanford.edu/ai-index-2018. 94 p.
2. IJCAI 2019 Workshop on Explainable Artificial Intelligence (XAI) (2019). https://sites.google.com/view/xai2019/home

3. Anshakov, O.M., Gergely, T.: Cognitive Reasoning: A Formal Approach. Cognitive Technologies. Springer, Heidelberg (2010). https://doi.org/10.1007/978-3-540-68875-4. https://www.springer.com/gp/book/9783540430582
4. Attewell, P., Monaghan, D.: Data Mining for the Social Sciences: An Introduction. Data Mining for the Social Sciences (2015)
5. van Benthem, J.: Logic and reasoning: do the facts matter? Studia Logica **88**(1), 67–84 (2008). https://doi.org/10.1007/s11225-008-9101-1
6. Corbin, J., Strauss, A.: Basics of Qualitative Research: Techniques and Procedures for Developing Grounded Theory, 4th edn. SAGE Publications, Thousand Oaks (2015)
7. Fayyad, U., Piatetsky-Shapiro, G., Smyth, P.: From data mining to knowledge discovery in databases. AI Mag. **17**(3), 37–37 (1996). https://doi.org/10.1609/aimag.v17i3.1230. https://www.aaai.org/ojs/index.php/aimagazine/article/view/1230
8. Fielding, N.G.: Qualitative research and our digital futures. Qual. Inq. **20**(9), 1064–1073 (2014). https://doi.org/10.1177/1077800414545237
9. Finn, V.K.: Toward structural cognitology: phenomenology of consciousness form the point of view of artificial intelligence. Russ. J. Commun. **2**(1–2), 81–104 (2009)
10. Finn, V.K.: On the class of JSM reasoning that uses the isomorphism of inductive inference rules. Sci. Tech. Inf. Process. **44**(6), 387–396 (2017). https://doi.org/10.3103/S0147688217060041
11. Finn, V.K.: On the heuristics of JSM research (additions to articles). Autom. Doc. Math. Ling. **53**(5), 250–282 (2019). https://doi.org/10.3103/S0005105519050078
12. Finn, V.K., Mikheyenkova, M.A.: Plausible reasoning for the problems of cognitive sociology. Log. Log. Philos. **20**(1–2), 111–137 (2011). https://doi.org/10.12775/LLP.2011.006. https://apcz.umk.pl/czasopisma/index.php/LLP/article/view/LLP.2011.006
13. Finn, V.: Iskusstvennyj Intellekt: metodologija, primenenija, filosofija [Arificial Intelligence: Methodology, Applications, Philosophia], p. 448. URSS, Moscow (2018)
14. Hammersley, M.: What is Qualitative Research? Continuum/Bloomsbury, London (2013). http://www.bloomsbury.com/uk/what-is-qualitative-research-9781849666091/
15. Josephson, J.R.: Smart inductive generalizations are abductions. In: Flach, P.A., Kakas, A.C. (eds.) Abduction and Induction: Essays on their Relation and Integration. Applied Logic Series, pp. 31–44. Springer, Dordrecht (2000). https://doi.org/10.1007/978-94-017-0606-3
16. Klimova, S.G., Mikheyenkova, M.A.: Formal methods of situational analysis: experience from their use. Autom. Doc. Math. Linguist. **46**(5), 183–194 (2012). https://doi.org/10.3103/S0005105512050032
17. Luhmann, N.: Social Systems. Stanford University Press, Stanford (1996). http://www.sup.org/books/title/?id=2225
18. Marx, A., Rihoux, B., Ragin, C.: The origins, development, and application of Qualitative Comparative Analysis: the first 25 years. Eur. Political Sci. Rev. **6**(1), 115–142 (2014). https://doi.org/10.1017/S1755773912000318. https://www.cambridge.org/core/journals/european-political-science-review/article/origins-development-and-application-of-qualitative-comparative-analysis-the-first-25-years/88705E347335A40769AA83787748D35F
19. McCarthy, J.: Epistemological problems of artificial intelligence. In: Webber, B.L., Nilsson, N.J. (eds.) Readings in Artificial Intelligence, pp. 459–465. Morgan Kaufmann, January 1981. https://doi.org/10.1016/B978-0-934613-03-3.50035-0. http://www.sciencedirect.com/science/article/pii/B9780934613033500350

20. McCarthy, J.: From here to human-level AI. Artif. Intell. **171**(18), 1174–1182 (2007). https://doi.org/10.1016/j.artint.2007.10.009. http://www.sciencedirect.com/science/article/pii/S0004370207001476
21. McCarthy, J.: The well-designed child. Artif. Intell. **172**(18), 2003–2014 (2008). https://doi.org/10.1016/j.artint.2008.10.001. http://www.sciencedirect.com/science/article/pii/S0004370208001380
22. Mikheenkova, M.A., Finn, V.K.: Myslitel'nye i poznavatel'nye procedury v kognitivnoj sociologii [mental and cognitive procedures in cognitive sociology]. In: VIII mezdunarodnaja konferencija po kognitivnoj nauke: tezisy dokladov [VIIIth International Conference on Cognitive Science: Abstracts], pp. 1133–1136. Institut Psihologii RAN, Moscow (2018). https://cogconf.ru/materialy-konferentsii/. 1368 p
23. Mikheyenkova, M.A.: On the logical tools of intelligent sociological data analysis. Sci. Tech. Inf. Process. **37**(6), 386–397 (2010)
24. Mikheyenkova, M.A.: On the approach to intelligent data analysis in the social sciences. In: Golenkov, V.V. (ed.) Open Semantic Technologies for Intelligent Systems. Research Paper Collection, vol. 4, pp. 129–132. Belarusian State University of Informatics and Radioelectronics (2020). https://proc.ostis.net/ru/digital-proceedings/. 356 p
25. Mikheyenkova, M.A., Klimova, S.G.: Knowledge discovery in social research. Autom. Doc. Math. Ling. **52**(6), 318–329 (2018). https://doi.org/10.3103/S0005105518060079. https://doi.org/10.3103/S0005105518060079
26. Mill, J.: A System of Logic Ratiocinative and Inductive, Being a Connected View of the Principles of Evidence and the Methods of Scientific Investigation. Parker, Son and Bowin, London, England (1843). http://www.gutenberg.org/files/27942/27942-h/27942-h.html
27. Molina, M., Garip, F.: Machine learning for sociology. Annu. Rev. Sociol. **45**(1), 27–45 (2019). https://doi.org/10.1146/annurev-soc-073117-041106. https://www.annualreviews.org/doi/10.1146/annurev-soc-073117-041106
28. Parsons, T.: On theory and metatheory. Humboldt J. Soc. Relat. **7**(1), 5–16 (1979). https://www.jstor.org/stable/23261746
29. Piatetsky-Shapiro, G.: Data mining and knowledge discovery 1996 to 2005: overcoming the hype and moving from "university" to "business" and "analytics". Data Mining Knowl. Discov. **15**(1), 99–105 (2007). https://doi.org/10.1007/s10618-006-0058-2
30. Polya, G.: Mathematics and Plausible Reasoning (Reprint of 1954 Princeton University Press Edition). Martino Fine Books, Eastford (2014)
31. Popper, K.: Evolutionary epistemology. In: Evolutionary Theory: Paths into the Future, chap., pp. 239–255. John, Chichester (1984). 294 p
32. Popper, K.. In Search of a Better World. Lectures and Essays from Thirty Years. Routledge, London, pp. 64–81 (1995). https://www.routledge.com/In-Search-of-a-Better-World-Lectures-and-Essays-from-Thirty-Years/Popper/p/book/9780415135481
33. Rickert, H.: Kulturwissenschaft und Naturwissenschaft. Celtis Verlag, Berlin (2014)
34. Silver, C., Lewins, A.: Using Software in Qualitative Research: A Step-by-Step Guide, 2nd edn. 55 City Road, London (2019). https://doi.org/10.4135/9781473906907. https://methods.sagepub.com/book/using-software-in-qualitative-research-2e

35. Sloane, M., Moss, E.: AI's social sciences deficit. Nat. Mach. Intell. **1**(8), 330–331 (2019). https://doi.org/10.1038/s42256-019-0084-6. https://www.nature.com/articles/s42256-019-0084-6
36. Sorokin, P.A.: Fads and Foibles in Modern Sociology and Related Sciences, no. viii. Greenwood Press, Westport (1976). 357 p. http://www.catalog.hathitrust.org/Record/000697211
37. Wright, G.V.: Explanation and Understanding. Cornell University Press, Ithaca (1971)

Ontological Approach for Standards Development Within Industry 4.0

Valery Taberko[1] , Dzmitry Ivaniuk[1] , Daniil Shunkevich[2(✉)] ,
and Oleksandr Pupena[3]

[1] JSC "Savushkin Product", Brest, Republic of Belarus
{tab,id}@pda.savushkin.by
[2] Belarusian State University of Informatics and Radioelectronics,
Minsk, Republic of Belarus
shunkevich@bsuir.by
[3] National University of Food Technologies, Kyiv, Ukraine
pupena_san@ukr.net

Abstract. In this paper, we propose an approach to automating the processes of creating, developing and applying standards based on OSTIS Technology. The problems of modern approaches to the development, maintenance and application of standards are considered in detail, special attention is paid to standards in the field of Industry 4.0, such as ISA-88 and ISA-95, their role in the context of Industry 4.0 and problems specific to standards in this field are considered. The paper proposes an approach to the development of standards based on the ontological approach and involving the transformation of the standard into a knowledge base developed by a distributed team of developers directly in the process of its use. It is proposed to use OSTIS Technology as the basis for building this kind of system. We consider a prototype information system for employees of a batch production enterprise that implements the proposed approach, as well as examples of the integration of such a system with production systems.

Keywords: Standards · Ontologies · Industry 4.0 · OSTIS · ISA-88

1 Introduction

This work evolves the ideas discussed in [17] and in particular contains a more detailed analysis of existing works related to the use of ontologies as a means of formalizing standards in the context of Industry 4.0 was carried out. In addition, the paper presents a new version of tools for organizing the process of the standard development and maintaining, as well as tools for integrating of the knowledge base describing the standard and the software used in the enterprise.

Each developed sphere of human activity is based on a number of standards formally describing its various aspects – a system of concepts (including terminology), a typology and sequence of actions performed during the application

© Springer Nature Switzerland AG 2020
V. Golenkov et al. (Eds.): OSTIS 2020, CCIS 1282, pp. 64–80, 2020.
https://doi.org/10.1007/978-3-030-60447-9_5

process of appropriate methods and means, a model of a production facility, type and composition of project documentation accompanying activities and more.

The presence of standards allows us to solve one of the key problems that is relevant for any technology, especially for rapidly developing computer information technologies, the **compatibility problem** [6]. Compatibility can be considered in various aspects, from the consistency of terms in the interaction of process participants to the consistency of actions performed during the technology application. The latter ensures that the results of the same actions performed by different participants coincide.

Despite the development of information technology, at present the vast majority of standards are presented either in the form of traditional linear documents, or in the form of web resources containing a set of static pages linked by hyperlinks. This approach to the presentation of standards has a number of significant drawbacks, that finally leads to the fact that the overhead costs of maintaining and applying the standard actually exceed the benefits of its application [13].

2   State of the Arts

Analysis of the work allowed to formulate the most important and general problems associated with the development and application of modern standards in various fields [13, 18]:

- duplication of information within the document describing the standard;
- the complexity of maintaining the standard itself, due, among other things, to the duplication of information, in particular, the complexity of terminology changing;
- the problem of internationalization of the standard – in fact, translating the standard into several languages makes it necessary to support and coordinate independent versions of the standard in different languages;
- inconvenience of applying the standard, in particular, difficulties while searching for the necessary information, and, as a consequence, complexity of studying the standard;
- inconsistency in the form of various standards among themselves, as a result – the complexity of the automation of processes of standards development and application;
- the complexity of the automation of checking the conformity of objects or processes with the requirements of a particular standard;
- and others.

These problems are mainly related to the presentation of standards. The most promising approach to their solution is the transformation of each specific standard into a knowledge base, which is based on a set of ontologies corresponding to this standard [2, 6, 13, 18, 19]. This approach allows us to significantly automate the development processes of the standard and its application.

The task of any standard in the general case is to describe an agreed system of concepts (and related terms), business processes, rules and other laws, methods for solving certain classes of problems, etc. *ontologies* are successfully used to formally describe this kind of information. Moreover, at present, in a number of areas, instead of developing a standard in the form of a traditional document, the corresponding ontology is being developed [4,7,11,12]. This approach provides obvious advantages in terms of automating the standards agreeing and application processes. In addition, there are a number of works related to coreference resolution of ontologies and, accordingly, standards presented in the form of ontologies [5], as well as the automation of the processes of building ontologies based on natural language texts, in particular, standards [14].

As an example, we consider the standard **ISA 88** [8] – the fundamental standard for batch production. The standard is widely used at enterprises in America and Europe, it is actively implemented in the territory of the Republic of Belarus, however, it has a number of disadvantages listed below.

Another popular standard in the context of industry 4.0 is **PackML** (Packaging Machine Language) [10]. **PackML** is an industry standard (in fact) for describing control systems for filling machines. Its main purpose is to simplify the development of such systems, abstract from hardware implementation and provide a single interface for interaction with the SCADA and MES levels. This standard defines both software elements (software modules for industrial controllers) and general principles for the development of packaging lines.

These and other standards are currently distributed in the form of documents. Gradually, scientists and practitioners are considering the creation and use of ontologies in the maintenance and use of standards. Work [9] gives great survey of current state of art in ontologies approach in context of Industry 4.0.

Given that in the field of enterprise management, the ISA-95 and ISA-88 standards are fundamental, it is reasonable that the first work in this direction of automation is devoted to ontologies specifically for these standards. However, we managed to find only two works [2,19], which deal with the problems of ontologies for the standards of the ISA-88 series. The authors of [2] speak of the almost complete absence of research in this direction. The authors of these works confirm the relevance of the development and use of ontologies in the standards.

So, the work [19] addressed the use of ontologies in the context of the Manufacturing Operation Management (MOM) areas, for which the ISA-95 standard is responsible, and batch production processes, for which ISA-88 is responsible. The authors note that although the standards are genetically similar, there are many contradictions, such as the difference in terms for the same concepts and vice versa, while this problem is relevant for both different standards and within the same standard. The relationship between standards cannot be traced. It was also noted that, for example, to define the concept of "recipe", the standard does not offer a sufficiently clear unambiguous description. In addition, even fundamental equipment models do not have clear descriptions of the separation of entities between levels. The construction of an appropriate ontology would allow harmonizing standards at least at the level of these problems. The authors describe the experience of using the OWL2 language and the Protege editor to describe recipes using the PFC graphical language.

The authors of [2] also confirm the theses of their colleagues. They also note that the problem of developing and using of standards without the use of ontologies has three main problems. The first is the ambiguity of the natural language, generating inaccuracies in spelling. The second is a misinterpretation of the standard when reading it, which is associated with an understanding of the issue and previous experience. The third problem is related to the fact that a person who directly applies the standard (code developer) and a person who reads the standard are usually different people and when forming requirements, an additional link appears with an error in knowledge transferring. In this regard, the authors in their work propose two methodologies (automatic and semi-automatic), which involve the formation on the basis of an ontology standard that is directly used by all project stakeholders. In the process of creating the ontology, three editions of the 1st part of ISA-88, as well as other parts of the standard, were taken as a basis. When creating an ontology, a lot of problems were found in the standard:

- missing concepts;
- use of synonymy;
- misuse of adjectives;
- duplicate descriptions;
- indirect definitions that are deduced only by common sense;
- contradictions.

Some of these problems are found only in the old version of the standard. In turn, there are contradictions between the parts of the standard. With a semi-automatic approach, ontologies were built by automatically analyzing the text, however, drawings could not be processed automatically.

The authors of [2] and this article felt the problems of interpreting the standard from their own experience, sometimes understanding of some descriptions came only when getting acquainted with software that implements this functionality.

Problems with the incompatibility of ISA-88 and ISA-95 standards as well as insufficient formalization led to the appearance of a new version of ISA-88-2010, in which definitions were clarified, new ones were added and a certain attempt was made in agreement with ISA-95. The experience of using the ISA-88 and ISA-95 standards by the authors of this work revealed the following problems associated with versions of the standards:

- the American version of the standard – *ANSI/ISA-88.00.01-2010* – is already updated, the third edition from 2010;
- at the same time, the European version adopted in 1997 – *IEC 61512-1* – is based on the old version *ISA-88.01-1995*;
- Russian version of the standard – *GOST R IEC 61512-1-2016* – is identical to *IEC 61512-1*, that is, it is also outdated;
- Russian version of the standard - *GOST R IEC 61512-1-2016* - also raises a number of questions related to the not very successful translation of the original English terms into Russian;

The development of the standard itself is also problematic: 15 years have passed between the 1st and last edition of the 1st part of the ISA-88 standard. Obviously, people could change in the technical committee, and their interpretation of the primary foundations may also differ.

An additional problem of translation into another language is added to the problem of understanding standards and their interpretation. Considering that people who are not competent enough in the subject domain can participate in the translation of standards, the translated version may generally contradict the original by more than 50%. If there is an ontology for the standard, the translation issue remains secondary and is automated. It should also be noted that for different batch-productions there are also different terms, i.e. different language communities use the same standard, which requires the localization of one standard for different productions. At the same time, when changing only one concept, the standard must be read out once again for the correct translation or localization.

The absence of a strict description of the standard in any of the semantic languages makes it almost impossible to verify the correctness and completeness of the standard itself, and to verify the decision of compliance with the standard.

It should also be noted that batch production control systems also need support. The presence of an online help system enables new employees to learn not only on the basis of a specific implementation, but also to learn the general principles of building a standard. The standard is written in a language that is difficult to understand even for experienced developers, and therefore the presence of an appropriate ontology would make it easier to train employees. This kind of system is considered in the framework of this article.

3   Proposed Approach

The approaches discussed above can partially solve the problems associated with the presentation of standards. However, the problem that remains relevant is not with the form, but with the essence (semantics) of standards – the problem of inconsistency of the system of concepts and terms between different standards, which is relevant even for standards within the same field of activity.

To solve this problem and the problems listed above, it is proposed to use OSTIS Technology, one of the key tasks of which is to solve the problem of syntactic and semantic compatibility of computer systems [6], in particular, the compatibility of various types of knowledge [1] and various problem solving models [15].

As part of this work, we will consider the experience of using this technology in building an information and reference system for the standard for batch production ISA-88 [8] together with employees of JSC "Savushkin Product". The system was initially considered as a reference and training system for employees but now it is transformed into an international open-source project, the purpose of which is to create an up-to-date, constantly developed knowledge base that describes the specified standard. Work [16] considered the initial version of the formal description of the standard and fragments of the enterprise departments using the OSTIS Technology means.

Subsequently, part of the descriptions presented, not directly related to the enterprise, was allocated to the above-mentioned separate system dedicated to the ISA-88 standard. The current version of the system is available online at http://ostis.savushkin.by.

4   ISA-88 Standard

The *ISA-88* (short for ANSI/ISA-88) standard is based on the previously developed standard NAMUR N33 and helps in solving several fundamental problems, such as the lack of a single model of batch production, the difficulty of requirements agreeing, the complexity of integrating solutions from various suppliers, the complexity of the management of batch production. To solve these problems, it was necessary to define common models, terminology, data structures and process description language. The structure of the standard corresponds to the mentioned tasks and includes four parts:

- ANSI/ISA-88.00.01-2010, Batch Control Part 1: Models and Terminology – defines standard models and terminology for formalizing requirements for batch production control systems, its equivalent is IEC 61512 1;
- ANSI/ISA 88.00.02 2001, Batch Control Part 2: Data Structures and Guidelines for Languages – defines data models for production management, data structures for information exchange, as well as a form for recording recipes;
- ANSI/ISA 88.00.03 2003, Batch Control Part 3: General and Site Recipe Models and Representation – defines models for presenting generalized recipes and exchanging such recipes between departments of the enterprise, as well as between the enterprise and its partners;
- ANSI/ISA 88.00.04 2006, Batch Control Part 4: Batch Production Records – defines data models and an indicative system model for recording, storing, retrieving and analyzing data on the progress of periodic production.

5   System Architecture and Use Cases

It is proposed to use OSTIS Technology and the corresponding set of models, methods and tools for developing semantically compatible intelligent systems as a basis for automating the processes of creating, developing and applying of standards. The basis of OSTIS Technology is a unified version of the information encoding language based on semantic networks with a basic set-theoretic interpretation, called the SC-code [6].

The use of SC-code and models for the presentation of various types of knowledge built on its basis will provide such opportunities as:

- automation of standardization processes by a distributed team of authors;
- the ability to fix conflicting points of view on the same problem in the discussion process and even in the process of applying the developed standard;
- the possibility of evolution of the standard directly in the process of its application;
- absence of information duplication at the semantic level;
- independence of the system of concepts from terminology, as a result – from the natural language in which the standard was originally created;
- the ability to automate standard verification processes, including identifying inconsistencies, information holes, logical duplications, etc.;
- improving the efficiency of using the standard, providing the ability to solve various problems without the need to convert the standard to any other format, in particular, the ability to automate the process of verifying compliance with anything necessary standards;
- and others.

The architecture of each system based on OSTIS Technology (ostis-system) includes a platform for interpreting semantic models of ostis-systems, as well as a semantic model of ostis-system described using SC-code (sc-model of ostis-system). In turn, the sc-model of ostis-system includes the sc-model of the knowledge base, the sc-model of the problem solver and the sc-model of the interface (in particular, the user interface). The principles of organization and designing of knowledge bases and problem solvers are discussed in more detail in [1] and [15], respectively.

Let us consider in more detail the composition of each of the above components in the framework of the system under the ISA-88 standard.

5.1   System Knowledge Base

According to the principles of OSTIS Technology, the basis of the knowledge base of any ostis-system is the hierachical system of subject domains and their corresponding ontologies. The principles of developing knowledge bases of ostis-systems are discussed in more detail in [1]. In turn, among the indicated subject domains, a family of top-level subject domains is distinguished, due to which the compatibility of various types of knowledge in various ostis-systems is ensured, and the development time of new knowledge bases is significantly reduced due to the reuse of existing components.

Within the framework of the system under consideration, the following set of subject domains that correspond to the ISA-88 standard (Fig. 1) is distinguished:

Each subject domain corresponds to its structural specification, which includes a list of concepts studied within this domain (Fig. 2):

In turn, each concept of the standard is described with the necessary level of detailing (Fig. 3). The system user can ask various questions to any entities in the knowledge base, including entities whose names are mentioned in natural language texts that are part of the knowledge base.

Subject domain of batch manufacturing enterprises
⇒ private subject domain*:
- Subject domain of physical models of batch manufacturing enterprises
- Subject domain of process models of batch manufacturing enterprises
- Subject domain of procedural control models of batch manufacturing enterprises
- Subject domain of batch control activities

Fig. 1. ISA-88 standard subject domains hierarchy.

Subject domain of physical models of batch manufacturing enterprises
⇒ main identifier*:

> Subject domain of physical models of batch manufacturing enterprises ···

⇐ private subject domain*:
Subject domain of batch manufacturing enterprises
∈ key sc-element:
Section. Subject domain of physical models of batch manufacturing enterprises
∋ maximum class of explored objects':
equipment_entity
∋ explored_relation':
contains*
∋ not maximum class of explored objects':
- process cell
- unit
- equipment_module
- control_module
- enterprise
- site
- area
- equipment relation

Fig. 2. Subject domain specification.

process cell
⇒ main identifier*:

> process cell ···

⇐ inclusion*:
equipment_entity
∈ key sc-element:
- This term applies to both the *physical equipment* and the *equipment entity*. ···

- A logical grouping of *equipment* that includes the *equipment* required for production of one or more *batches*. It defines the span of logical control of one set of process *equipment* within an *area*.

∈ not maximum class of explored objects':
Subject domain of physical models of batch manufacturing enterprises

Fig. 3. Concept specification within the standard.

In addition, an important advantage of using OSTIS Technology to develop standards development support systems is an availability of methods and tools for the collective development of knowledge bases [1], which support the development of a standard presented in the form of a knowledge base by a distributed team of developers.

5.2   System Problem Solver

The ostis-system problem solver according to the principles of OSTIS Technology is a hierarchical system of agents interacting with each other exclusively through the semantic memory of this ostis-system (sc-agents) [15]. This approach provides the modifiability of the solver and the possibility of integrating various problem solving models within the solver.

For the support system for the development and use of standards the urgent task is to search for various information in the knowledge base by employees of the enterprise, both experienced and new employees. Actual are not only requests for definitions of various concepts, but also more complex requests, for example, the search for similarities and differences between various entities. In addition, the presentation of the standard in the form of a knowledge base allows using the appropriate sc-agents to automatically detect duplication of information, contradictions and lack of necessary information (information holes).

The approach used to build knowledge bases and problem solvers makes it possible to unify the principles of information processing, and, as a result, reduce the number of necessary sc-agents. So, for example, questions of the form

- "What subclasses does the given class have?";
- "What components is the specified entity divided into?";
- "What parts does the given object consist of?";
- "What are the varieties of a given entity?";
- etc.

can be reduced to the generalized question "What entities are particular with respect to a given entity?", for the processing of which, therefore, it is enough to implement only one sc-agent. However, this does not prohibit having within the user interface a set of more specialized commands with names that are understandable to the end user.

5.3   System User Interface

The important component for a system that describes a standard is the user interface. Usually users of the system are employees who are far from semantic technologies, and often information technologies in general. Due to that the task of building an interface is urgent, which, on the one hand, would be easy to use and visual, on the other hand, would be universal (able to display different types of knowledge).

By default, system responses to the user are displayed in SCn-code, which is a hypertext version of the external representation of SC-code texts and can be read as linear text. The information in the above figures is displayed as SCn-texts in a mode intended for the end user. For a more experienced user, a mode with a more detailed display of information is also provided.

An important feature of knowledge bases built on the basis of SC-code is the separation of the entities themselves and external identifiers (names) corresponding to the specified entities. Due to this, each entity can be associated with an arbitrary number of names in different languages, which, in turn, provide a multilingual standard without the need for duplication of information.

So, for the current version of the system according to the ISA-88 standard, it turned out to be relevant to have versions of the system in Russian, English, Ukrainian and German. Figure 4 presents the start page of the system in German. As can be seen from the presented examples, only the displayed terms change, the structure of the information remains similar for different languages.

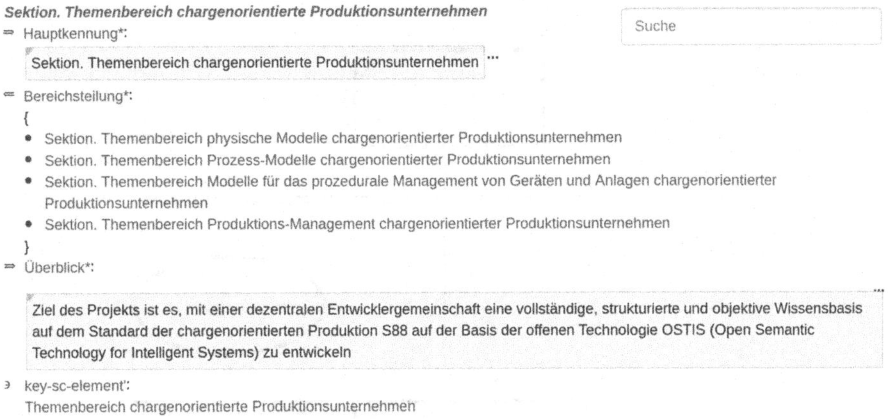

Sektion. Themenbereich chargenorientierte Produktionsunternehmen
⇒ Hauptkennung*:

> Sektion. Themenbereich chargenorientierte Produktionsunternehmen ···

⇒ Bereichsteilung*:

{
- Sektion. Themenbereich physische Modelle chargenorientierter Produktionsunternehmen
- Sektion. Themenbereich Prozess-Modelle chargenorientierter Produktionsunternehmen
- Sektion. Themenbereich Modelle für das prozedurale Management von Geräten und Anlagen chargenorientierter Produktionsunternehmen
- Sektion. Themenbereich Produktions-Management chargenorientierter Produktionsunternehmen
}

⇒ Überblick*:

> Ziel des Projekts ist es, mit einer dezentralen Entwicklergemeinschaft eine vollständige, strukturierte und objektive Wissensbasis auf dem Standard der chargenorientierten Produktion S88 auf der Basis der offenen Technologie OSTIS (Open Semantic Technology for Intelligent Systems) zu entwickeln

Suche

³ key-sc-element':
Themenbereich chargenorientierte Produktionsunternehmen

Fig. 4. Start page in German.

Thus, the proposed approach also allows us to describe the syntax and semantics of external languages, which makes it possible to construct unified visualization tools not only for universal languages (variants for external representation of SC-code texts), but also for specialized languages, such as PFC. The Fig. 5 shows an image of a chart in PFC language, to the elements of which it is possible to ask various questions, as well as to any other elements within the knowledge base.

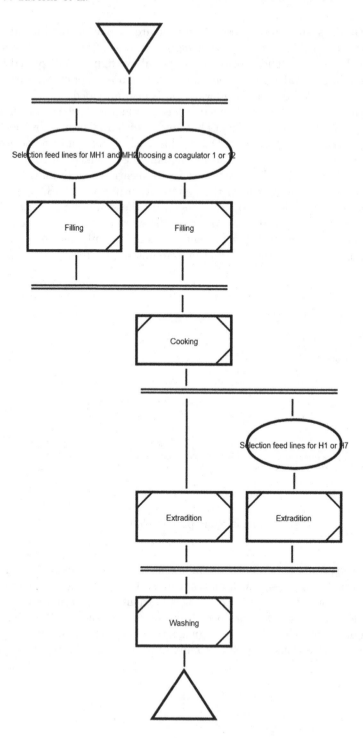

Fig. 5. An example chart in PFC

In addition, the OSTIS Technology means allow to store and, very importantly, specify any external files, for example, images, documents, etc. within the framework of the knowledge base. The Fig. 6 shows the description in the knowledge base of the procedure image in the PFC language, which is part of the ISA-88 standard.

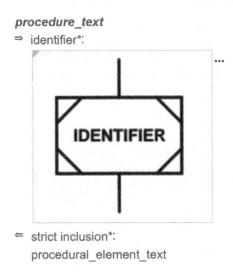

Fig. 6. Image specification in the knowledge base.

6   Integration of Third-Party Solutions with a Knowledge Base

A standard system built on the basis of OSTIS Technology can be easily integrated with other systems in the workplace. To integrate the ISA-88 standard system with other systems running on JSC "Savushkin Product", a web-oriented approach is used – the ostis-system server is accessed with the use of the following queries:

http :// ostis . savushkin . by? sys_id=procedure

where "sys_id=procedure" defines a term (the name of an entity) whose value we want to find out (in this example, in fact, the answer to the question "What is a "procedure"?"). This approach makes it relatively easy to add support of the knowledge base for current control systems projects, for this it is enough to indicate the names corresponding to the entities in the knowledge base within the control system.

In addition, it is possible to ask more complex and intelligent questions with several arguments, for example, "What is the difference between the concepts of "process operation" and "process action"?

The corresponding query to the ostis-system server looks like:

http://ostis.savushkin.by?command_id=ui_command_difference &arg1=process_operation&arg2=process_action

Thus, an interactive intelligent help system for control systems projects is implemented, allowing employees to simultaneously work with the control system and ask questions to the system directly during the work.

Figure 7 shows an illustration of the display of information in the form of a HMI page (from the control system project).

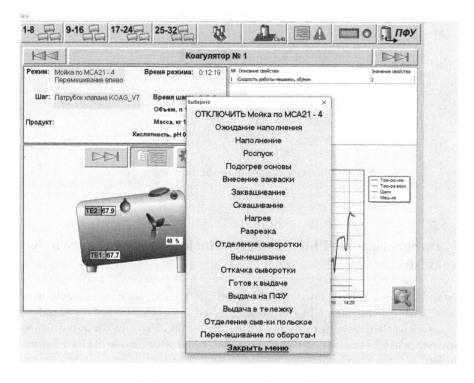

Fig. 7. Example HMI from SCADA [16].

Figure 8 shows a web page that displays the same information as a PFC chart (from the knowledge base).

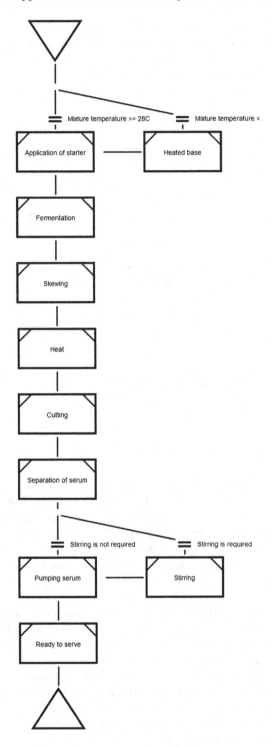

Fig. 8. Corresponding PFC chart from OSTIS.

Another example is the integrated help subsystem within corporate Add-In EasyEPLANner [3] for CAD EPLAN. It helps to describe technological objects (Tank, Boiler, etc.), operations, etc. according to the ISA-88 standard. Figure 9 shows a short preview of the project functionality.

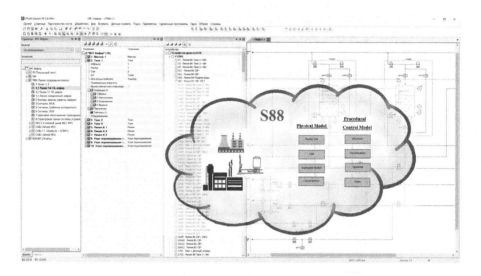

Fig. 9. Add-In project EasyEPLANner

7   Conclusion

The paper considers an approach to automating the processes of creating, developing and applying standards based on OSTIS Technology. Using the example of the ISA-88 standard used at the Savushkin Product enterprise, the structure of the knowledge base, the features of the problem solver and the user interface of the support system for these processes are considered. It is shown that the developed system can be easily integrated with other enterprise systems, being the basis for building an information service system for employees in the context of Industry 4.0.

The approach proposed in the work allows us to provide not only the ability to automate the processes of creation, agreeing and development of standards, but also allows us to significantly increase the efficiency of the processes of applying the standard, both in manual and automatic mode.

As part of the further development of the obtained results, the authors plan to attract the international community to the development of the knowledge base and the entire prototype of the system according to the ISA-88 standard, for which the tools of collective development of knowledge bases proposed in the framework of OSTIS Technology will be used.

Acknowledgment. Authors would like to thank the research teams of the Departments of intelligent information technologies of the Belarusian State University of Informatics and Radioelectronics and the Brest State Technical University.

References

1. Davydenko, I.: Semantic models, method and tools of knowledge bases coordinated development based on reusable components. In: Golenkov, V. (ed.) Open Semantic Technologies for Intelligent Systems, vol. 2, pp. 99–118. BSUIR, Minsk (2018)
2. Dombayci, C., Farreres, J., Rodríguez, H., Espuña, A., Graells, M.: Improving automation standards via semantic modelling: application to ISA88. ISA Trans. **67** (2017). https://doi.org/10.1016/j.isatra.2017.01.008
3. EasyEPLANner project on GitHub. https://github.com/savushkin-r-d/EasyEPLANner/. Accessed June 2020
4. El-Sappagh, S., Franda, F., Ali, F., Kwak, K.S.: SNOMED CT standard ontology based on the ontology for general medical science. BMC Med. Inf. Decis. Making **18**(1) (2018). https://doi.org/10.1186/s12911-018-0651-5
5. Garanina, N., Sidorova, E., Kononenko, I., Gorlatch, S.: Using multiple semantic measures for coreference resolution in ontology population. Int. J. Comput. **16**(3), 166–176 (2017). https://www.computingonline.net/computing/article/view/900
6. Golenkov, V., Guliakina, N., Davydenko, I., Eremeev, A.: Methods and tools for ensuring compatibility of computer systems. In: Golenkov, V. (ed.) Open Semantic Technologies for Intelligent Systems, vol. 4, pp. 25–52. BSUIR, Minsk (2019)
7. Heravi, B.R., Lycett, M., de Cesare, S.: Ontology-based standards development: application of OntoStanD to ebXML business process specification schema. Int. J. Account. Inf. Syst. **15**(3), 275–297 (2014). https://doi.org/10.1016/j.accinf.2014.01.005
8. ISA-88 standard. https://www.isa.org/isa88/. Accessed June 2020
9. Kumar, V.R.S., et al.: Ontologies for industry 4.0. Knowl. Eng. Rev. **34** (2019). https://doi.org/10.1017/s0269888919000109
10. Mušič, G.: A low-cost PackML-based control solution for a modular production line. IFAC-PapersOnLine **48**(10), 184–189 (2015). https://doi.org/10.1016/j.ifacol.2015.08.129
11. Schulz, S., Martínez-Costa, C.: How ontologies can improve semantic interoperability in health care. In: Riaño, D., Lenz, R., Miksch, S., Peleg, M., Reichert, M., ten Teije, A. (eds.) KR4HC/ProHealth -2013. LNCS (LNAI), vol. 8268, pp. 1–10. Springer, Cham (2013). https://doi.org/10.1007/978-3-319-03916-9_1
12. Schulz, S., Stegwee, R., Chronaki, C.: Standards in healthcare data. In: Kubben, P., Dumontier, M., Dekker, A. (eds.) Fundamentals of Clinical Data Science, pp. 19–36. Springer, Cham (2019). https://doi.org/10.1007/978-3-319-99713-1_3
13. Serenkov, P., Solomaho, V., Nifagin, V., Minova, A.: Koncepcija infrastruktury standartizacii kak bazy znanij na osnove ontologij [the concept of a standardization infrastructure as an ontology-based knowledge base]. Novosti. Standartizacija i sertifikacija. [News. Standardization and certification.] (5), pp. 25–29 (2004)
14. Shu, C., Dosyn, D., Lytvyn, V., Vysotska, V., Sachenko, A., Jun, S.: Building of the predicate recognition system for the nlp ontology learning module. In: 10th IEEE International Conference on Intelligent Data Acquisition and Advanced Computing Systems: Technology and Applications (IDAACS), vol. 2, pp. 802–808 (2019)

15. Shunkevich, D.: Agent-oriented models, method and tools of compatible problem solvers development for intelligent systems. In: Golenkov, V. (ed.) Open Semantic Technologies for Intelligent Systems, vol. 2, pp. 119–132. BSUIR, Minsk (2018)
16. Taberko, V.V., et al.: Ontological design of prescription production enterprises based on ontologies. In: Golenkov, V. (ed.) Open Semantic Technologies for Intelligent Systems, vol. 1, pp. 265–280. BSUIR, Minsk (2017)
17. Taberko, V.V., Ivaniuk, D.S., Shunkevich, D.V., Pupena, O.N.: Principles for enhancing the development and use of standards within Industry 4.0. In: Golenkov, V. (ed.) Open Semantic Technologies for Intelligent Systems, vol. 4, pp. 167–174. BSUIR, Minsk (2020)
18. Uglev, V.: Aktualizacija soderzhanija standartov proektirovanija slozhnyh tehnicheskih ob'ektov: ontologicheskij podhod [updating the content of design standards for complex technical objects: ontologic approach]. Ontologija proektirovanija. [Ontology of designing] (1), pp. 80–86 (2012)
19. Vegetti, M., Henning, G.: ISA-88 Formalization. A Step Towards its Integration with the ISA-95 Standard. vol. 1333, February 2015

Neuro-Symbolic Artificial Intelligence: Application for Control the Quality of Product Labeling

Vladimir Golovko[1,2], Aliaksandr Kroshchanka[1], Mikhail Kovalev[3(✉)],
Valery Taberko[4], and Dzmitry Ivaniuk[4]

[1] Brest State Technical University, Brest, Belarus
`kroschenko@gmail.com`
[2] Pope John Paul II State School of Higher Vocational Education in Biala Podlaska,
Biala Podlaska, Poland
`gva@bstu.by`
[3] Belarusian State University of Informatics and Radioelectronics, Minsk, Belarus
`michail.kovalev7@gmail.com`
[4] JSC "Savushkin Product", Brest, Belarus
`{tab,id}@pda.savushkin.by`

Abstract. The paper presents the implementation of an intelligent decision support system (IDSS) to solve a real manufacturing problem at
JSC "Savushkin Product". The proposed system is intended to control
the quality of product labeling, based on neuro-symbolic artificial intelligence, namely integrating deep neural networks and semantic models.
The system perform localization and recognition of images from a high-
speed video stream and is based on several deep neural networks. Semantic networks fulfill intelligent processing of recognition results in order to
generate final decision as regards the state of the production conveyor.
We demonstrate the performance of the proposed technique in the real
production process. The main contribution of this paper is a novel view
at the creation of a real intelligent decision support system, which combines bio inspired approach, namely neural networks and conventional
technique, based on a knowledge base.

Keywords: Deep neural networks · Object detection · Knowledge
base · Integration · Inference · IDSS · Neuro-symbolic

1 Introduction

Artificial intelligence (AI) is a key challenge in the domain of computer science
and has been successfully applied to many problems in real life, namely speech
recognition, computer vision, natural language processing, data visualization,
etc. [1, 7–11, 14, 16–18, 22–24, 27]. There exist two main approaches in the area of
artificial intelligence, namely bio-inspired and symbolic AI.

This paper deals with an integration of bio-inspired and symbolic AI for control the quality of product labeling. The most popular and effective technique

© Springer Nature Switzerland AG 2020
V. Golenkov et al. (Eds.): OSTIS 2020, CCIS 1282, pp. 81–101, 2020.
https://doi.org/10.1007/978-3-030-60447-9_6

concerning bio-inspired approach is deep learning. The new semantic technique, named OSTIS (Open Semantic Technology for Intelligent Systems) was proposed last decade as symbolic AI [26]. Therefore, in this work deep neural and semantic networks are used as bio-inspired and symbolic AI accordingly. In general, symbolic AI is based on symbolic (logical) reasoning, which tries to model human thinking, permits to decide problems that can be formalized and plays an important role in human knowledge [25,37]. It should be noted, that logical thinking is the generation of the human brain and because the brain consists of different structures of neural networks, the symbolic thinking is closely connected with bio-inspired AI. The main drawback of neural networks is their black box nature [3].

The advantage of neural networks is that they can deal with unstructured data. Symbolic artificial intelligence is very convenient if symbolic reasoning rules can be generated. However symbolic AI can face big problems when we deal with the unstructured data. That is the main limitation of symbolic approach. The idea of neuro-symbolic AI is to integrate advantages of both neural networks and logical rules. The fusion of neural networks and symbolic approaches can make an intelligent system more smarter by breaking the world into symbols [2,4,5,15].

Symbolic approach can also influence the learning quality of neural networks through incorporation of domain knowledge into deep learning.

In this paper, we propose the implementation of the intelligent decision support system based on the integration of neural networks and semantic models. We have been using deep neural networks for initial analysis of product labeling. After that the semantic network, using symbolic reasoning, generates a final decision as regards the operation of the production line, namely incorrect labeling, unreadable labeling, no paint and so on. This system was developed for JSC "Savushkin product".

The rest of the paper is organized as follows. In Sect. 2 we formulate the problem and list main failures, which can appear on the production line. In Sect. 3 we give a short overview of our previous works and existing approaches to quality control of labeling. In Sect. 4 we propose a neuro-symbolic approach to control the quality of product labeling. In Sect. 5 we describe the hardware part of the system. Section 6 is devoted to the neural networks models, which have been used in the implementation of the system. In this section we present results of the separate char's detection. In Sect. 7 we give a description of a decision making module based on the OSTIS technology. Finally, the paper ends with conclusion in Sect. 8.

2   Problem Formulation and Goals

An important task in real manufacturing is to check the correctness and quality of the labeling printed on the product. As it was mentioned earlier we consider a neuro-symbolic approach to quality control of product labeling at JSC "Savushkin Product". Let's examine this problem in more detail.

The source data is a video stream obtained by an RGB camera mounted above the manufacturing tape. In our example, this stream is characterized by a speed of 76 frames per second. An example of a frame from a stream is shown in Fig. 1.

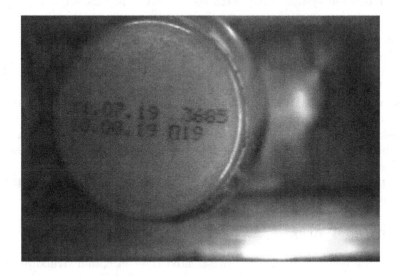

Fig. 1. Example of a frame from a video stream

The solution to this problem includes:

- labeling detection and recognition;
- the identification of labeling problems;
- search for the causes of these problems;
- search for the decision to these problems;
- generation of the solution automatically to repair the problems encountered, if possible.

It should be noted that labeling problems can be as follows:

- **no paint.** If empty bottles start to go, then the printer has run out of paint. The system can also refer to it (since the printer is connected to the network) and check the availability of paint.
- **camera shift.** The system knows that the batch has started filling, but there are no positive recognition results from the camera.
- **incorrect labeling.** The labeling is recognized, passed to the system, but it does not match the standard – this means that an error occurred when setting the labeling text and it is necessary to stop the filling process and notify the operator.

- **unreadable labeling.** Labeling is not recognized – several digits are not recognized, so the printer nozzles are clogged – it is needed to stop the filling process and notify the operator to clean the printer nozzles. In this case, it is needed to remove bottles with incorrect labeling from the conveyor.

The intelligent system being developed should satisfy the following requirements:

- **High-speed operation.** Manufacturing processes are very fast, so the search for incorrectly marked products and its rejection also must be very fast.
- **Ability to explain.** It is necessary to identify not only incorrect labeling, but also to explain the reasons for this situation.
- **Autonomy.** The system should minimize human involvement in the quality control process. Of course, there may be situations when system can't handle problem without operator help, but even in such situations, the system must be able to instruct the operator and be able to explain the reasons for certain actions.
- **Adaptability.** It is necessary to have the ability to adapt the system to recognize labeling to any other products.

3   Related Works

In our previous works [12, 13] we investigated the conceptual structure of the gybrid intellectual system. Sometimes we paid attention to concrete models, which are parts of integrated system [11]. The presented work is divided into two parts. The first one contains the research of the hybrid intelligent system designing. The second improves the efficiency of neural networks models to labeling detection and classification. There are several main approaches to build the hybrid intelligent system.

The proposed intelligent neuro-symbolic system should be able to find and propose decisions concerning emerging problems, as well as justify these decisions. Therefore, the proposed approach is based on the experience of building IDSS during designing this system [39].

Classic DSS can be defined as an interactive automated system that helps the decision maker (DSS) use data and models to identify and solve problems and make decisions [34]. Intelligent DSS extends the DSS conception by using intelligent models.

The proposed system goes beyond the definition of IDSS, since the system can not only offer, but also apply decisions.

As mentioned earlier, the proposed solution is based on neuro-symbolic AI. At present neuro-symbolic AI is a relatively new, but actively developing area of AI [41]. In this field, we consider some ways to integrate different methods of connectionist and symbolic approaches. As a rule, translation algorithms from symbolic representation to connectionist representation and vice versa are used to provide neural implementation of logic, logical characteristics of a neural system, or to build hybrid learning systems that combine the features of connectionism and symbolic artificial intelligence [2].

We examine the last option and as a result we have a cyclical interaction between parts of the system, which are implemented using different approaches (Fig. 2).

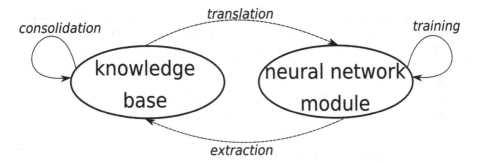

Fig. 2. Diagram of cyclical interaction

In general, this cycle is described as:

- transfer from "logic" (symbolic AI) to connectionist network;
- machine learning;
- transfer from the connectionist network back to "logic".

Logic refers to various symbolic models, for instance non-monotonic, modal, temporal, epistemological, intuitionistic logic, first-order logic, higher-order logic, deductive reasoning, and so on.

As for the connectionist network the different kind of neural networks can be used.

The use of this loop with a different set of specific models for implementing "logic" and connectionist networks can be found in many works on the neuro-symbolic field [13,32,35]. Hot topic for building a symbolic part in such systems is how to represent the rules and knowledge on which these rules will work.

Another focus of our work is improving the efficiency of neural networks models for different computer vision subtasks.

The quality control task of labeling at enterprises similar to the enterprise of JSC "Savushkin Product" is often solved manually. A human periodically selectively checks a part of the product. This approach has the following disadvantages:

- only part of products are checked;
- there is a possibility that a human will not notice a slight discrepancy between the checked labeling and the standard one;
- the use of monotonous manual labor.

At the moment, developments to automation these activities are underway and are being implemented, but in most cases we are only talking about identifying problems with labeling, but not at all about finding the causes and solutions to these problems.

For example, Omron [29] sensors are often used. These sensors are equipped with a camera and are able to recognize product labeling on high-speed tape. Using these sensors allows to automate the work of a person for quality control, but there are the following disadvantages:

- Recognition quality isn't high enough. Sensors are based on Optical Character Recognition (OCR), an approach used for document recognition that is highly dependent on the image quality of the text. Due to the high speed of the industrial tape, it is not always possible to get a high-quality photo of the labeling.
- Need to buy specialized software for system configuration.
- No built-in system for finding and fixing labeling problems.

4   The Proposed Approach

Symbolic part of the proposed system uses semantic networks as an ontology-based knowledge base to represent knowledge. A distinctive feature of the system is that the rules and knowledge are represented in the same knowledge base using the same tools. This is achieved by using the OSTIS [6] technology.

OSTIS technology uses knowledge representation and processing models focused on unifying and working with knowledge at the semantic level. This is achieved due to the knowledge integration model presented in the technology and the unified semantic representation of the knowledge model(SC-code) [6]. As a result, we get the ability to integrate different solution models in an uniform environment, which distinguishes it from, for example, Semantic Web [19].

The main principles and models used in this approach include:

- knowledge integration model and unified semantic-based knowledge representation model [12], based on the SC code [6];
- principles of situational control theory;
- ontological model of events and phenomena in knowledge processing processes;
- multi-agent approach [38];
- hybrid knowledge processing models [36].

Based on the fact that search and decision-making is carried out using knowledge, the proposed system can be defined as a knowledge-based ISPR [33].

The main components of the system are as follows:

- **Machine vision module.** The task of the module is localization and recognition product labeling on the image and transfer to the results of this recognition to the decision-making module. Also, this module stores all trained artificial neural networks (ANNs), the description of which is stored in the KB. In the future, the module should be able to switch between trained ANNs if the engineer sets the appropriate configuration of the KB.

- **Decision-making module (DMM).** Consists of the KB and the problem solver. The KB contains all the necessary knowledge for making and implementing decisions, such as logical rules, statements, current labelings, device states, and so on. The problem solver contains a set of internal and external agents that work with the KB. These agents are used for inference for finding decisions, calling external programs for implementing decisions, and preparing decision for the engineer's terminal.
- **Robotic subsystem control module.** This module has access to the subsystem that directly carries out the labeling of products. The task of this module is implementation of system decisions that can be taken without the involvement of the engineer, such as labeling updates, switching the subsystem on and off, etc.
- **Engineer's terminal.** The user interface module that can be used to track decisions made by the system, including decisions that require the attention of an engineer. The terminal provides full access to the KB, so the engineer has the ability to manually configure the system for certain tasks. For example, they can indicate to the system the fallacy of its reasoning and correct the rule by which it made an wrong decision.

The Fig. 3 shows the general diagram of interaction of the labeling quality control system modules.

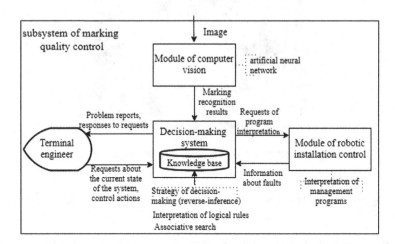

Fig. 3. The general diagram of interaction of the labeling quality control system modules [13]

5   System Hardware

Let's consider the description of system hardware. It consists of the following modules.

PLCnext. Testing of given program solution was produced based on controller PLCnext RFC 4072S (Fig. 4). This hardware platform is open solution of modern automation systems, which satisfy requirements of IIoT [30].

Controller PLCnext RFC 4072S has next technical parameters: processor Intel® Core™i5-6300U 2 × 2.4 GHz, USB-interface, 4 Ethernet ports with different values of data transmitting speed. This model has degree of protection IP20. Additionally can be acquired software, fan module and SD-cards 2/8 GB for store programs and configurations [31].

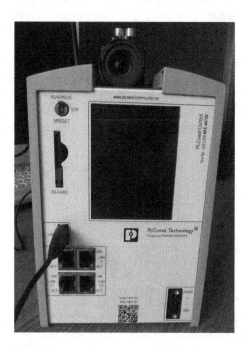

Fig. 4. Controller RFC 4072S with connected camera DFK 22AUC03

During testing of this hardware platform, we have dealt with the following problems:

- small amount of storage available to work in this model of controller (only 2 GB of free space on original SD card);
- limited version of OS;
- limitations in current firmware.

First and second problem has been solved by installing a larger non-original SD card with a pre-installed Debian OS.

6   Machine Vision Module

6.1   Labeling Detection Problem Statement

If we want to detect objects in real time, then the problem of fast frame processing by neural networks appears. In-time completion of processing is not possible in case of each frame processing. In our task time window for processing one frame from a video stream is only 0.013 s or 13 ms. At present, neural network models, which are capable of objects detection for a such time interval using a mobile device or a specialized controller, don't exist. Therefore, it is necessary to evaluate the significance of separate frames for performing detection.

On the other hand, bottles move along the manufacturing tape with a certain frequency (about 3 pieces per second), which means that the neural network can process not every frame of the video stream, but only some and ignore the rest. This circumstance increases the time interval during which the processing should be performed, to a value of 250–300 ms.

The process of labeling recognition includes additional tasks such as testing labeling printing. The first task is to determine the presence of labeling on the cap. The second task is to determine the presence of labeling distortions, which arise during the printing process, the absence of labeling parts, etc. And, finally, the third task is the actual detection of the numbers in the labeling, the formation of output information (the date of manufacturing of the goods, numbers in the consignment, etc.) and the determination of the correctness of this data in accordance with a predefined pattern. The main labeling defects are shown in Fig. 5.

The presence of several subtasks involves the use of a group of neural networks, each of which performs its own part of the work.

6.2   Architecture of the Recognition Module

Our recognition module is an extension of the idea described in [11]. The developed labeling recognition module consists of three neural networks (Fig. 6).

The first network is a simple classifier based on a convolutional neural network, which determines the position of the bottle in the frame. We have selected four classes of position by distance from the center of the frame. Class 1 describes the minimal distance from the center of the frame. Only frames of this class are transferred for further analysis to other models. Class 2 and 3 describe the average and maximal distance. Finally, class 4 is needed for the case when the cap with the labeling is not in the frame (for example, an empty line is viewed).

The architecture of the classifier is shown in Fig. 7. It consists of 5 layers and has 4 output neurons according to the number of classes that determine the position of the bottle in the frame. All layers use the ReLU activation function except for the 3rd and last layers. They use linear and softmax activation functions, respectively. Also, max pooling is applied after the first and second convolutional layers with stride = 2.

Fig. 5. Main labeling defects

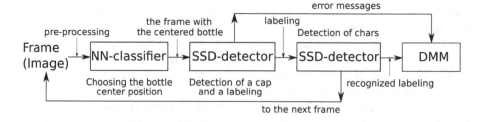

Fig. 6. Pipeline of the labeling recognition module

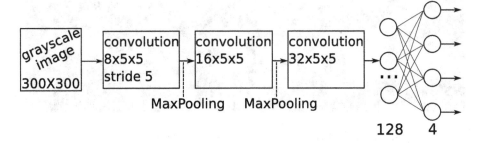

Fig. 7. Structure of classifier for evaluating bottle position

In case the frame was classified as class 1, it's transmitted further to the second neural network.

The second model is a detector and searches for caps and labelings in the frame. Here, an SSD network based on the MobileNet v1 [20] classifier was chosen as the architecture.

At the stage of detection of the cap and labeling, an analysis is made of the presence of a defect associated with the absence of labeling. This is made trivial: if object **cap** has been detected without object **labeling**, then it has assumed that a defect occurs. If a defect has been identified, the module notifies the operator. If no defects were found in the labeling, the frame is transferred to the next neural network.

Finally, the third neural network is also SSD-MobileNet v1, which detects individual digits in the labeling. After that, the formation of the final recognition result is performed.

The use of two serial networks for the detection of individual objects is explained by the fact that the original image has a high resolution and is scaled to 300×300 pixels before being fed to the detector. This conversion makes the detection of individual digits almost impossible due to their relatively small size. To eliminate this drawback, the image of the labeling in the original dimensions with the necessary scaling is fed to the input of the second detector.

DMM, as mentioned above (see Sect. 4), is the decision-making system, which implements the logic of the knowledge base and the problem's solver.

6.3 Training Datasets: Preparing and Main Features

To create a training dataset for the classifier, we have used the neural network model Faster R-CNN (based on the pre-trained ResNet50 classifier). This model has better detection efficiency compared to the SSD-MobileNet model, but it is slower [21]. This network was used to detect the caps in the frame. A trained detector was used to split the available dataset to bottle position classes. The Euclidean distance from the center of the cap to the center of the frame was used as a measure of distance. Thus, classes 1–4 were formed for classifier (Fig. 8). The resulting dataset includes 6189 images, 1238 of which make up the testing dataset.

Fig. 8. Distance of the bottle from the center of the frame (4 classes)

After the classifier was trained, the final classification accuracy was about 92%.

Both detectors (for detection of caps/labelings and individual digits) were trained based on pre-trained models.

During the learning of the detector of caps and labelings, a prepared dataset was used, which includes 637 images in the training part and 157 in the testing part accordingly.

The following learning procedure was used to train the digit detector. At the beginning, the SSD model was pre-trained on images from SVHN dataset of house numbers for 80 epochs (several images from this dataset are shown in Fig. 9). As regards pre-training, a variant of this dataset was used, which includes 33402 images in the training part and 13068 in the test part. After pre-training, we have continued to train the neural network using a dataset of labelings. This dataset contains 780 images in the training part and 196 in the test part. The training continued until we got the best results (approximately 90 epochs). Examples of images used for training are presented in Fig. 10.

Fig. 9. Examples of images from SVHN dataset [28]

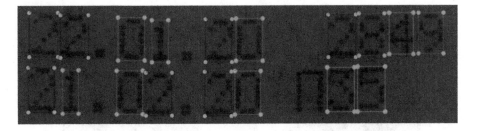

Fig. 10. Image from training dataset of detector 2

6.4   Results

The use of the SSD model allows to achieve a detection efficiency of 99% (mAP = 0.99) for caps and labelings detection and 89.3% (mAP = 0.8928) for individual digits. Additionally, the processing speed allows to detect objects in the video stream at a speed of 76 frames per second. Efficiency of the detection of individual digits are presented in the Table 1.

Table 1. Detection efficiency of individual classes of digits

Class label	AP
0	0.8972
1	0.8611
2	0.9000
3	0.8970
4	0.8900
5	0.8928
6	0.8931
7	0.8818
8	0.9523
9	0.8625
mAP	0.8928

The result of detection by the first and second detector is shown in Fig. 11 and 12.

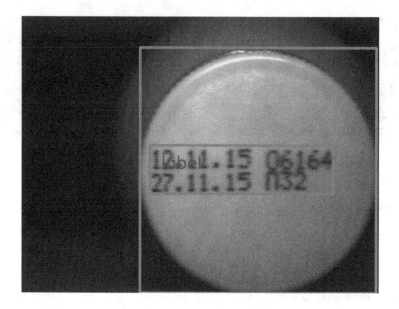

Fig. 11. Example of cap labeling detection

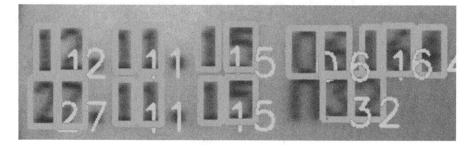

Fig. 12. Example of digits detection

7   Decision Making Module

7.1   Knowledge Base

KB designed using OSTIS technology is divided into subject domains, which in turn have its own ontologies. The proposed system has next subject domains:

- Subject domain of product labeling;
- Subject domain of neural network models;

Each subject domain that described in the KB has ontology in KB.

The Subject Domain of Product Labeling. This subject domain contains a description of all necessary information about the product and quality control of its labeling, such as:

- product brand;
- the recognized labeling;
- the standard labeling;
- number of consecutive unmarked products;
- the level of paint in the printer;
- and etc.

The Fig. 13 shows a fragment from this subject domain that describes the quality control point for labeling the bottles of some yogurt. This fragment contains information that machine vision module didn't recognize the labeling of bottle, which is currently being controlled. Moreover, at this control point, this is the fourth bottle with an unrecognized labeling. For this control point, there is a limit on the number of consecutive bottles with the wrong labeling,

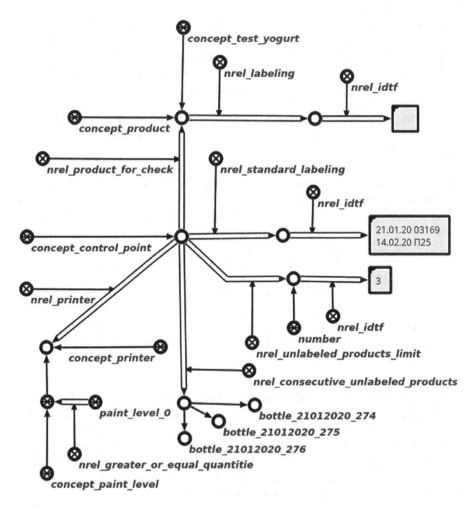

Fig. 13. Fragment of subject domain of product labeling for some yogurt bottles

which is equal to three. Also, the control point knows a printer, which prints the labeling and the level of paint in it. In this case, this level is zero.

This information will be enough for a human to conclude on the reasons for the missing of labeling. Below we will consider the mechanism by which the system will make a similar conclusion.

This subject domain also contains a set of implicative and equivalence bundles, which we will call logical rules for short. According to these rules, the reverse inference [40] is used to make the decision or a set of decisions. Inference uses the "if" part as search patterns in the KB. When matching the "if" part of a statement was found, the system generates the knowledge described in the "then" part of the implicative bundle of the used logical rule. For logical rules, presented in the form of equivalence tuples, the mechanism of its using is similar, with the only difference that in place of the "if-then" parts there can be any part of the equivalence tuple.

It should be noted that the logical rule can also be the specifications of agents or programs. These specifications are represented in the form of the implicative tuple, in which "if" part describes the input data, and "then" part describes the output data. When making the inference, the problem solver will use these logical rules on a par with the rest, but when using these logical rules, the appropriate agent or program will be called.

Each logical rule has the number of times it is used by inference. This technique will allow the system to self-learn and speed up the inference for trivial situations [13].

The Fig. 14 shows an example of a logical rule that can be written in natural language like this: *If the product is not marked, but it is critically bad marked, and the paint level in the printer is less than or equal to 0, then it is needed to stop the production tape and send a message that the printer has run out of paint.*

Applying of this logical rule to the KB which containing the fragment shown in the Fig. 13 will lead to the fact that the system will be able to conclude on the reasons for the missing of labeling.

One of the most important features of the system is the ability to explain made or proposed decisions. For this purpose, the inference makes a decision tree in the course. Decision tree stores the input recognition data, the recognized labeling, the chain of applied logical rules and the applied (proposed for application by the engineer) decision.

Subject Domain of Neural Network Models. The description of this subject domain will help the specialist when setting up the system for a specific task. Based on this knowledge, the system will be able to offer one or another trained ANN available in the machine vision module. In this regard, there is a need to describe the entire hierarchy of subject domain of neural networks models, proposed in [12], in the KB. This subject domain contains description of the following information about the trained ANN:

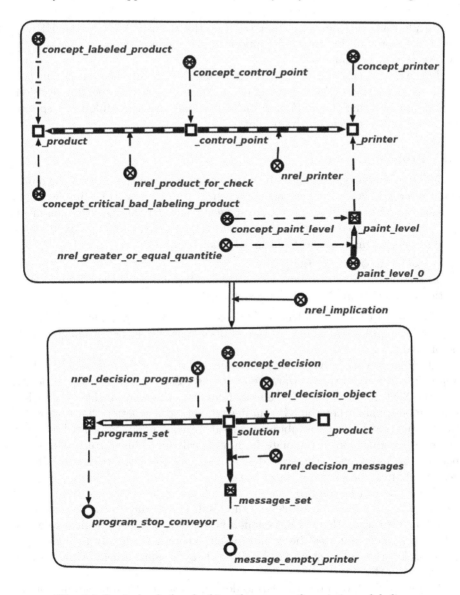

Fig. 14. Logical rule for checking the reasons for missing a labeling

- type of input data;
- set of recognized classes or output data type;
- class of tasks solved by ANN;
- architecture;
- average operating time;
- the quality of recognition.

In addition, this detailed description of the trained ANN in the KB can be used to provide information support to the engineer who will update the architecture or retrain the ANN.

In the future, this part of the KB can be used to expand the system's authority from supporting decision-making on labeling control to supporting decision-making on selecting the configuration of machine vision module for a specific hardware and a specific hardware platform.

7.2 Problem Solver

In OSTIS technology, problem solvers are constructed on the basis of the multi-agent approach. According to this approach, the problem solver is implemented as a set of agents called *sc-agents*. All sc-agents interact through common memory, passing data to each other as semantic network structures (sc-texts) [36].

The general tasks of the problem solver of IDSS are:

- access to knowledge in the KB;
- processing (analysis, verification, and generation)of knowledge; item interaction with other modules of the system.

The main task of the solver is implementation of reverse inference. In this way, the system knows in advance the set of reasons why incorrect labelings may be printed.

At the start work, solver creates sets of logical rules(by pattern search), whose applying will lead to the appearance of the necessary semantic construction in the KB. Next, it tries to apply the most frequently used logical rule. The logical rule can be applied when the KB contains semantic construction that isomorphic to the construction that was obtained by substituting nodes associated with the processed product into a template from a logical rule. This pattern is the first part of the logical rule, the second part describes the knowledge that will be generated after applying this logical rule.

If the rule can be applied, the system will generate knowledge from second part of rule and will add the rule and the result of its using to the decision tree.

In the case when there is not enough knowledge to apply a logical rule, the solver recursively initiates the work of itself, where it is already trying to find logical rules, the applying of which will lead to the appearance of the missing knowledge in the KB.

If the applying of any logical rule does not lead to the appearance of the necessary semantic constructions in the KB, the agent reports that it can't find the decisionfor this problem.

In the future, we consider an option in which the system will be able to generate logical rules itself, based on patterns in the course of the system's operation or on cases of manual correction of problems.

8 Conclusion

In this paper we have addressed the key aspects of the development of an intelligent decision support system to control the quality of product labeling. The proposed system based on neuro-symbolic artificial intelligence, namely integrating deep neural networks and semantic models.

The implementation of the proposed IDSS significantly improves quality control in manufacturing, since such a system is able not only to identify a problem with products, but also to help find the causes of these problems, and even, in some cases, to solve them independently.

The quality of detection of individual digits can be improved with the increase of the training dataset, this is a subject of future work. The second aspect that affects the quality of detection is the location of the labeling. It was noticed that when the labeling is in a horizontal orientation, the quality of detection is higher than in case of rotated labeling. Therefore a study of the possibility of using neural network models to select the correct labeling orientation is required.

A prospective development of the system is the addition of software functionality to support the engineer when scaling the solution to any other product or on another hardware platform. The engineer should be able to set the configuration of the machine vision module, as well as receive recommendations on this configuration from the system. Recommendations will be based on the specification of the task and the hardware capabilities of the platform. This requires a description of the ontology of neural network models and hardware platforms.

References

1. Bengio, Y.: Learning deep architectures for AI. Found. Trends Mach. Learn. **2**, 1–127 (2009)
2. Besold, T.R., et al.: Neural-symbolic learning and reasoning: a survey and interpretation, November 2017. https://arxiv.org/pdf/1711.03902.pdf. Accessed June 2020
3. Castelvecchi, D.: Can we open the black box of AI? Nat. News **538**(7623), 20–23 (2016)
4. d'Avila Garcez, A., et al.: Neuralsymbolic learning and reasoning: contributions and challenges. In: McCallum, A., Gabrilovich, E., Guha, R., Murphy, K. (eds.) Proceedings of the AAAI 2015 Propositional Rule Extraction under Background Knowledge 11 Spring Symposium on Knowledge Representation and Reasoning: Integrating Symbolic and Neural Approaches. AAAI Press Technical Report SS-15-03 (2015)
5. d'Avila Garcez, A., Lamb, L., Gabbay, D.: Neural-symbolic cognitive reasoning. Cognitive Technologies. Springer, Heidelberg (2009). https://doi.org/10.1007/978-3-540-73246-4
6. Golenkov, V., Guliakina, N., Davydenko, I., Eremeev, A.: Methods and tools for ensuring compatibility of computer systems. In: Golenkov, V. (ed.) Open Semantic Technologies for Intelligent Systems, vol. 2, pp. 25–52. BSUIR, Minsk (2019)
7. Golovko, V.A.: Deep learning: an overview and main paradigms. Opt. Mem. Neural Netw. **26**(1), 1–17 (2017). https://doi.org/10.3103/S1060992X16040081
8. Golovko, V., Bezobrazov, S., Kroshchanka, A., Sachenko, A., Komar, M.: Convolutional neural network based solar photovoltaic panel detection in satellite photos. In: Proceedings of Intelligent Data Acquisition and Advanced Computing Systems: Technology and Applications (IDAACS), 9th IEEE International Conference, Bucharest, Romania, no. 2, pp. 14–19 (2017)

9. Golovko, V., Komar, M., Sachenko, A.: Principles of neural network artificial immune system design to detect attacks on computers. In: Proceedings of the 10th International Conference on Modern Problems of Radio Engineering, Telecommunications and Computer Science, TCSET 2010, p. 237 (2010)

10. Golovko, V., Kroshchanka, A., Treadwell, D.: The nature of unsupervised learning in deep neural networks: a new understanding and novel approach. Opt. Mem. Neural Netw. **25**(3), 127–141 (2016). https://doi.org/10.3103/S1060992X16030073

11. Golovko, V., Kroshchanka, A., Mikhno, E.: Brands and caps labeling recognition in images using deep learning. In: Ablameyko, S.V., Krasnoproshin, V.V., Lukashevich, M.M. (eds.) PRIP 2019. CCIS, vol. 1055, pp. 35–51. Springer, Cham (2019). https://doi.org/10.1007/978-3-030-35430-5_4

12. Golovko, V.A., et al.: Integration of artificial neural networks and knowledge bases. In: Golenkov, V. (ed.) Open Semantic Technologies for Intelligent Systems, vol. 2, pp. 133–145. BSUIR, Minsk (2018)

13. Golovko, V.A., Ivashenko, V.P., Taberko, V.V., Ivaniuk, D.S., Kroshchanka, A.A., Kovalev, M.V.: Principles of decision making building systems based on the integration of neural networks and semantic models. In: Golenkov, V. (ed.) Open Semantic Technologies for Intelligent Systems, vol. 2, pp. 91–102. BSUIR, Minsk (2019)

14. Golovko, V., Savitsky, Y., Laopoulos, T., Sachenko, A., Grandinetti, L.: Technique of learning rate estimation for efficient training of MLP. In: Proceedings of the IEEE-INNS-ENNS International Joint Conference on Neural Networks, IJCNN 2000, pp. 323–328 (2000)

15. Hammer, B., Hitzler, P.: Perspectives of neural-symbolic integration. Studies in Computational Intelligence, vol. 77. Springer, Heidelberg (2007). https://doi.org/10.1007/978-3-540-73954-8

16. Hatzilygeroudis, I., Prentzas, J.: Integrating (rules, neural networks) and cases for knowledge representation and reasoning in expert systems. Expert Syst. Appl. **27**, 63–75 (2004)

17. Hatzilygeroudis, I., Prentzas, J.: Neuro-symbolic approaches for knowledge representation in expert systems. Int. J. Hybrid Intell. Syst. **1**(3–4), 11–126 (2014)

18. Hinton, G.: Deep neural network for acoustic modeling in speech recognition. IEEE Signal Process. Mag. **29**, 82–97 (2012)

19. Hitzler, P., Krötzsch, M., Rudolph, S.: Foundations of semantic web technologies. Chapman & Hall/CRC Textbooks in Computing. Chapman & Hall/CRC, Boca Raton (2009)

20. Howard, A.G., et al.: Mobilenets: efficient convolutionalneural networks for mobile vision applications, April 2017. https://arxiv.org/pdf/1704.04861.pdf. Accessed June 2020

21. Hui, J.: Object detection: speed and accuracy comparison (Faster R-CNN, R-FCN, SSD, FPN, RetinaNet and YOLOv3) May 2018. https://medium.com/@jonathan_hui/object-detection-speed-and-accuracy-comparison-faster-r-cnn-r-fcn-ssd-and-yolo-5425656ae359. Accessed June 2020

22. Komar, M., Yakobchuk, P., Golovko, V., Dorosh, V., Sachenko, A.: Deep neural network for image recognition based on the Caffe framework. In: Proceedings of the 2018 IEEE 2nd International Conference on Data Stream Mining and Processing, DSMP 2018, pp. 102–106 (2018)

23. Krizhevsky, A., Sutskever, I., Hinton, G.: ImageNet classification with deep convolutional neural networks. In: Proceedings of the International Conference on Advances in Neural Information Processing Systems (NIPS-2012), Lake Tahoe, no. 25, pp. 1090–1098 (2012)

24. LeCun, Y., Yoshua, B., Hinton, G.: Deep learning. Nature **521**(7553), 436–444 (2015)
25. Lehmann, F.: Semantic networks. Comput. Math. Appl. **23**(2–5), 1–50 (1992)
26. Mao, J., Gan, C., Kohli, P., Tenenbaum, J.B., Wu, J.: The neuro-symbolic concept learner: interpreting scenes, words, and sentences from natural supervision. In: ICLR (2004)
27. Mikolov, T., Deoras, A., Povey, D., Burget, L., Cernocky, J.: Strategies for training large scale neural network language models. In: IEEE Workshop Automatic Speech Recognition and Understanding, Waikoloa, pp. 195–201 (2011)
28. Netzer, Y., Wang, T., Coates, A., Bissacco, A., Wu, B., Ng, A.: Reading digits in natural images with unsupervised feature learning. In: NIPS Workshop on Deep Learning and Unsupervised Feature Learning (2011)
29. Omron documentation. https://robotics.omron.com/browse-documents. Accessed June 2020
30. Phoenix contact — control technology and software - intelligent automation. https://www.phoenixcontact.com/assets/2018/interactive_ed/101_86135/index. html#4. Accessed June 2020
31. Phoenix contact — safety controller - rfc 4072s–1051328. https://www. phoenixcontact.com/online/portal/us?uri=pxc-oc-itemdetail:pid=1051328& library=usen&tab=1. Accessed June 2020
32. Pinkas, G., Lima, P., Cohen, S.: A dynamic binding mechanism for retrieving and unifying complex predicate-logic knowledge. In: Villa, A.E.P., Duch, W., Érdi, P., Masulli, F., Palm, G. (eds.) ICANN 2012. LNCS, vol. 7552, pp. 482–490. Springer, Heidelberg (2012). https://doi.org/10.1007/978-3-642-33269-2_61
33. Power, D.: Decision Support Systems: Concepts and Resources for Managers. Expert Systems with Applications, p. 251. Greenwood Publishing Group, Westport (2002)
34. Saraev, A., Shcherbina, O.A.: System analysis and modern information technologies. In: Proceedings of the Crimean Academy of Sciences, pp. 47–59. SONAT, Simferopol (2006)
35. Sarker, M.K., Xie, N., Doran, D., Raymer, M., Hitzler, P.: Explaining trained neural networks with semantic web technologies: first steps, October 2017. https:// arxiv.org/pdf/1710.04324.pdf. Accessed June 2020
36. Shunkevich, D.: Agent-oriented models, method and tools of compatible problem solvers development for intelligent systems. In: Golenkov, V. (ed.) Open Semantic Technologies for Intelligent Systems, vol. 2, pp. 119–132. BSUIR, Minsk (2018)
37. Sowa, J.: Semantic networks. In: Encyclopedia of artificial intelligence. Expert Systems with Applications (1987)
38. Tarasov, V.: Ot mnogoagentnih sistem k intellektualnim organizaciyam filosofiya psihologiya informatika, p. 352 (2002)
39. Tariq, A., Rafi, K.: Intelligent decision support systems. Inf. Knowl. Manage. **2**(6) (2012). ISSN 2224–5758 (Paper) ISSN 2224–896X (Online)
40. Vagin, V., Zagoryanskaya, A., Fomina, M.: Dostovernii i pravdopodobnii vivod v intellektualnih sistemah, p. 704 (2008)
41. Workshop series on neural-symbolic learning and reasoning. http://www.neural-symbolic.org/. Accessed June 2020

Decision-Making Systems Based on Semantic Image Analysis

Natallia Iskra[1]([⊠])(iD), Vitali Iskra[2](iD), and Marina Lukashevich[1](iD)

[1] Belarusian State University of Informatics and Radioelectronics, Minsk, Belarus
{niskra,lukashevich}@bsuir.by
[2] Omnigon Communications LLC, New York, NY, USA
iskra.vitaly@gmail.com

Abstract. In this paper principles of decision-making systems construction are considered. An approach to image analysis based on semantic model is proposed and studied. The results show an improvement in processing speed and image captioning quality based on Visual Genome dataset.

Keywords: Decision-making · Video surveillance · Neural networks · Semantic analysis · Image captioning

1 Introduction

Image semantic analysis has been an important research direction of computer vision, which is a key technology for image processing. The main concept of semantic analysis is to classify each pixel in an image according to its own category and finally, to get a prediction result map containing "semantic" information. Image semantic analysis is related to research and applications in many fields, for example, medicine, industry and civilians and has achieved very significant results but its application in underwater scenes is less frequent than its application in other fields.

The human interpretation of the image is based on a clear understanding of the meaning of both the scene itself and its individual elements as well as semantic connections between these elements. Paying attention to the objects of the scene and their relative position, we understand the situation well. All this happens quickly and naturally. However, for artificial vision systems, such an interpretation is still a challenge today.

2 Decision-Making System

In recent years great progress has been made in the field of image classification, where the task is to assign a label (or class) to each image. Further development in image analysis went in two directions:

V. Golenkov et al. (Eds.): OSTIS 2020, CCIS 1282, pp. 102–120, 2020.
https://doi.org/10.1007/978-3-030-60447-9_7

– the improvement of the results in the field of automatic detection of multiple objects in an image (identification of object labels and the locations of the objects);
– semantic description of the image, which, given a set of objects from the image, would allow to obtain a sequence of words describing more complex concepts than simply listing the objects in the image, thus creating a text (including the one in simplified natural language) describing relations between the objects in the image.

Solving the problem of understanding and interpreting images today requires the integration of methods from these areas. Thus, in the framework of certain modern approaches a graph model that reflects semantic relations between objects is constructed based on the results of automatic detection. A promising direction for further development in this area is the use of more advanced semantic means, both for describing the results of image analysis (objects and relations), and directly in the analysis process. Such tools currently are knowledge bases and ontologies.

Integration of knowledge about the image and the objects represented on it into the knowledge base will allow, on the one hand, to improve the accuracy of understanding through the context and information available in the knowledge base, and on the other hand, to supplement the results of the analysis with new knowledge, that is not clearly presented in the analysis results, but can be generated on the basis of these results and information from the knowledge base. As part of this work, an approach to semantic image analysis based on the integration of a model using convolutional neural networks and information representation and processing tools within the framework of an Open semantic technology for intelligent systems design is considered.

Currently, the majority of works related to image analysis, including semantic analysis, are devoted to solving image recognition tasks, which involves object detection, classification, and sometimes building semantic links between objects. The result of solving this problem is a description of the depicted objects, which can be both formal and natural-language based. For the formal representation of the identified relations between objects it is convenient to use models based on semantic networks.

However, building complex intelligent system, especially autonomous one, implies the ability of not only processing the images, acquired by the system from the external sources, but also the ability of the system to understand the information that can be obtained by

The task of image analysis in decision-making systems using technical vision today is acute. Automatic image interpretation is a non-trivial task. For example, for a video surveillance system, it would be relevant not only to record and save video, but also to analyze what is happening, as well as to signal any suspicious situations - violations, incidents, actions that require an immediate response.

The approach to image analysis considered in this paper proceeds as follows:

Step 1. Individual objects detection. These can be the objects that are significant in the context of the system (for example, traffic participants, road markings and signs in traffic monitoring systems), areas that outline objects (bounding boxes), or more precise object-by-pixel selection.

Step 2. Building a semantic model. At this stage, relations between objects and/or attributes of individual objects are formalized.

Step 3. Model interpretation. According to the constructed model, a textual description of what is happening (an annotation of the image or image caption, for example, for keeping a surveillance log) can be obtained, or specific situations on the image that are of interest (for example, cases of traffic rules violation, traffic accidents, etc.) can be determined. In this case, the interpretation of the model will consist in highlighting only those relationships and attributes that can signal of an abnormal situation.

The most important part in a situational analysis implementing is the construction of an interpretable image model. Modern approaches to models construction have a large number of limitations. In this article, the main focus is on the methodology for constructing this model, the selection of an algorithm for detecting objects in an image, as a preliminary stage of building a model, as well as the principles of quality analysis of the constructed model and decision-making based on it. To represent the obtained model and implement the decision-making process on the basis of the obtained model, it is proposed to use the approaches developed in the framework of OSTIS Technology.

3   Methods Overview

3.1   Object Detection in Images

The first step during the image analysis is to process the source image and detect the objects automatically. During this step one of the following tasks is performed as a rule [1]:

- Semantic Segmentation – for every pixel in the source image determine its class and category;
- Classification and Localization – determine the class of a single object in the image and its exact location;
- Object Detection – define a class and a rectangular area bounding each of the objects in the image;
- Instance Segmentation – on the image with multiple objects determine the contours (all visible pixels) and the class of each of the objects.

From the standpoint of a semantic model construction last two tasks are of the most interest.

Among the existing modern object detection algorithms, including those based on deep learning methods, the most relevant approaches are:

- Sliding Window [18];
- Region Proposals [6];
- Single Shot Detection [16].

Each of the approaches has its own advantages and disadvantages, in terms of their relevance to application in systems that include image analysis [10].

The most popular approach for image semantic analysis is deep learning. We combine deep learning-based works into the following categories based on their main technical contributions:

- Fully convolutional networks;
- Convolutional models with graphical models;
- Encoder-decoder based models;
- Multi-scale and pyramid network based models;
- R-CNN based models (for instance segmentation);
- Dilated convolutional models and DeepLab family;
- Recurrent neural network based models;
- Attention-based models;
- Generative models and adversarial training;
- Convolutional models with active contour models;
- Other models.

To construct the model, described in this paper, it seems to be the most promising to use methods, based on the group of neural networks architectures with region proposals, so-called R-CNN, and their development:

- R-CNN [6] – represents a model of sequential image processing pipeline: generation of a set of regional proposals, the use of a pre-trained convolutional neural network with a final layer of support vectors and linear regression for a more accurate regions estimation;
- Fast R-CNN [5] – a model in which, to speed up the performance of the previous processing pipeline, a selection of regions and the union of all neural network models into one are used;
- Faster R-CNN [19] – to accelerate the model even further, a selective search of regions is used;
- Mask R-CNN [9] – unlike previous models, this one uses a binary mask to determine not just a rectangular region - a candidate for objects, but specific pixels belonging to the object, which, in essence, is the solution to the image segmentation problem described above.

3.2   Semantic Model

Within the framework of modern approaches as the basis of the semantic image model the so-called Scene Graph [21] is widely used. A scene graph is a data structure that describes the contents of a scene, which, in turn, can be specified by an image or its textual description. In the scene graph instances of objects their attributes and relationships between objects are encoded.

Formally, a scene graph is defined as follows: let C be a set of object classes, A – a set of attribute types, R – a set of relation types. A scene graph is defined as $G = (O, E)$, where $O = \{o_1, \ldots, o_n\}$ – a set of objects – nodes of a graph,

$E \in O \times R \times O$ – a set of graph edges. Every object is represented by $o_i = \{c_i, A_i\}$, where $c_i \in C$ – the class of the object, and $A_i \in A$ – its attributes.

A scene graph can be grounded to an image. Let B be a set of rectangular areas, each of which delineates a certain object in the image (they are generally called Bounding Boxes), then the grounding of the scene graph $G = (O, E)$ to the image is the function $\gamma : O \rightarrow B$, or γ_o.

To conduct the experiments the dataset Visual Genome[1] [15] is commonly used. It consists of 108 077 labelled images, for which 5.4 millions of the textual descriptions and scene-graphs for the whole images and their sections (regions) were produced using crowd sourcing. All the scene graphs are grounded to either textual descriptions, or images (regions), or both.

The example of scene graph – region grounding in Visual Genome is shown in Fig. 1).

Fig. 1. An example of an image from Visual Genome with grounding [15].

Grounding scene graphs to a textual descriptions (each object, attribute and relation) in Visual Genome corresponds to WordNet synset [17]. WordNet – network word representation, that is structured according to semantic relations. In WordNet each word is represented as a set of its synonymous meanings, which are called synsets. Each synset comprises of a triplet <word> · <pos> · <number>, where word – is a word itself, pos – its part of speech (n – noun, v – verb, a – adjective, r – adverb), number – index of the meaning in the set. E.g. the term "person" in WordNet is represented by three meanings person.n.01, person.n.02 and person.n.03. Textual grounding of the object "person" in Visual Genome corresponds to the synset person.n.01. In WordNet there are relations of synonymy, antonymy, "part – whole" (meronym – holonym), "general – specific" (hypernym – holonym).

Using a graph representation to describe an image model has a number of significant advantages compared to more traditional approaches to image captioning aimed toward a natural language description (considered in [2] and other

---

[1] Available at: https://visualgenome.org.

works). The graph representation is more unambiguous (invariant) and is much better suited for automatic processing, and, in particular, the interpretation of such a model.

However, despite these advantages, the currently used approach to the scene graph construction has a number of disadvantages that make it difficult to interpret image models presented in this form. The key disadvantage, in our opinion, is the lack of any semantic unification (standardization) in the principles of building scene graphs, in particular, in the principles of distinguishing relations and attributes (and, generally speaking, in this case, there is no clear boundary between the concepts of relation and attribute), in the framework of even one data set, as well as the lack of syntactic unification in the representation of scene graphs in various approaches. In addition, in modern approaches to the construction of scene graphs, as a rule, the problem of internationalization still remains.

In turn, the lack of unification in the representation of scene graphs makes it impossible to build universal processing tools for such graphs, in particular, means for verifying and decision making based on scene graphs.

An ontological approach is currently used as the basis for solving the problem of unification in various fields. In this paper, to implement this approach, it is proposed to use the OSTIS Technology, within the framework of which a unified standard for coding information (SC-code) is proposed [7], the problem of unification of the principles for representing different types of knowledge [4] and the problem of integrating various models for problem solving [20] are solved.

We list some of the advantages of OSTIS Technology that are relevant in the context of solving the problem posed in this paper:

- unification of the representation of semantic image models;
- ensuring the independence of the image model from the external language in which the preliminary description was made;
- the possibility of structuring the model according to various criteria, as well as the possibility of representing meta-information, which, in particular, will allow us to select image regions that are more or less significant for solving the current problem;
- the availability of verification tools and adjustments to the image model, partially considered in [11], which make it possible to verify the model itself for its internal consistency and adequacy of the subject area, and in the future will automatically evaluate the degree of conformity of the automatically obtained model to standard models developed by experts;
- the presence of a large amount of source data that has been accumulated at the moment and which may be useful for further research makes the task of automating the transition from scene graphs, for example, from the Visual Genome dataset, to a unified semantic representation in relevant SC-code.

4 Semantic Model Construction Technique

To build a semantic image model in the form of a scene graph, we must first detect the objects in the image, and then for each pair of objects decide whether they have a relations and which ones [22]. The selection of relations can be greatly simplified by using external knowledge bases (general purpose or specialized for a specific domain) [11]. In both cases, for the image on which n objects are found, it is necessary to consider $(n^2 - n)$ relations. In this paper it is proposed to simplify the solution by identifying the so-called salient (significant or the most relevant) objects [3], and to further consider $(n - 1)$ relationships. This approach corresponds to the scenario of tracking certain objects or situations in surveillance systems.

Frequency analysis of Visual Genome data shows that the most frequent relationships between objects in images are spatial relationships: the "on" relationship occurs 642,150 times, the "in" relation – 218,166, "behind" - 39,833. In addition, due to the hierarchical structure of WordNet grounding, spatial relationships can be described in more detail: for example, "car in a parking lot" or "car is parked in a parking lot". Indeed, when looking at an image, a person first of all notes how the objects are located relative to each other in space. In automatic processing it is also possible to determine semantic spatial relations between objects [12]. In addition, reducing the set of relations of the image model to spatial relations will allow at the current stage to significantly simplify the process of constructing and interpreting the model, while maintaining the ability to assess the anomalies and oddities.

The technique for automatic model construction for spatial relations is presented in Fig. 2.

In Fig. 2 the system of all possible spatial relations is visualized: the area of the salient object (subject) is filled, all the other areas are the options for the location of the object of interest (object), for which, using the decision tree in Fig. 3, the type of spatial relationship in the form "subject-relation-object" will be determined.

It should be noted that for the names of types of relations in this model prepositions are used (and prepositions, as it was described above, are not represented in WordNet), i.e. at this stage, grounding to WordNet is not possible, but at the next step (for interpretation), synsets containing these prepositions and their meanings (be.v.01, along.r.01, etc.) will be used.

In the decision tree the rectangles show the blocks corresponding to a certain type of relationship, while more general relationships that need to be specified are highlighted (similar to hypernyms from WordNet). When constructing a tree to speed up the process of final decision-making, the rules (shown in the figure by rhombus's) were formulated in accordance with the statistical data of the Visual Genome analysis, so that a more frequent case would be to the left of the tree. So, in the initial dataset, the"near" relationship is found more often than other spatial relationships (26,316 times), the "above" is significantly more common than the "below" – 13,767 times and 3,349 times respectively etc.

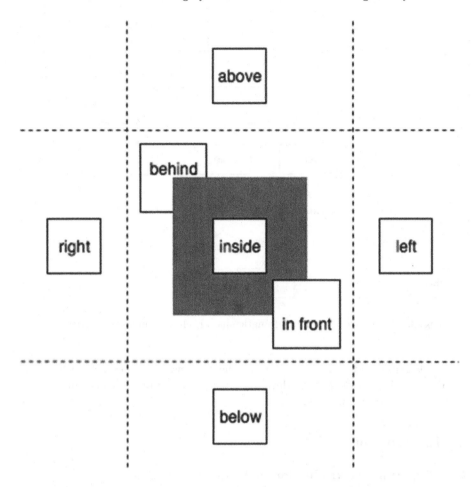

Fig. 2. Spatial relations system.

The implementation of the method used for the experiments described below first detects objects using the Faster R-CNN method, determining the classes of objects and their bounding boxes. The salient object is determined as the object with the largest bounding box.

In natural images the boundaries of the object regions, as a rule, intersect. If the intersection of the regions of the salient object and the object of interest is less than 50% of the area of the object of interest region, the relations corresponding to the decision rule are selected from the set "top", "bottom", "left", "right" (that is, it is considered that there is no intersection). At an intersection of more than 50%, the ratio is selected based on a comparison of the pixel masks of the objects obtained by applying Mask R-CNN to the object regions: if there are more pixels of a significant object in the intersection zone, the "back" relation is selected, and the "in front" relation is the opposite case.

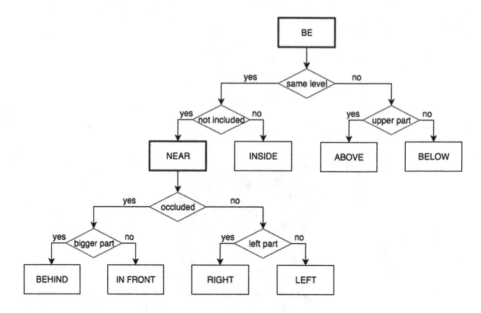

Fig. 3. The decision tree for automatic spatial relations model construction.

To describe spatial relationships in the framework of OSTIS Technology, a corresponding ontology was developed, the description of which and usage examples are presented in [12].

5   Experiments

5.1   Experimental Evaluation of Model Construction

For experimental evaluation of the semantic model construction technique from Visual Genome dataset the subset of images was selected. It is a sample of images in which each of the relations under consideration is represented by 50 regions with a grounding to the image (i.e. 50 regions for the relation "above", 50 regions for "below", etc. – the total of 350 regions). The examples of the images are given in Fig. 4 and 5.

In the experiment, relationships in the selected regions are automatically determined and the results are compared with the reference (given in the dataset) and evaluated by experts (see Table 1).

Fig. 4. The example of the region grounding for "crowd behind car".

Fig. 5. The example of the region grounding for "car below trees".

5.2   Experimental Evaluation of Model Interpretation

To experimentally evaluate the interpretation of the constructed model for the set of regions, textual descriptions of the regions are generated by replacing the relationships with the most common synonyms from WordNet (for example, "car below tree" turns into "car parked under tree") and the resulting annotations are compared with the reference using the METEOR metric [2].

The annotation results are also compared with the results obtained using a combined neural network [14] and purely convolutional neural network [13] approaches to annotating image regions without constructing a semantic model (Table 3).

As mentioned earlier, the description of the image model in the form of natural language text has a number of significant drawbacks. The rejection of such a description and the transition to graph representation leads to the need for a transition from classical text metrics (e.g. METEOR [2]) to metrics that allow us to evaluate the similarity of graph models.

A graph representation makes it possible to simplify the comparison of two models at the syntactic level, however, problems related to the semantic data presented remain urgent, which in the textual presentation faded into the background due to the large number of problems associated with the presentation form.

In general, we can distinguish the following levels of complexity of situations that arise when comparing graph image models:

- the system of terms and the system of concepts (logical ontology) coincide. In this case, the comparison is reduced to the search for isomorphic fragments, however, the problem of assessing the significance of each fragment remains relevant;
- the system of terms does not coincide, but the system of concepts coincides, i.e. the same concepts are used, but they can be named differently (for example, in the context of a street situation, the meaning of the words "car" and "automobile" will coincide). In this case, the identification and gluing of the same concepts, named differently, is additionally required. In the general case, this problem concerns not only concepts, but also specific entities;
- the system of concepts does not match. In this case, the alignment of systems of concepts is additionally required, in this case involving the definition of concepts used in the evaluated model through the concepts used in the example model.

The indicated levels relate to the case when strict coincidence of models is evaluated to the level of specific objects and concepts, however, when interpreting a model it is often enough to use a generalized model (for example, in a situation "a person sits on a chair" and a "person sits in an armchair" it is often important that a person sits and it doesn't matter where). Thus, the task of generalizing models with subsequent comparison is also relevant. In classical textual approaches, a similar problem is partially solved by identifying synonyms.

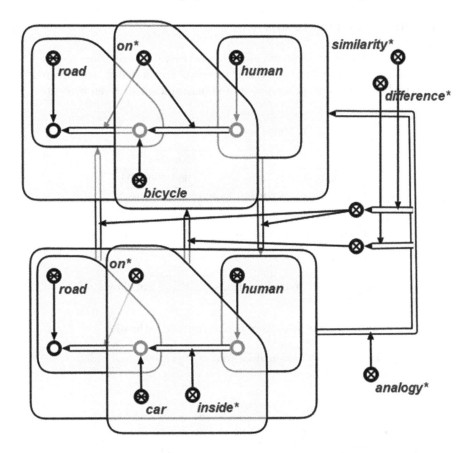

Fig. 6. Representation of similarities and differences in SCg.

Using OSTIS Technology to represent image models and construct relevant metrics has several advantages, in particular, one of them is the availability of means for structuring information and representing meta-information. Figure 6 shows an example representation of similarities and differences for the two pieces of information presented in SCg-code[2].

Note that the development of graph metrics based on OSTIS Technology will allow them to be used for other tasks, for example, to assess the quality and completeness of a student's response in intelligent training systems, to assess the contribution of each developer to a common knowledge base, etc.

---

[2] Available at: http://ims.ostis.net/.

6   Results and Discussion

In Table 1 the results of semantic model construction evaluation are shown. Object detection is considered correct, if the class labels match, the differences in bounding boxes estimation are considered insignificant in given context.

Table 1. Model construction evaluation.

	Number	%
Set size (relations/objects)	350/700	100
Object detection (RCNN-based)	687	98.1
Relations (dataset match)	335	95.7
Relations (visual analysis)	340	97.18

In Table 2 the results of spatial relations matching are shown.

Table 2. The analysis of spatial relations estimation.

Spatial relation	Visual analysis (out of 50)	Model (out of 50)
BEHIND	49	44
IN FRONT	48	45
RIGHT	50	50
LEFT	50	50
INSIDE	50	50
ABOVE	49	48
BELOW	49	48

In Table 3 the results of image captioning evaluation are shown.

Table 3. Region captioning results evaluation.

Coder model	METEOR
CNN + RNN [14]	0.305
TCN [13]	0.290
Semantic model (this paper)	0.515

As shown in Table 3, the use of a semantic model for encoding information from an image significantly exceeds neural network models when constructing meaningful phrases that describe regions. According to the METEOR metric, which takes into account not only the structure of the annotation, but also its semantic variations, the proposed method shows the results by more than 60% better than the neural network approaches.

7   Decision Making Based on Semantic Model

To make decisions on the basis of the proposed model at this stage (with a small number of classes of objects and relations between them), a general mechanism can be used, which was examined in detail, in particular, in [8]. The specified technique assumes a reliable logical conclusion based on the logical rules and ontology of contingencies available in the knowledge base, where for each class some recommendations are assumed.

Let us consider in more detail the example of decision-making. The Fig. 7 shows the image from the surveillance camera, on which the regions of objects detected are highlighted. For convenience, some regions are omitted (in the current implementation, the detector on this image detected 25 people, 7 cars, 4 umbrellas, 2 backpacks and 4 bags).

Fig. 7. The example of the image for decision-making.

According to the technique described above, a salient object, i.e. the key subject of the relationship, is an instance of the id1 class "pedestrian crossing" (label "crosswalk", synset crossing.n.05). In the current implementation, this is due to the fact that it has the largest size, but subsequently the application of the ontological approach will also allow contextual information to be taken into account.

The following objects of the corresponding classes were detected in the image:

– id2, id5, id6 – class "car"
– id3, id4, id7, id8, id9 – class "person"

According to the technique for constructing a model based on existing inter-sections of regions, the following relationships between pairs of objects are esti-mated:

1. id2 ->id1: "on"
2. id3 ->id1: "on"
3. id4 ->id1: "below"
4. id5 ->id1: "on"
5. id6 ->id1: "above"
6. id7 ->id1: "inside"
7. id8 ->id1: "below"
8. id9 ->id1: "on" (detection error due to camera placement)

In the form of SCg language this model is presented as in Fig. 8.

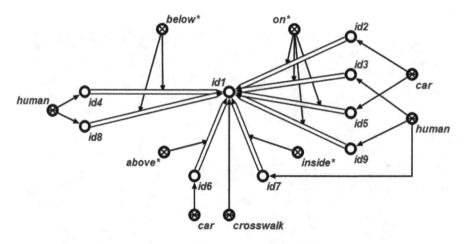

Fig. 8. Semantic model of image in SCg.

Based on estimated relations the following captions can be generated:

1. car on crosswalk - car is parked on crosswalk
2. person on crosswalk - person is crossing the road on crosswalk

Based on the of detected objects and relations, decisions in this example are made in the context of "people cross the road, cars let pedestrians pass". Thus, normal (regular) situations for "person" with respect to "crosswalk" – "on" and "inside", for "car" with respect to "crosswalk" – the opposite.

The example of formal rule in SCg language is shown in Fig. 9.

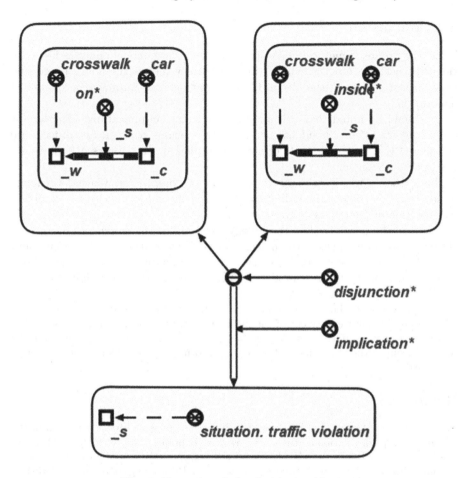

Fig. 9. Example rule for decision making.

Using a rule base, applying the simple inference mechanisms, the following contingencies can be distinguished:

1. traffic rules violation: car on the crosswalk – in pairs 1 and 4
2. traffic rules violation: a person is using a crosswalk – in pairs 4 and 7

Rule Violation in pair 8 will not be determined at the moment, due to the camera placement. To prevent this mistakes, it is possible to detect not regions, but masks, however, in this case, image processing will take much longer.

8   Conclusion

Thus, the proposed method of constructing a semantic model analyzes less relationships between objects, which can significantly reduce the image processing time on test sets from the Visual Genome dataset and improve the quality of annotation.

It should be noted that this approach contains simplifications - the largest of the objects is considered salient and only relations between two objects are considered (i.e. only fragments of a scene-graph), also attributes of objects are not taken into account.

In further work, it is planned to use more complex approaches to determining a salient object (including based on specific subject area), the complete construction and analysis of graph scenes.

In turn, the use of OSTIS Technology to represent the model and implement the decision-making mechanism makes it possible to ensure the modifiability and scalability of the system, built on the basis of the approaches proposed in this paper, which in the future will allow to eliminate the described limitations.

Acknowledgment. The research presented in this paper was conducted in close collaboration with the Department of Intelligent Information Technologies of Belarusian State University of Informatics and Radioelectronics. Authors would like to thank the research group of the Department of Intelligent Information Technologies for productive cooperation.

References

1. Agarwal, S., Terrail, J.O.D., Jurie, F.: Recent advances in object detection in the age of deep convolutional neural networks. arXiv preprint arXiv: 1809.03193 (2018)
2. Banerjee, S., Lavie, A.: METEOR: an automatic metric for MT evaluation with improved correlation with human judgments. In: Proceedings of the ACL Workshop on Intrinsic and Extrinsic Evaluation Measures for Machine Translation and/or Summarization, Ann Arbor, Michigan, pp. 65–72. Association for Computational Linguistics, June 2005. https://www.aclweb.org/anthology/W05-0909
3. Borji, A., Cheng, M.-M., Hou, Q., Jiang, H., Li, J.: Salient object detection: a survey. Comput. Visual Media **5**(2), 117–150 (2019). https://doi.org/10.1007/s41095-019-0149-9
4. Davydenko, I.: Semantic models, method and tools of knowledge bases coordinated development based on reusable components. In: Golenkov, V. (ed.) Open Semantic Technologies for Intelligent Systems, pp. 99–118. BSUIR, Minsk (2018)
5. Girshick, R.: Fast R-CNN. In: 2015 IEEE International Conference on Computer Vision (ICCV), pp. 1440–1448 (2015). https://doi.org/10.1109/ICCV.2015.169
6. Girshick, R., Donahue, J., Darrell, T., Malik, J.: Rich feature hierarchies for accurate object detection and semantic segmentation. In: 2014 IEEE Conference on Computer Vision and Pattern Recognition, pp. 580–587 (2014). https://doi.org/10.1109/CVPR.2014.81
7. Golenkov, V., Guliakina, N., Davydenko, I., Eremeev, A.: Methods and tools for ensuring compatibility of computer systems. In: Golenkov, V. (ed.) Otkrytye semanticheskie tekhnologii proektirovaniya intellektual'nykh system [Open semantic technologies for intelligent systems], pp. 25–52. BSUIR, Minsk (2019)

8. Golovko, V., Kroshchanka, A., Ivashenko, V., Kovalev, M., Taberko, V., Ivaniuk, D.: Principles of decision-making systems building based on the integration of neural networks and semantic models. In: Golenkov, V. (ed.) Otkrytye semanticheskie tekhnologii proektirovaniya intellektual'nykh system [Open semantic technologies for intelligent systems], pp. 91–102. BSUIR, Minsk (2019)
9. He, K., Gkioxari, G., Dollár, P., Girshick, R.: Mask R-CNN. IEEE Trans. Pattern Anal. Mach. Intell. **42**(2), 386–397 (2020). https://doi.org/10.1109/TPAMI.2018.2844175
10. Hursov, P.S., Iskra, N.A.: Algoritmy detektsii ob'ektov dlya analiza izobrazhenii [Object detection algorithms for image analysis]. In: Informatsionnye tekhnologii i sistemy: materialy mezhdunarodnoi nauchnoi konferentsii [Information Technologies and Systems: materials of the international scientific conference], pp. 128–129. Minsk (2019). (in Russian)
11. Iskra, N., Iskra, V., Lukashevich, M.: Neural network based image understanding with ontological approach. In: Otkrytye semanticheskie tekhnologii proektirovaniya intellektual'nykh system: materialy mezhdunarodnoj nauchno-tekhnicheskoj konferencii [Open semantic technologies for intelligent systems: materials of the international scientific and technical conference], Minsk, pp. 113–122 (2019)
12. Iskra, N.A., Mezhen', A.L., Shunkevich, D.V.: Ontologiya predmetnoj oblasti prostranstvennyh sushchnostej dlya sistemy semanticheskogo analiza izobrazhenij [Ontology of the subject area of spatial entities for the system of semantic image analysis]. In: Informatsionnye tekhnologii i sistemy: materialy mezhdunarodnoi nauchnoi konferentsii [Information Technologies and Systems: of the international scientific conference], Minsk, pp. 112–113 (2019). (in Russian)
13. Iskra, N., Iskra, V.: Temporal convolutional and recurrent networks for image captioning. In: Ablameyko, S.V., Krasnoproshin, V.V., Lukashevich, M.M. (eds.) PRIP 2019. CCIS, vol. 1055, pp. 254–266. Springer, Cham (2019). https://doi.org/10.1007/978-3-030-35430-5_21
14. Johnson, J., Karpathy, A., Fei-Fei, L.: Densecap: fully convolutional localization networks for dense captioning. In: 2016 IEEE Conference on Computer Vision and Pattern Recognition (CVPR), pp. 4565–4574 (2016). https://doi.org/10.1109/CVPR.2016.494
15. Krishna, R., et al.: Visual genome: connecting language and vision using crowdsourced dense image annotations. Int. J. Comput. Vision **123**(1), 32–73 (2017). https://doi.org/10.1007/s11263-016-0981-7
16. Liu, W., et al.: SSD: single shot MultiBox detector. In: Leibe, B., Matas, J., Sebe, N., Welling, M. (eds.) ECCV 2016. LNCS, vol. 9905, pp. 21–37. Springer, Cham (2016). https://doi.org/10.1007/978-3-319-46448-0_2
17. Miller, G.A.: WordNet: An Electronic Lexical Database. MIT Press, Cambridge (1998)
18. Müller, J., Fregin, A., Dietmayer, K.: Disparity sliding window: object proposals from disparity images. In: 2018 IEEE/RSJ International Conference on Intelligent Robots and Systems (IROS), pp. 5777–5784 (2018). https://doi.org/10.1109/IROS.2018.8593390
19. Ren, S., He, K., Girshick, R., Sun, J.: Faster R-CNN: towards real-time object detection with region proposal networks. IEEE Trans. Pattern Anal. Mach. Intell. **39**(6), 1137–1149 (2017). https://doi.org/10.1109/TPAMI.2016.2577031
20. Shunkevich, D.: Agent-oriented models, method and tools of compatible problem solvers development for intelligent systems. In: Golenkov, V. (ed.) Open Semantic Technologies for Intelligent Systems, pp. 119–132. BSUIR, Minsk (2018)

21. Xu, D., Zhu, Y., Choy, C.B., Fei-Fei, L.: Scene graph generation by iterative message passing. In: 2017 IEEE Conference on Computer Vision and Pattern Recognition (CVPR), pp. 3097–3106 (2017). https://doi.org/10.1109/CVPR.2017.330

22. Yang, J., Lu, J., Lee, S., Batra, D., Parikh, D.: Graph R-CNN for scene graph generation. In: Ferrari, V., Hebert, M., Sminchisescu, C., Weiss, Y. (eds.) Computer Vision - ECCV 2018, pp. 690–706. Springer, Cham (2018). https://doi.org/10.1007/978-3-030-01246-5_41

Intelligent Voice Assistant Based on Open Semantic Technology

Vadim Zahariev⬤, Daniil Shunkevich(✉)⬤, Sergei Nikiforov⬤,
and Elias Azarov⬤

Belarusian State University of Informatics and Radioelectronics,
Minsk, Republic of Belarus
{zahariev,shunkevich,azarov}@bsuir.by, nikiforov.sergei.al@gmail.com

Abstract. The paper considers the approach to building a personal assistant based on the open semantic technology (OSTIS). The key idea of our approach is the transition from processing a message in speech form to a formalized representation of the meaning in a knowledge base with the least number of intermediate stages. Knowledge base is built on the basis of a semantic network implemented using OSTIS technology. In this case, many tasks of the syntactic, semantic and pragmatic levels of natural language processing, for example, such as recognition of named entities (NEM) and definition of a part of speech (POS), dialogue management (intentions identifications and directives forming), can be performed directly in the knowledge base of the intelligent assistant. This will make it possible to effectively solve such problems as managing the global and local context of the dialogue, resolving linguistic phenomena such as anaphores, homonymy and eleptical phrases, correctly formulating answers to questions that are complex in structure and content, posed by the user during the dialogue.

Keywords: Dialogue system · Intelligent personal assistant · Voice interface · Semantic network · Spoken language understanding

1 Introduction

This work is a development of the article [30]. This work is distinguished by a deeper study of the architecture of the problem solver and user model description tools.

Speech is one of the most natural and convenient forms of transferring information between people. This fact leads to a steady trend in the use of speech interface technologies in the development of modern software. At the present time, no one doubts that this form of human-machine interaction will play a significant role in the construction of intelligent systems of the future.

Voice user interface is most often implemented as a part of virtual assistant software. In the literature, such applications are commonly referred to as intelligent personal assistant (IPA) or intelligent virtual assistant (IVA) [5,20,22].

© Springer Nature Switzerland AG 2020
V. Golenkov et al. (Eds.): OSTIS 2020, CCIS 1282, pp. 121–145, 2020.
https://doi.org/10.1007/978-3-030-60447-9_8

These programs are able to conduct a dialogue with the user in natural language and carry out input-output of information in both text and speech form.

Universal speech assistants "Alexa" [2], "Siri" [25], "Google Assistant" [12], "Cortana" [8], "Alice" [1], developed by the world's largest companies such as "Amazon", "Apple", "Google", "Microsoft", "Yandex" are widely used in modern smartphones and operating systems. The trends of their development are such that they have turned from stand-alone applications into platforms that can be deployed on devices of different manufacturers, and on the basis of which various services (in the form of so-called skills, data of assistants) built on the basis of intelligent information technologies can be delivered to the user [21,23]. This fact allows manufacturers of both electronics and software to open new niches in consumer markets using the latest advances in artificial intelligence technologies.

Analytical agencies predict that the combined annual growth rate of the global market for products built using speech assistant technologies will be more than 30%, increasing from $1.2 billion in 2018 to $5.4 billion by 2024 [10]. According to their estimates, this trend will be due to both an increase in the total number of smartphones and the expansion of the standard functions of speech interfaces: managing the dialogue context, personalization, the ability to conduct dialogue in several languages, or respond in both text mode and voice modes.

2 Analysis of Existing Solutions and Problem Statement

Consider the architecture and principles of the voice assistant, peculiar to most modern solutions. In our description, we will focus on the voice assistant "Alexa" from the company "Amazon". This product is currently the most popular assistant (with the exception of mobile phones) in the speech technology market (about 65%) [3], based on a modern stack of speech technologies. Many other major players in the speech market such as "Google" ("Google Assistant"), "MicroSoft" ("Cortana"), "Yandex" ("Alice") are trying to adopt solutions specific to "Alexa" [14] in their products. Therefore, the architecture under consideration can be considered typical.

Modern voice assistant forms a distributed software and hardware system consisting of two main parts: front end and back end (Fig. 1).

The front end part is deployed on a specialized device or installed as an application on the user's device. The client is responsible for issues related to capturing and playing back audio information, pre-processing, wake-word system triggering activation, encoding and decoding data, and generating backend requests. Access to the server part is carried out through the corresponding program interface, most often REST [6].

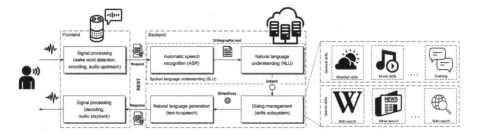

Fig. 1. Dialogue system architecture

The back end part includes following main components.

- spoken language understanding subsystem (SLU), which consists of automatic speech recognition module (ASR) and natural language understanding (NLU) module;
- dialogue management module (DM) includes a subsystem of "Skills" (general type like weather, music, navigation and specialized like web search, wiki, news etc.).
- natural language messages generator (NLG) module.

Let's review server components in detail. The Speech Understanding Subsystem (SLU) converts the input signal into some semantic equivalent of the spoken phrase - "intent", which reflects the meaning of the spoken phrase and the user's expectations. This subsystem includes:

The automatic speech recognition module (ASR) of speech implements the process of converting speech into text. Acoustic and linguistic models are used to describe this process. Algorithms that implement the corresponding models make it possible to determine fragments of the speech wave in the audio signal equal to the basic phonetic units of the target language and form a phonetic text from them. Then a spelling text is obtained which is based on the relevant rules of morphology and grammar. Modern ASR implementations involve the use of a combining statistical methods such as hidden Markov models (HMM) of neural network methods based on convolutional (CNN) and recurrent neural networks (LSTM-RNN) [7,26].

The natural language understanding module (NLU) implements a natural language text processing sequence that includes the main stages: tokenization, defining the boundaries of sentences, parts of speech tagging, named entities recognition, syntactic and semantic analysis. At the output of this module, an entity is formed called "intent", which is a structured formalized user request. It conveys the main meaning of what was said and the wishes of the user. A frame model of utterances is used to form an "intention", as a result of which an object is formed which is transferred to the next module.

The dialogue management manager (DM) is a module that directly controls the dialogue, its structure and progress, fills the general context, contains knowledge about a specific subject domain in the form of compact fragmented ontologies in the semantic network and the rules for responding to them which are known as "skills". It receives the input data from the SLU component in the form of incoming "intentions" and must select the necessary "skill" block, then attains the global state of the dialogue process and transfers the output data to the generation module in the form of a "directive" object. The Fig. 2 shows examples of the description of intent and "directive".

The natural language generation module (NLG) synthesizes the voice response message in accordance with the available signal and speaker voice model and text of the response message which is located in the "directive" object. In connection with the steady tendency towards personalization of devices and programs, the possibility of adapting systems to the voice of a new speaker is one of the interesting features that we would like to consider in our work and which is not available in current solutions on the market. According to research [19] the voice of a person known to the listener is perceived 30% better than the voice of an unfamiliar person. Changing the speaker's voice during the speech synthesis process allows you to attract the attention of system users to key information in a voice message, to emphasize especially important events or moments. It helps to improve the ergonomics of the system.

```
{
    "intent": "GetHoroscope",
    "sign": "libra",
    "date": "2019-12-31"
}
```
a) Intent object example

```
{
    "namespace": "Speech",
    "name": "speak",
    "text": "The horoscope
    for Libra."
}
```
b) Directive object example

Fig. 2. Intent and directive object example

It should be noted that this architecture has proven itself in all modern solutions. However, the current situation in the market of voice assistants, from our point of view, has several unresolved problems and limitations:

– The main parts (semantic processing of information in the NLU and DM modules) of the system are proprietary closed. Developers and researchers do not have the ability to make changes to the knowledge base, supplement and modify existing ontologies. There is only the opportunity to use these modules as a service without directly participating in their development. Also, scientific and practical details related to the methods of formalization and processing of knowledge were not disclosed, which does not allow comparing the proposed solutions with alternative technologies and implementations.

- All common voice assistants have an exclusively distributed implementation, where the main part is located on the server side. There are no alternative, the so-called "on the eadge" solutions that allow you to deploy the system in an independent local environment, for example, on your servers in your own data center or directly on the client device. Such a method would make it possible to ensure stable operation of the system in cases where there is no stable Internet connection and could also be in demand if the user does not want to transmit their personal data to companies in the form of voice fragments and descriptions of their requests in the system in form of "intentions" objects (intent) and "directives". This thesis is of particular relevance in connection with the increasing incidence of leakage of personal information from large companies [16, 17].

In this regard, from our point of view, the urgent task is to build a voice assistant based on open semantic technologies that allow a large group of developers to participate in the design and extend the knowledge base. To solve this problem, it is necessary to formulate a number of requirements for such an assistant.

Analysis of the user needs (including various companies) allows us to present the following set of functional requirements to the developed speech assistants:

- speaker independent recognition, the ability to correctly recognize messages from various interlocutors, possibly with speech dysfunctions;
- in a situation where the message is not understood by the system or clarification of any parameters is required, the system should be able to ask the interlocutor clarifying questions;
- the ability to recognize a speaker by voice, as a result - the ability to conduct a dialogue simultaneously with a group of interlocutors;
- the ability to work in conditions of noise interference;
- the ability to accumulate and take into account the history of the dialogue with the same interlocutor for a long time (to build and store a portrait of the interlocutor);
- the ability to take into account the current state of the user, including his emotions, as well as such individual characteristics as gender, age, etc.;
- the speech assistant can receive information about the interlocutor not only directly from the dialogue, but also have predefined information about him that is of interest in the context of the current dialogue;
- the speech assistant can conduct a dialogue of an infotainment nature (to answer user questions or conduct a conversation without a specific goal), and to pursue a specific goal that affects the dialogue process (for example, to calm or amuse a person to talk to).

The development of speech assistants that meet these requirements is hindered by a number of problems. Some problems were considered and partially solved by the authors in previous works:

– in [28], the problem of identifying and eliminating ambiguities (including those associated with speech defects, noise, etc.) in a speech signal due to a knowledge base is considered;
– in [29], an approach to the description of the context of the dialogue with the possibility of its consideration in the analysis of voice messages is considered;

In this paper, the main attention will be paid to the principles of dialogue organization (situational dialogue management), description of the user model, as well as mechanisms for adapting the dialogue process to the characteristics of a specific user and specific subject domain.

An important feature that distinguishes dialogue system (in specific domain area) from universal voice assistents is the lack of the need to understand the meaning of the message completely; more often, to generate the required response, it is enough to determine the type of message and select some keywords. This feature significantly reduces the complexity of the problem being solved and will be taken into account further when detailing the proposed approach.

2.1   Analysis of the Functionality of Close Analogues

Consider the capabilities of the speech assistant "Replika" from the "uka" company, due to the similarity of solved tasks [27].

"Replica" is a companion system designed to partially solve the problem of loneliness, through dialogue on topics related to the user's life. This allows people who for any reason find it difficult to communicate with people to partially satisfy their need for communication.

Dialogue with this system can be conducted both in text and in voice version, however, all processing is carried out on the message text. In the case of a voice message, an intermediate stage of translation from speech to text is added.

Among the features of this system, it is necessary to note the use of generalized answers in cases where it is not possible to precisely determine the subject of the message.

During the first dialogs, the system tries to find out as much information as possible about the user, which can be further used during the dialogue. This information is stored and taken into account in the future, as evidenced by the periodic mention by the system of the problems previously mentioned by the user during subsequent dialogs.

The use of information obtained during previous dialogs is an advantage of this system, as this improves the quality of the dialogue.

1. Only a distributed implementation, which involves sending and storing personal user data on remote servers, which may be unacceptable for a certain part of users.
2. The accumulation of knowledge about the user, obtaining it exclusively during dialogs, takes a rather long time, during which the system cannot correctly perform all its functions.
3. Currently, the system supports only English.

3   Proposed Approach

OSTIS Technology and the corresponding set of models, methods and tools for developing semantically compatible intelligent systems as the basis for building voice assistants are proposed here. The basis of OSTIS Technology is a unified version of the information encoding based on semantic networks with set-theoretic interpretation, called the SC code [11].

The architecture of each system built on OSTIS Technology (ostis-systems) includes a platform for interpreting semantic models of ostis-systems, as well as a semantic model of ostis-systems using SC-code (sc-model of ostis-systems). In turn, the sc-model of the ostis-system includes the sc-model of the knowledge base, the sc-model of the task solver and the sc-model of the interface (in particular, the user interface). The principles of engineering and designing knowledge bases and problem solvers are discussed in more detail in [9] and [24], respectively.

Models and tools application proposed by OSTIS Technology will provide, in addition to the advantages indicated in the above works, the opportunity to

- create, store and analyze the user's portrait, including both long-term information and its current state;
- save and analyze the history of the dialogue with each interlocutor;
- clearly distinguish the part of the dialogue management, depending only on the meaning of the messages and not depending on the language in which the dialogue is conducted, and the part depending on the language of dialogue;
- integrate the subject-independent part of the knowledge base with the subject-dependent part within each system, which will allow you to flexibly take into account the characteristics of the subject domain when conducting dialogue.

Further in the text, we will assume that the dialogue is carried out in Russian, however, most of the models presented do not depend on the language in which the dialogue is conducted. To write formal texts within the framework of the work, we will use options for external display of SC-code constructions such as SCg (graphic version) and SCn (hypertext version).

4   System Architecture

The general dialogue scheme can be written as follows:

- The user delivers a voice message;
- The speech analysis module, based on the dictionary of speech identifiers available in the knowledge base of the system, selects keywords within the message and correlates them with entities in the knowledge base;
- Based on the rules available in the knowledge base, the system classifies the received message;
- Based on the rules available in the knowledge base, the system generates a new message addressed to the current interlocutor (possibly non-atomic);
- The speech synthesis module generates a fragment of the speech signal corresponding to the new message and voices it;

4.1 Speech Analysis

To perform the processing of the speech signal inside the ASR module, it is necessary to fulfill it analysis and parametric description, i.e. represent as a sequence of characteristic vectors of the same dimension.

The proposed signal model and method for its evaluation has a number of distinctive features. They are a discrete Fourier transform or determination of the autocorrelation function of a signal in a short fragment. The method under consideration does not impose strict restrictions associated with the observance of the stationary conditions of the signal parameters on the analysis frame. This allows one to obtain a high temporal and frequency resolution of the signal, as well as a clearer spectral picture of the energy localization at the corresponding frequencies Fig. 3, and as a result, a more accurate estimate of the signal parameters (on average by 10–15%).

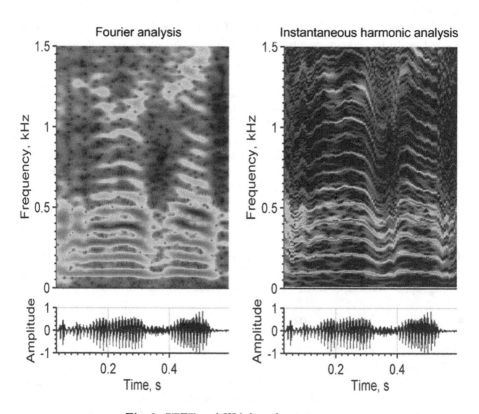

Fig. 3. STFT and IHA based spectrograms

The speech signal is divided into overlapping fragments, each of which is described by a set of parameters: the spectral envelope, the instantaneous fundamental frequency (if the fragment is voiced) and the type of excitation, which can be voiced, unvoiced or mixed.

The quasiperiodic component of the speech signal is represented as the sum of sinusoids or the real part of complex exponentials with continuous amplitude, frequency and phase, and noise as a random process with a given power spectral density (PSD):

$$s(n) = \sum_{p}^{P} A_p(n) cos\phi_k(n) + r(n)$$

$$= Re[\sum_{p}^{P} A_p(n) \exp j\phi_p(n)] + r(n)$$

(1)

where P – number of sinusoids (complex exponentials), $A_p(n)$ – instantaneous amplitude of the p-th sinusoid, $\phi_p(n)$ – instantaneous phase of the p-th sine waves $r(n)$ – aperiodic component. The instantaneous frequency $F_p(n)$, located in the interval $[0, \pi]$ (π corresponds to the Nyquist frequency), is a derivative of the instantaneous phase. It is assumed that the amplitude changes slowly, which means limiting the frequency band of each of the components. Using the obtained harmonic amplitudes of the voiced and PSD unvoiced components, a common spectral envelope is formed.

This set of parameters is extracted from a speech signal using an algorithm consisting of the following steps:

- estimation of the instantaneous fundamental frequency using the error-resistant algorithm for tracking the instantaneous fundamental frequency "IRAPT (Instantaneous Robust Algorithm for Pitch Tracking)" [4];
- deformation of the time axis of the signal to ensure the stationary frequency of the fundamental tone;
- estimation of instantaneous harmonic parameters of a speech signal using a DFT modulated filter bank - each harmonic of the fundamental tone of voiced speech falls into a separate channel of the filter bank, where it is converted into an analytical complex signal from which the instantaneous amplitude, phase and frequency are extracted;
- based on the analysis of the obtained instantaneous frequency values, various regions of the spectrum are classified as periodic and aperiodic;
- harmonics belonging to periodic spectral regions are synthesized and subtracted from the original signal;
- the remainder is transferred to the frequency domain using the short-term Fourier transform;
- parameters of the synthesized harmonics and the PSD of the remainder are combined into one common spectral envelope and translated into a logarithmic scale;
- adjacent spectral envelopes are analyzed to determine how to excite the entire analyzed fragment of the signal.

Each spectral envelope is represented as a vector of logarithmic energy values equally spaced on the chalk scale. For a speech signal with a sampling frequency of 44.1 kHz, a 100-dimensional vector is used. The characteristic vector consists of the fundamental tone frequency values, the spectral envelope and the sign of vocalization of the current speech fragment. The dimension of the vector determines a compromise between the quality of signal reconstruction and computational complexity. Based on practical experiments, it was found that the selected dimension is sufficient for the reconstruction of natural speech.

4.2   Knowledge Base

The basis of the knowledge base of any ostis-system (more precisely, sc-models of the knowledge base) is a hierarchical system of subject domains and their corresponding ontologies. The Fig. 4 shows the upper hierarchy of the knowledge base part that relates directly to voice assistants.

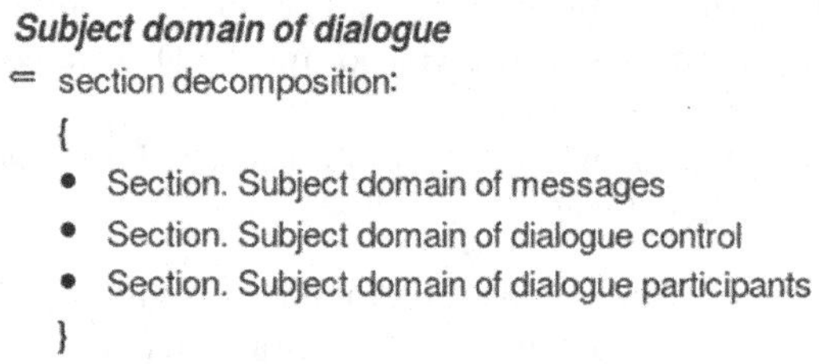

Subject domain of dialogue
⇐ section decomposition:
   {
   • Section. Subject domain of messages
   • Section. Subject domain of dialogue control
   • Section. Subject domain of dialogue participants
   }

Fig. 4. The hierarchy of subject domains.

Consider in more detail the concepts studied in each of these subject domains and examples of their use.

4.3   Message Subject Domain

The Fig. 5 shows the top level of message classification according to various criteria, independent of the subject domain.

An atomic message refers to a message that does not include other messages, in turn, Non-atomic message is a message that includes other messages. At the same time, a non-atomic message can consist of one sentence, but have several semantic parts, for example, "Can I log in if I am not 16 years old?" (age is reported and a question is asked) or "Hello, my name is Sergey." (the name is communicated and a greeting is expressed).

In turn, the presented classes can be further divided into more private ones. The Fig. 6 shows the classification of interrogative sentences.

message

⇒ inclusion*:

- incentive message
- interrogative message
- declarative message

⇐ subdividing*:

- {
  - daytime message
  - evening message
  - morning message
  }
- {
  - message with respectful treatment
  - message with standard treatment
  }
- {
  - exclamatory message
  - non-exclamatory message
  }
- {
  - non-atomic message
  - atomic message
  }
- {
  - undefined language message
  - english language message
  - russian language message
  }

Fig. 5. Typology of messages.

interrogative message

⇐ subdividing*:

{

- complete dictal question
- partial dictal question
- complete modal question
- partial modal question

}

Fig. 6. Typology of interrogative messages.

4.4   Subject Domain of Dialogue Participants

To present information about the participants in the dialogue, an appropriate domain model and ontology have been developed.

Figure 7 and 8 shows a fragment of the description in the knowledge base of a specific known system user. The above description contains both long-term information about the user, which will be saved after the dialogue is completed (gender, name, etc.) and short-term, which can be updated with each new dialogue - information on age, location, mood, etc.

4.5   Dialog Management Area

Within the subject domain of dialogue management, rules are presented according to which the analysis of user messages and the generation of response messages are carried out.

In accordance with the above general plan of work, the system distinguishes several categories of rules:

– voice message classification rules;
– rules for generating new messages within the current dialogue;
– voice message generation rules;

To simplify processing, some rules can be written not in the form of logical statements, but with the help of additional relations (for example, keywords that define the class of messages) and their corresponding knowledge processing agents. This hybridization of declarative and imperative recording options is widely used within the framework of OSTIS Technology in order to increase the efficiency of information processing while maintaining consistency of presentation at a basic level.

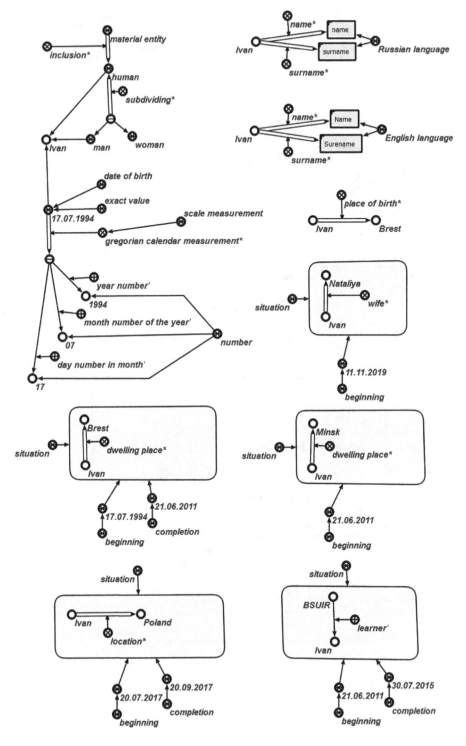

Fig. 7. Known system user description (biographical information).

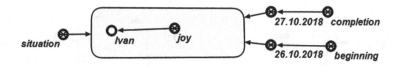

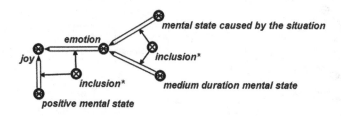

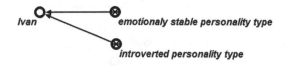

Fig. 8. Known system user description (emotional condition).

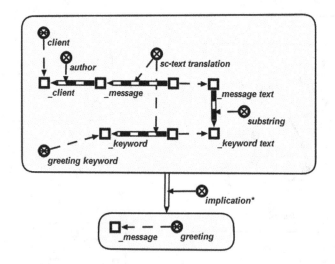

Fig. 9. Example rule for classifying a message.

Figure 9 shows an example of a simple rule for classifying messages based on keywords. The shown rule systemizes a message as a welcome class if it contains the appropriate words.

Figure 10 provides a formal definition of an atomic message.

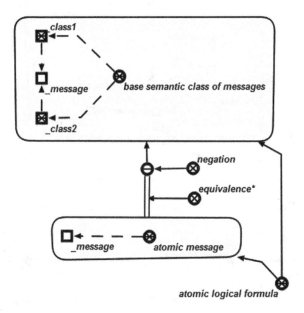

Fig. 10. Definition of an atomic message.

Figure 11 shows a rule requiring you to find out the name of the interlocutor, if it is still not known to the system.

4.6   Subject-Dependent Fragments of the Knowledge Base

If necessary, the subject-independent part of the knowledge base can be supplemented with any information clarifying the specifics of a particular subject domain, if it is necessary to improve the quality of the dialogue. The Fig. 12 shows a fragment of the knowledge base for the speech assistant-waiter of a cafe. The given fragment of the knowledge base includes a description of some drinks composition and confectionery products available in the menu, as well as information about the order made by a specific client.

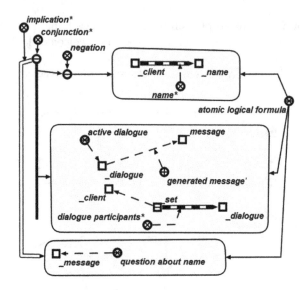

Fig. 11. Rule of generating a question about a name.

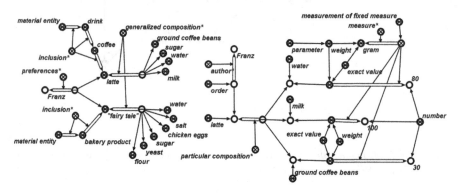

Fig. 12. An example of a knowledge base fragment, depending on the subject domain.

4.7   Problem Solver

The task solver of any ostis-system (more precisely, the sc-model of the ostis-system task solver) is a hierarchical system of knowledge processing agents in semantic memory (sc-agents) that interact only by specifying the actions they perform in the specified memory.

The top level of the agents hierarchy for the speech assistant task solver in SCn is as follows:

Voice Assistant Problem Solver
⇐ *abstract sc-agent decomposition*:*
{
- *Logical Rule Enforcement Agent*
- *Voice Message Analysis Agent*
  ⇐ *abstract sc-agent decomposition*:*
  {
  - *Keyword selection agent in a voice message*
  - *Keyword selection agent from a set of words in a speech message*
  - *Translation agent of fragments of a speech message to a knowledge base*
  }
- *Message processing agent within the framework of semantic memory*
  ⇐ *abstract sc-agent decomposition*:*
  {
  - *User Message Processing Agent*
    ⇐ *abstract sc-agent decomposition*:*
    {
    - *Message management agent*
    - *Text formalization agent*
    - *Building a sequence of tokens in a message agent*
    - *Syntactic analysis agent*
    - *Disambiguation agent*
    - *Message classification agent*
    - *User message argument allotment agent*
    - *Message processing agent*
    }
  - *System message generation agent*
    ⇐ *abstract sc-agent decomposition*:*
    {
    - *Message generation agent*
    - *Message text generation agent*
    - *Message text composition agent*
    }
  }
- *Voice Concatenation Agent*
- *Voice Message Generation Agent*
}

4.8   Speech Synthesis

One of the requirements for the developed voice assistant indicated in this article is adaptation to a specific speaker. Changing the speaker's voice in the process of speech synthesis allows you to attract the attention of system users to key information in a voice message, emphasize important events or moments, according to studies. The voice of a person known to the listener is perceived 30% better than the voice of an unknown person. In this paper, we would like to show the applicability of the developed methods for signal synthesis with personalized speaker properties, namely, building a personal speaker model that will get you around to synthesize speech with the voice of the selected target speaker.

The voice model of the speaker is based on a neural network, built on the principle of an automatic encoder. An automatic encoder is a multilayer neural network that converts multidimensional data into lower dimensional codes and then restores them in their original form. It was shown in [13] that data reduction systems based on neural networks have much broader capabilities, because, unlike the principal component analysis method, they permit nonlinear transformations to be performed.

The used artificial neural network configuration is shown in Fig. 13.

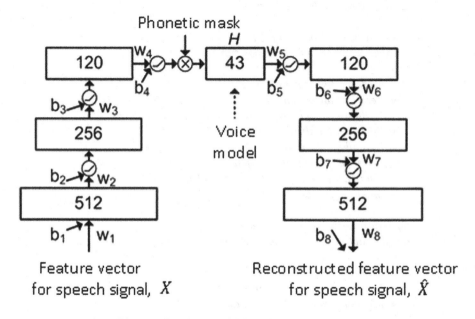

Fig. 13. Speaker model based on auto-encoder

The auto-encoder performs next mapping function:

$$H = (w_4 RL(w_3 RL(w_2 RL(w_1 X + b_1) + b_2) + b_3) + b_4) \otimes M \qquad (2)$$

where X is characteristic vector of the speech signal, H – vector of reduced dimension, M – phonetic mask vector, w_{1-4} and b_{1-4} – weight coefficients and offsets of the corresponding network signals, $\otimes$ – stands for element-wise multiplication. The network uses a piecewise linear activation function $RL(x) = max(0, x)$, since it is shown that it provides a more effective internal representation of speech data compared to the logistic one and allows you to speed up the learning process [15]. At the output of the encoder, lower dimensional codes are generated, which are constrained in order to perform phonetic binding. The restriction is imposed by multiplying the signal H by a phoneme mask, which is a sparse matrix, and formed on the basis of the phonetic marking of the speech corpus.

The decoder reconstructs the reduced-dimensional codes into the characteristic vectors $\hat{X}$. The corresponding display function is as follows:

$$\hat{X} = (w_8 RL(w_7 RL(w_6 RL(w_5 H + b_5) + b_6) + b_7) + b_8) \tag{3}$$

The next number of neurons in each hidden layer of the neural network was used: 512-256-120-43-120-256-512. Network training involves several steps:

- preliminary segmentation of the teaching speech corps into phonemes;
- initialization of network parameters and preliminary training;
- training of the encoder/decoder system;

As a result of training, a voice model is formed, which includes a model of each individual phoneme and the transitions between them contained in the training sample. For more details, the process of model formation is presented in [18].

5   Example of Working

The scenario of the system is proposed:

1. The user asks a question like "What is X?" (the typology of questions is still limited to one class of questions);
2. The speech signal analysis module selects a fragment corresponding to the name of entity X in the request and finds an entity with that name (*exactly how - see the question above*) in the knowledge base;
3. The module for analyzing a speech signal in a formal language (in SC-code) forms a query to the knowledge base of the form "What is X?" for the found entity;
4. Ostis-system generates a response that is displayed to the user visually (in SCn, SCg). A subset of the answer (natural language definition or explanation for a given entity) goes to the speech synthesis module;
5. The speech synthesis module voices the received natural language text.

This dialog can be used as an example:

- "Welcome. What is your name?"
- "Hello Andrey."
- "How is it going?"
- "Great!"
- "We can offer drinks and rolls. What do you prefer?"
- "I would like to order a latte."
- "Great choice, expect. Have a nice day."

Figures 14, 15, 16, 17, 18, 19 and 20 show fragments of the knowledge base that sequentially reflect changes in it after processing each message in the dialog.

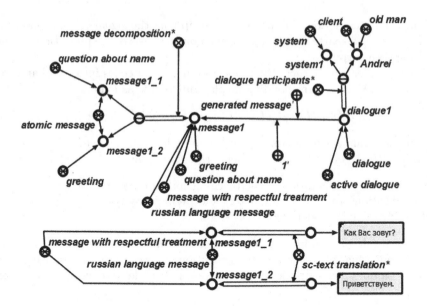

Fig. 14. The portion of the knowledge base after the system generates a greeting and a question about the name.

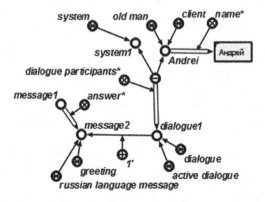

Fig. 15. A part of the knowledge base after receiving and processing the user's answer to the question about the name.

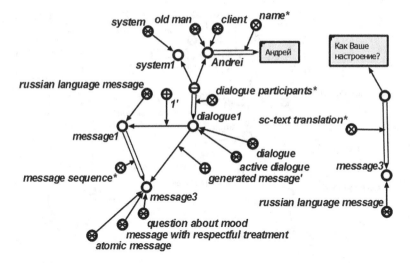

Fig. 16. Section of the knowledge base after the system generates a question about the user's mood.

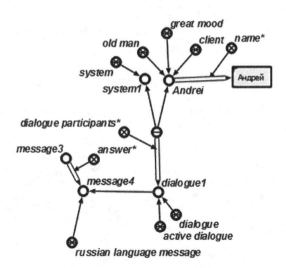

Fig. 17. Section of the knowledge base after receiving and processing the user's response to a question about mood.

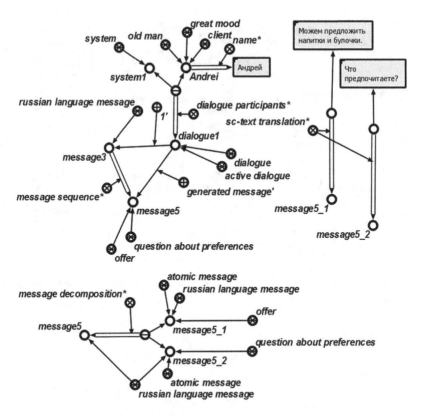

Fig. 18. Knowledge base part after generating a system message containing a suggestion and a question about preferences.

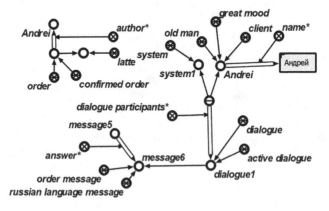

Fig. 19. Knowledge base part after receiving and processing a user message containing order information.

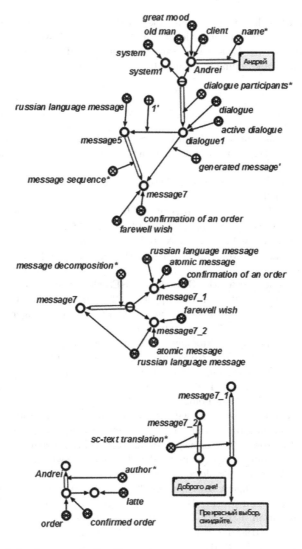

Fig. 20. Knowledge base part after the system generates a message containing an order confirmation and a farewell message.

6   Conclusion

An approach to the development of intelligent speech assistants based on the integration of modern approaches to speech signals processing and semantic dialogue management models is proposed. Obtained results, in particular, developed set of ontologies, can be applied to the lay-out of speech assistants for various purposes wit the possibility to be adapted to the characteristics of a specific subject domain.

Acknowledgment. The authors would like to thank the scientific teams from the departments of intellectual information technologies, control systems and electronic computing facilities of the Belarusian State University of Informatics and Radio Electronics for their help and valuable comments.

References

1. Alice - a voice assistant from Yandex. https://yandex.ru/alice. Accessed May 2020
2. Amazon Alexa Official Site: What Is Alexa? https://developer.amazon.com/alexa. Accessed June 2020
3. Amazon Echo & Alexa Stats. https://voicebot.ai/amazon-echo-alexa-stats. Accessed Jan 2020
4. Azarov, E., Vashkevich, M., Petrovsky, A.: Instantaneous pitch estimation based on RAPT framework. In: European Signal Processing Conference (2012)
5. Azvine, B., Nauck, D.D., Azarmi, N. (eds.): Intelligent Systems and Soft Computing. LNCS (LNAI), vol. 1804. Springer, Heidelberg (2000). https://doi.org/10.1007/10720181
6. Bülthoff, F., Maleshkova, M.: RESTful or RESTless – current state of today's top web APIs. In: Presutti, V., Blomqvist, E., Troncy, R., Sack, H., Papadakis, I., Tordai, A. (eds.) ESWC 2014. LNCS, vol. 8798, pp. 64–74. Springer, Cham (2014). https://doi.org/10.1007/978-3-319-11955-7_6
7. Corona, R., Thomason, J., Mooney, R.: Improving black-box speech recognition using semantic parsing. In: Proceedings of the Eighth International Joint Conference on Natural Language Processing (vol. 2: Short Papers), pp. 122–127. Asian Federation of Natural Language Processing, Taipei, Taiwan, November 2017. https://www.aclweb.org/anthology/I17-2021
8. Cortana helps you achieve more with less effort. Your personal productivity assistant helps you stay on top of what matters, follow through, and do your best work. https://www.microsoft.com/en-us/cortana. Accessed June 2020
9. Davydenko, I.: Semantic models, method and tools of knowledge bases coordinated development based on reusable components. In: Golenkov, V. (ed.) Open Semantic Technologies for Intelligent Systems, pp. 99–118. BSUIR, Minsk (2018)
10. Global Voice Assistant Market By Technology, By Application, By End User, By Region, Competition, Forecast & Opportunities, 2024. https://www.businesswire.com/news/home/20190916005535/en/Global-Voice-Assistant-Market-Projected-Grow-1.2. Accessed Dec 2019
11. Golenkov, V., Guliakina, N., Davydenko, I., Eremeev, A.: Methods and tools for ensuring compatibility of computer systems. In: Golenkov, V. (ed.) Open Semantic Technologies for Intelligent Systems, pp. 25–52. BSUIR, Minsk (2019)
12. Google Assistant, your own personal Google. https://assistant.google.com/. Accessed May 2020
13. Hinton, G.E., Salakhutdinov, R.: Reducing the dimensionality of data with neural networks. Science **313**(5786), 504–7 (2006)
14. Hoy, M.B.: Alexa, Siri, Cortana, and more: an introduction to voice assistants. Med. Ref. Serv. Q. **37**, 81–88 (2018). https://doi.org/10.1080/02763869.2018.1404391
15. Zeiler, M.D., et al.: On rectified linear units for speech processing. In: 2013 IEEE International Conference on Acoustics, Speech and Signal Processing, pp. 3517–3521 (2013)

16. Matyus, A.: Facebook faces another huge data leak affecting 267 million users. https://www.digitaltrends.com/news/facebook-data-leak-267-million-users-affected. Accessed Dec 2019
17. OFlaherty, K.: Data Leak Warning Issued To Millions Of Google Chrome And Firefox Users. https://www.forbes.com/sites/kateoflahertyuk/2019/07/19/data-leak-warning-issued-to-millions-of-google-chrome-and-firefox-users. Accessed Dec 2019
18. Petrovsky, A., Azarov, E.: Instantaneous harmonic analysis: techniques and applications to speech signal processing. In: Ronzhin, A., Potapova, R., Delic, V. (eds.) SPECOM 2014. LNCS (LNAI), vol. 8773, pp. 24–33. Springer, Cham (2014). https://doi.org/10.1007/978-3-319-11581-8_3
19. Polzehl, T., Schoenenberg, K., Möller, S., Metze, F., Mohammadi, G., Vinciarelli, A.: On speaker-independent personality perception and prediction from speech. In: 13th Annual Conference of the International Speech Communication Association 2012, INTERSPEECH 2012, pp. 258–261 (2012)
20. Pospelov, D.: Intelligent interfaces for computers of new generations. Electron. Comput. (3), 4–20 (1989). (in Russian)
21. Rubin, F.: Amazon's Alexa and Google assistant try making themselves the talk of CES 2020. https://www.cnet.com/news/amazon-alexa-and-google-assistant-try-making-themselves-talk-of-ces-2020/. Accessed Jan 2018
22. Santos, J., Rodrigues, J.J.P.C., Casal, J., Saleem, K., Denisov, V.: Intelligent personal assistants based on internet of things approaches. IEEE Syst. J. 12(2), 1793–1802 (2018). https://doi.org/10.1109/JSYST.2016.2555292. https://ieeexplore.ieee.org/document/7473837/
23. Sarikaya, R.: The technology behind personal digital assistants: an overview of the system architecture and key components. IEEE Signal Process. Mag. 34, 67–81 (2017). https://doi.org/10.1109/MSP.2016.2617341
24. Shunkevich, D.: Agent-oriented models, method and tools of compatible problem solvers development for intelligent systems. In: Golenkov, V. (ed.) Open Semantic Technologies for Intelligent Systems, pp. 119–132. BSUIR, Minsk (2018)
25. Siri. https://www.apple.com/siri/. Accessed May 2020
26. Tang, H., et al.: End-to-end neural segmental models for speech recognition. IEEE J. Sel. Top. Signal Process. 11(8), 1254–1264 (2017). https://doi.org/10.1109/jstsp.2017.2752462
27. The AI companion who cares. https://replika.ai/. Accessed May 2020
28. Zahariev, V.A., Azarov, E.S., Rusetski, K.V.: An approach to speech ambiguities eliminating using semantically-acoustical analysis. In: Golenkov, V. (ed.) Open Semantic Technologies for Intelligent Systems, pp. 211–222. BSUIR, Minsk (2018)
29. Zahariev, V.A., Lyahor, T., Hubarevich, N., Azarov, E.S.: Semantic analysis of voice messages based on a formalized context. In: Golenkov, V. (ed.) Open Semantic Technologies for Intelligent Systems, pp. 103–112. BSUIR, Minsk (2019)
30. Zahariev, V.A., Shunkevich, D.V., Nikiforov, S.A., Lyahor, T., Azarov, E.S.: The principles of building intelligent speech assistants based on open semantic technology. In: Golenkov, V. (ed.) Open Semantic Technologies for Intelligent Systems, pp. 197–206. BSUIR, Minsk (2020)

Ontological Approach for Chinese Language Interface Design

Longwei Qian$^{(\boxtimes)}$ ⓘ, Mikhail Sadouski ⓘ, and Wenzu Li ⓘ

Department of Intelligent Information Technology, Belarusian State University
of Informatics and Radioelectronics, Minsk, Republic of Belarus
qianlw1226@gmail.com, mishachess@mail.ru, wzzggml@gmail.com

Abstract. The natural language user interface is a subclass of user
interfaces that allows user and system to communicate using natural
language. It is the development direction of the user interface of the
intelligent system. The key technology for implementation of natural
language user interface is the computer processing of natural language
text. Due to the diversity and complexity of natural language, its understanding hasn't completely achieved yet. By comparing Chinese language
with other European languages, this article describes the characteristics
of Chinese language and the difficulties in Chinese language processing. After an analysis of current mainstream natural language processing
methods, it was shown that the knowledge base plays an important role
in the natural language processing model. The knowledge base is the
basis for natural language processing. This article proposes a method
of computer processing of Chinese language text based on Chinese linguistic ontology and domain ontologies. The ontologies are used to build
a unified semantic model of Chinese linguistic knowledge and domain
knowledge for the processing of Chinese language text. In this way the
Chinese linguistic knowledge is integrated in the Chinese language processing model, the application of Chinese linguistic knowledge makes the
Chinese language processing model more interpretative.

Keywords: Chinese language processing · Ontology · Knowledge
base · Natural language user interface

1 Introduction

The article is based on the paper [16], that describes the core role of the natural
language processing and an approach for the creation of natural language user
interface. The main point is to build natural language processing model for
natural language user interface through knowledge base and problem solver.
The analysis of natural language generation and implementation details can be
found in the original article.

© Springer Nature Switzerland AG 2020
V. Golenkov et al. (Eds.): OSTIS 2020, CCIS 1282, pp. 146–160, 2020.
https://doi.org/10.1007/978-3-030-60447-9_9

1.1   Interaction Between User and Computer System

User interface is a significant part of any computer system. Interaction through the interface forms the first opinion about the system as a wholeness and shows its functionality.

The dialog between user and system is represented as a message exchanging. Each message enters the system in some external form and should be mapped into the system internal language [17]. Natural language is one of the most widely used external form. In the knowledge-based system the knowledge base is the internal form for knowledge representation. In this article the message exchanging will be the transfer between natural language text and the knowledge base. The natural language user interface is a key concept of this article and will be described in details further.

1.2   Disadvantages for Traditional User Interface

In the traditional graphical and command operation interfaces the orders and operations are complex and unnatural. The users need understanding the functionality of each component in the user interface. It's not friendly for the users. They are expecting to use more convenient interactive ways. The users don't want to memorize complex commands and don't want any action to operate the computer. The natural language user interface is one of the most normal ways of human-computer interaction to satisfy user requirement. The natural language user interface could bring user more natural interactive experience. The development of natural language user interface is valuable for intelligent system.

1.3   Natural Language User Interface

In this article we will describe the natural language user interface for knowledge-based system. Essentially the implementation of natural language user interface is the processing of natural language text. The task of the natural language user interface is to transfer the natural language text into knowledge base, then to obtain the intermediate result through processing knowledge by problem solvers. The intermediate result is formed in knowledge representation, finally need to be transferred into natural language text for user.

Due to the complexity of natural language, it's difficult to transfer the natural language text into knowledge base. We need to acquire two types of information of natural language text through syntactic-semantic analysis, i.e. the entities of text (persons, places, organizations, events and so on), as well as relations between entities. The majority of natural language processing tasks can be viewed as resolving ambiguity [14]. For example, for the same entity "Apple" machine need to determine the entity belongs to "fruit" or is a "company".

1.4   Chinese Language Processing for User Interface

The computer processing of different natural languages has its own characteristics and specific difficulties. Chinese language and European languages belong to two different language systems. Most of natural language processing models are developed basing on English. The study of particular qualities of Chinese language can give subsequent understanding of problems in Chinese language processing and provide research ideas for other languages that are different from the European language system.

In the following chapters we will describe the problems and methods of Chinese language processing. To specify the Chinese language processing oriented on knowledge base, in this article we devise the ontological approach for Chinese language processing.

2   Analysis of Chinese Language Processing

Chinese language processing is a distinctive field dedicated to conducting relevant research on Chinese languages and characters [22]. In the past few decades some syntactic parsers were developed, such as Bikel Parser, Stanford Parser, Collins Parser [12]. The best syntactic analysis performance of these parsers on standardized Chinese language text is worse than European ones (English and Russian). Even if these are the application systems such as information retrieval and information extraction, which do not require deep syntactic analysis, it must overcome the obstacles of word segmentation and part-of-speech tagging in Chinese language processing [21].

2.1   Problems of Chinese Language Processing

The focus of problems for Chinese language processing is on the characteristics of Chinese language. The Chinese language is a sequence of hieroglyphs. Unlike the representation of European languages, the hieroglyph is displayed by a two-dimensional graphic that expresses the specific meaning. From word formation to syntactic analysis and even the shallow semantic analysis the Chinese language has characteristics that are clearly different from European languages. The reasons that make Chinese language processing different can mainly be divided into the following aspects [20]:

– the same part-of-speech can serve multiple syntactic components without morphological changes, i.e. in Chinese language text regardless of any syntactic component, served by each part-of-speech, its morphology does not change;
– the construction principles of Chinese sentences are basically consistent with the construction principles of phrases. According to the different composition methods, the structure of Chinese phrases can be divided into various types such as subject-predicate, verb-object, modifier-noun, joint and so on. The structure of Chinese sentences also have the same types as the structure of Chinese phrases;
– the writing habits in Chinese language. European languages such as English, Russian are basically written in words with natural spaces between the units. However, in Chinese language text there is no natural space to separate each word from another.

In order to partly solve these specific problems and make Chinese language processing methods reach a practical level it is necessary to construct the Chinese language processing model suitable for the characteristics of Chinese language.

2.2   State of Art in the Area of Chinese Language Processing

The current natural language processing methods are divided into the following directions [1]:

- the methods of establishing of a logical reasoning system relying on rules, knowledge base and Noam Chomsky's grammar theory;
- the machine learning methods based on large-scale corpus and on mathematical statistics and information theory.

In the early stage of natural language processing research, scientists believed that the process of natural language processing corresponds to the process of recognition of the language. Researchers began to study the rules that exist in natural language and implement these rules in an automated way to understand natural language. The goal of the rule-based method is to use limited and strict norms to describe an infinite language phenomenon. The formulation of rules requires the participation of linguists. So the rule-based method is largely affected by individual subjective factors.

The task of the statistics-based method is to construct a mathematical model based on large-scale corpus samples. This method uses natural language text as the original encoded information and then decodes the original information through the constructed mathematical model. The statistics-based method avoids the error situation caused by the subjective factors of manual writing norms in the rule-based methods and reduces the dependence of the system on human. However, it inevitably has the defects, because the performance of the model is too dependent on training samples and it lacks domain adaptive capabilities.

At present, whether the rule-based methods or the statistical-based methods, the methods and evaluation standards used in Chinese language processing are almost borrowed from European language processing methods such as English. The analysis process lacks the characteristics of Chinese language text [23].

2.3   Analysis of Existing Knowledge Bases for Chinese Language Processing

Faced with problems of Chinese language processing, Liu Zhiyuan from Tsinghua university proposed adding knowledge to the natural language processing model and researched the model driven by knowledge and data [15]. There are many well-known knowledge bases developed for natural language processing, for example common sense knowledge bases Freebase, DBpedia and so on; linguistic knowledge bases WordNet, VerbNet, et al. The various knowledge can reasonably explain natural language processing. Particularly the linguistic knowledge can provide basic features and key data resources for the algorithms.

In the field of Chinese language processing there are common sense knowledge bases CN-DBpedia [19], zhishi.me, et al. Many superb linguistic knowledge bases also has been developed so far in the field of Chinese language processing.

The "Grammatical Knowledge-base of Contemporary Chinese (GKB)" [2], developed by Institute of Computational Languages of Peking University, is an electronic dictionary advanced for the computer in order to automatically analyze and generate Chinese language sentence. It contains 73,000 Chinese words in accordance with the criteria of combining of grammatical function and meaning. Under the principle of grammatical function distribution the various grammatical attributes of each word are classified and described. The "GKB" describes the functions and complex features of each word in the Chinese language text as much as possible at the Chinese syntactic level.

The Chinese FrameNet ontology [11], developed by Shanxi University, is constructed by drawing on the ontological thought of the Framenet project and its strong semantic analysis capabilities. This ontology was expanded with the help of other knowledge bases, such as WordNet and VerbNet. These knowledge bases make the Chinese FrameNet ontology cover more Chinese word. Among them, the theta-role of the Verb in the VerbNet can be used to expand the frame elements and semantic types of the Chinese FrameNet ontology. The semantic frame is used to identify the relationships between word and a valence mode, that is provided to reflect the syntactic-level relationships. So that the computer can perform a deeper semantic analysis of natural language text.

The "HowNet" [7], developed by the professor Dong Zhengqiang, considers that the word or Chinese characters is the smallest linguistic unit, but not the smallest semantic one. It examines that the word can be described as a small semantic unit – sememe. The concepts in the world can be described by using the smallest semantic unit and various relationships. Using processing the Chinese language text, based on HowNet, it is possible to recognize the concepts and relationships of the Chinese language text and its specific meanings, so that the automatic analysis of the Chinese language text could be achieved.

Each of these knowledge bases has its own characteristics. They describe characteristics of Chinese language in certain aspects. But due to lack of a unified semantic model for structuring knowledges, it's impossible to enable the knowledge base to be presented on different levels of detailing [6]. These knowledge bases don't support collective development, it will increase laboriousness and time of their development and modernization. Generally they lack knowledge processing tools.

2.4   Proposed Approach for Chinese Language Processing

On the basis of developed Chinese linguistic knowledge bases, this article proposes ontological approach for Chinese language processing based on Open Semantic Technology for Intelligent Systems (OSTIS technology). The OSTIS technology is aimed at knowledge processing and various knowledge presentation for intelligent systems, it's focused on the development of knowledge-driven computer systems [10]. Within OSTIS technology the ontological approach is to construct Chinese linguistic ontologies and problem solvers for knowledge processing.

The Chinese linguistic knowledge could be described in terms of various levels of linguistics such as word, phrase and sentence. The ontologies are used to organize the knowledge in the field of Chinese linguistics reasonably. According to the OSTIS technology the structured ontologies is further used by problem solvers for Chinese language processing. Various levels of Chinese linguistic knowledge helps to get better analysis result of Chinese language text. The knowledge-driven Chinese language processing model can effectively improve the interpretability of Chinese language processing.

3   System Architecture for Chinese Language Processing in User Interface

The proposed approach for Chinese language processing is a kind of knowledge-based method with OSTIS technology. We will develop a unified semantic model for Chinese language processing in the user interface of ostis-system. The ostis-system is an intelligent system being developed basing on OSTIS technology [8]. Generally, the ostis-system is divided into knowledge base, problem solver and computer system interface [9]. Knowledge base of ostis-system is a finite information structure, which is a formal representation of all knowledge [6]. Problem solver of ostis-system is relied on the principle that the solver is treated as a hierarchical system of sc-agents that react to situations and events. The sc-agent is a certain object that can perform actions in semantic memory, in which the knowledge base is stored [18]. The system interface of ostis-system is a solution oriented on interface tasks [5]. It allows the users to address the various types of questions to their interface.

Traditionally for development of knowledge-based system the W3C standards are widely used. In this standards the particular language for ontologies description OWL [3] and knowledge representation language in the form of semantic networks RDF [4] were developed. For developing knowledge bases and for designing knowledge processing machines by this standards there are many disadvantages described in [6,18]. With the help of OSTIS technology the development of knowledge bases and design of knowledge processing machines had attempted to eliminate these problems.

Different with the concept "ontology" in W3C standards, in OSTIS technology the ontology is a type of knowledge, each of which is a specification of the corresponding subject domain. It is an effective method for structuring of the various fields of knowledge on different levels of detailing. The subject domain is the key concept for describing the structure of knowledge. Each subject domain focuses on the description of concepts and their connections of research object, i.e. ontologies. According to the principle of OSTIS technology, the construction of knowledge base of Chinese linguistics is a hierarchical system of the various subject domains of the Chinese linguistic knowledge and their corresponding ontologies. Compared to lack of compatibility with developed components of knowledge base by W3C standards, the reusable components of knowledge bases will be supported through a hierarchical system of the various subject domains.

In the W3C standards knowledge processing itself is carried out at the level of application, which is working with a repository of knowledge [18]. Sequentially reusing of solutions applicable to one system is not possible in most cases for the same reason. The hierarchical system of Chinese linguistic ontologies divided by subject domain make it possible to process knowledge locally to solve specific problems of Chinese language processing. In addition to the basic factual knowledge of Chinese linguistics, the rules (logical statements) and sc-agent programs for analysis of Chinese language text are also stored in the knowledge base. This kind of problem solver is designed based on ontology, it's possible to execute problem solutions in most cases for same reason. Further, speaking in this article about ontologies and knowledge bases, we will mean ontologies and knowledge bases built on the basis of the OSTIS technology.

It is proposed to use two main modules for the processing of natural language in user interface: user interface module and natural language processing module (see Fig. 1).

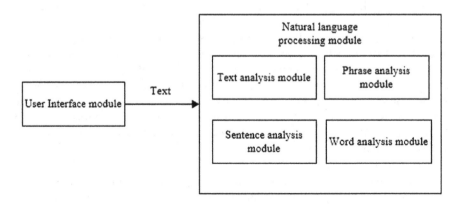

Fig. 1. Processing of natural language in user interface.

The user interface module obtains natural language text from user input. The natural language processing module uses syntactic-semantic analysis for the text understanding and its full process is described below:

– Text analysis. Using the subject domain of Chinese language text the syntactic and semantic structure of text will be analysed. The text is organized by the sequence of sentences. The independent analysis of each sentence is conducive to the text understanding;

- Sentence analysis. Using the subject domain of Chinese language sentence the syntactic and semantic structure of each sentence of text will be analyzed and as a result sentences will be separated to the specific phrases;
- Phrase analysis. The phrases couldn't provide complete information to understand a sentence. Through knowledge of subject domain of Chinese language phrase the syntactic and semantic analysis of phrase will be received and as a result separate words will be defined;
- Word analysis. Word analysis is the foundation of natural language text understanding. Because of the particularity of Chinese language text, the analysis of non-words in natural language text is also indispensable. The relevant knowledge for syntactic and semantic analysis of the word and the non-word will be described and processed by corresponding subject domains.

In the natural language processing module word analysis just be used for determination of syntactic function and semantic role of words in the text. For analysis of words' meaning it's not research focus in this article. After the natural language processing module the concepts and relations of text will be mapped into the domain knowledge base of ostis-system. The problem solver will processing these knowledge (for example, logical inference, solution search, so on) in the knowledge base to acquire the information users need.

Currently the knowledge-based natural language processing the syntactic-semantic analysis of natural language text and concept matching is carried out respectively. The syntactic and semantic information of concepts couldn't be simultaneously determined in the knowledge base. With the help of OSTIS technology we will develop the Chinese linguistic ontologise and problem solver for syntactic-semantic analysis and concept matching in knowledge base. These processes will be carried out locally in the knowledge base of ostis-system.

The development of Chinese linguistic ontologies is the basis for implementation of Chinese language processing in user interface of ostis-system. One of the goals of development of Chinese linguistic ontologies is to construct syntactic and semantic ontologies using the methods of domain ontology construction within OSTIS technology. The certain problem solver will be developed further to process specified ontologies to implement syntactic and semantic analysis of Chinese language text.

4   Knowledge Base Structure for Chinese Language Processing

The basis of ontological approach for Chinese language processing is to construct knowledge base of Chinese linguistics. The Chinese linguistic ontologies are backbone of knowledge base and will be described following. Within the framework of OSTIS technology Semantic Code (SC-code) is the basis for knowledge representation. It's used for developing the subject domain of Chinese linguistic and their corresponding ontologies. SC-code is the form of semantic network language with the basic set-theoretic interpretation. This is an internal language for coding knowledge in memory, which provides a unified semantically compatible representation of various subject domains and their corresponding ontologies [8]. SC-code could be used to represent any kind of knowledge and it could avoid duplication and redundancy of knowledge.

The following items are the general structure of the Chinese language subject domain represented in SCn-language (one of the ways for external dis play of SC-code text) [6].

Subject domain of Chinese language text
$\Rightarrow$ *particular SD**:
- *Subject domain of Chinese language syntax*
- *Subject domain of Chinese language semantic*

The *Subject domain of Chinese language syntax* describes the characteristics of the Chinese language syntax and functional characteristics of the syntactic components. The *Subject domain of Chinese language semantic* describes the semantic characteristics of word, the semantic relationships and the semantic structure in the Chinese language text. These subject domains could be used for the structural syntactic and semantic analysis of Chinese language text.

The key to the proposed method is the description of this specific subject domain and its corresponding ontology. The main elements of a particular subject domain are basic concepts studied in the subject domain and relationships. The relationships between these specific subject domains also need to be considered in the ontology. In general, the entire Chinese linguistic ontology forms a hierarchical and multilevel semantic model. This hierarchical sample is beneficial for management and application of various knowledge about Chinese language processing.

The focus of current research is on the subject domain of Chinese language syntax, which will be described in detail below.

In the *Subject domain of Chinese language syntax* the syntactic information of sentences, phrases, words and non-words in Chinese language text are need to be considered. These specific subject domain could provide linguistic ontologies that indicate the syntactic information.

The following is the structural fragment of the subject domain of Chinese language syntax represented in SCn-language.

Subject domain of Chinese language syntax
$\Rightarrow$ *private SD**:
- *Subject domain of Chinese language sentence*
- *Subject domain of Chinese language phrase*
- *Subject domain of Chinese language word*
- *Subject domain of non-word of Chinese language*

The detailed description of sentence analysis is an important basic intermediate stage connecting an analysis of text and word. The ontologies about sentence analysis is described in the subject domain of Chinese language sentence. The *Subject domain of Chinese language sentence* studies the types and patterns of

Chinese language sentence, determination of sentence components and their syntactic relationships in the sentence, i.e. the division of sentence components in a simple sentence and an accurate functional description of sentence components.

The structural fragment of the *Subject domain of Chinese language sentence* is represented in SCn-language below.

Subject domain of Chinese language sentence
∋ *maximum studied object class'*:
  Chinese language sentence
∋ *not maximum studied object class'*:
  • *simple sentence*
  • *compound sentence*
∋ *explored relation'*:
  • *subject'*
  • *object'*
  • *head predicate'*
  • *attribute'*
  • *center word'*
  • *adverbial modifier'*
  • *complement'*

simple sentence
⇐ *subdividing**:
  {
  • *subject-predicate sentence*
  • *non-subject-predicate sentence*
  • *special sentence*
  }

The structure of a simple subject-predicate sentence can be described by the logical statement. It's indicated in the logical ontologies of subject domain of Chinese language sentence. The logical statement can be used for syntactic analysis of simple sentence by problem solver (dividing the input sentence to the corresponding phrases and simple sentence generation). Figure 2 demonstrates the logical statement in SCg-language (one of the ways for external display of SC-code text) (see Fig. 2). The "simple sentence", the "noun phrase" and "verb phrase" are the concepts. The variable "x" is an instance of a simple sentence, the variable "a" is an instance of a noun phrase, the variable "b" is an instance of a verb phrase. The right part of Fig. 2 indicates that a specific noun phrase "a" and a specific verb phrase "b" can compose a specific simple sentence "x" with basic sequence according to subject-predicate relationship.

Phrase analysis is usually viewed as an intermediate result of sentence research. It's the basis of complete syntax analysis of sentence. For understanding sentence sometimes the various phrases of sentence could provide enough information. The phrase analysis can solve most of the problems associated with the ambiguity of processing individual words. The *Subject domain of Chinese language*

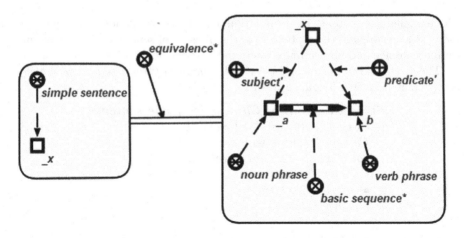

Fig. 2. Logical statement about subject-predicate sentence.

phrase indicates the types and patterns of Chinese language phrases, their internal structure and external functions. It also studies the syntactic relations in the internal structure of these phrases and syntactic relations between them.

The following is the structural fragment of the *Subject domain of Chinese language phrase* represented in SCn-language:

Subject domain of Chinese language phrase
∋ *maximum studied object class'*:
    phrase
∋ *not maximum studied object class'*:
 • *noun phrase*
 • *verb phrase*
 • *adjective phrase*
 • *numeral classifier phrase*
∋ *explored relation'*:
 • *subject'*
 • *object'*
 • *head predicate'*
 • *attribute'*
 • *center word'*

verb phrase
⇐ *subdividing*:
    {
 • *transitive verb phrase*
 • *intransitive verb phrase*
    }

Various basic phrase structures can be described by logical statement in logical ontologies. For example, an instance "x" of a verb phrase can be composed by an instance "a" of verb and an instance "b" of any other basic phrase or can be composed of an instance "a" of verb and an instance "b" of noun according to predicate-object relationship. It is represented in SCg-language in Fig. 3 (see Fig. 3).

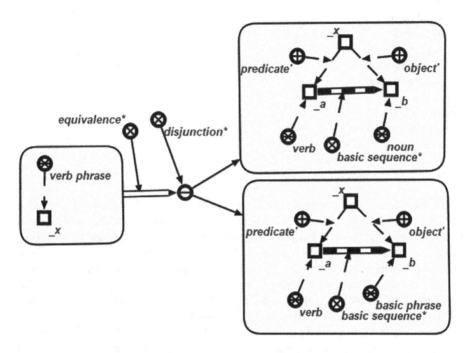

Fig. 3. Logical statement of a verb phrase.

The word is the most basis unit in the language text. The syntactic analysis of word is dependent on the specific language. Due to the problem of Chinese language writing habits, the definition (segmentation) of word is the first theoretical problem. In the field of Chinese language processing, the "Contemporary Chinese Language Word Segmentation Standard Used for Information Processing" has been proposed [13]. In this standard the word is represented as "segmentation unit". The precise definition is: "the basic unit for Chinese language processing with certain semantic or grammatical functions". The description of "segmentation unit" is focused on the computer processing of Chinese language. Generally, the *Subject domain of Chinese language word* indicates classifications of Chinese language word, its syntactic functions, capability of collocations. According to the knowledge of Chinese linguistics, it mainly indicates the related information of the "segmentation unit".

The following describes the structural fragment of the *Subject domain of Chinese language word* in SCn-language:

Subject domain of Chinese language word

∋ *maximum studied object class'*:
  Chinese language word
= the grammatical information of the segmentation unit in Chinese language
∋ *not maximum studied object class'*:

- *noun*
- *verb*
- *adjective*
- *adverb*
- *pronoun*
- *conjunction*
- *preposition*

verb

⇒ *inclusion**:

- *verb that does not take object*
- *verb that takes object*
- *verb that takes double object*

In European language text each language component is separated according to space, so it can be regarded as a word. However due to the characteristics of Chinese hieroglyph some language components couldn't be classified as words according to the definition of a word, such as Chinese characters, the idioms and the abbreviations. It's necessary to describe ontologies for non-word analysis in subject domain. The *Subject domain of non-word of Chinese language* contains description of non-word components in the Chinese language text. It indicates the features and syntactic functions of non-word.

Based on the ontological approach of OSTIS technology, the Chinese linguistic knowledge is structured for processing of Chinese language text. The main role of the knowledge base relied on ontology is to provide a common understanding of Chinese linguistic knowledge, determine commonly recognized concepts. The Chinese linguistic ontologies contain the main theories and basic principles of linguistic knowledge, as well as the rules for Chinese language processing. They could be used by problem solvers to implement common understanding for processing Chinese language text.

Based on constructed ontology of Chinese language syntax, it's possible to implement syntactic analysis of Chinese language text and generate Chinese language text that corresponding to the linguistic knowledge. However, for the deep processing of Chinese language text, it is necessary to establish semantic ontology of Chinese language in order to generate semantically equivalent fragments after syntactic processing into knowledge base. It is also used for generating reasonable and clear text in generation of Chinese language text. For Chinese language user interface we still need develop the problem solvers that could use ontologies to process knowledge in knowledge base.

5   Conclusion

Natural language processing is the key technology for implementation of natural language user interface. The proposed approach for Chinese language processing is intended to develop the semantic model of Chinese linguistic knowledge. Based on the linguistic ontology the proposed approach can make up for the lack of interpretability for natural language processing of statistical-based approaches. Based on OSTIS technology the natural language (external form) is automatically transformed into semantic equivalent fragments in the knowledge base. Compared with traditional user interface the information that user obtains is not accurate. The proposed approach can search for accurate information in the knowledge base and return it to the user. Obviously, the proposed approach in this article is the preliminary result of the research work of Chinese language processing based on ontology. The improvement of Chinese syntactic ontology, the development of Chinese semantic ontology is the focus of the next work. The representation of rules and methods for Chinese language processing in the knowledge base, the development of sc-agents for Chinese language processing using these knowledge need to be researched further.

References

1. 2018 natural language processing research report. Technical report. https://aminer. org. Accessed 6 July 2019
2. Modern Chinese grammar information dictionary, Peking University Open Research Data Platform. https://opendata.pku.edu.cn/dataverse/clkb. Accessed 12 Aug 2019
3. Owl implementations. https://www.w3.org/2001/sw/wiki/OWL/Implementati ons/. Accessed 23 Oct 2019
4. Rdf 1.1 concepts and abstract syntax. http://www.w3.org/TR/rdf11-concepts/. Accessed 23 Oct 2019
5. Boriskin, A.S., Koronchik, D.N., Zhukau, I.I., Sadouski, M.E., Khusainov, A.F.: Ontology-based design of intelligent systems user interface. In: 7th International Scientific and Technical Conference "Open Semantic Technologies for Intelligent Systems", Belarus, Minsk pp. 95–106 (2017)
6. Davydenko, I.T.: Ontology-based knowledge base design. In: 7th International Scientific and Technical Conference "Open Semantic Technologies for Intelligent Systems", Belarus, Minsk, pp. 57–72 (2017)
7. Dong, Z.D., Dong, Q.: Theoretical findings of HowNet. J. Chin. Inf. Process. **21**(4), 3–9 (2007)
8. Golenkov, V.V.: Ontology-based design of intelligent systems. In: 7th International Scientific and Technical Conference "Open Semantic Technologies for Intelligent Systems", Belarus, Minsk, pp. 37–56 (2017)
9. Golenkov, V.V., Shunkevich, D.V., Davydenko, I.T., Grakova, N.V.: Principles of organization and automation of the semantic computer systems development. In: 9th International Scientific and Technical Conference "Open Semantic Technologies for Intelligent Systems", Belarus, Minsk, pp. 53–90 (2019)
10. Golenkov, V.V., Gulyakina, N.A.: Project of open semantic technology for component design of intelligent systems. Ontol. Designing **1**(11), 42–64 (2014)

11. Jia, J.Z., Dong, G.: The study on integration of CFN and VerbNet, WordNet. New Technol. Libr. Inf. Serv. **6**, 6–10 (2008)
12. Jiang, M., Huang, Y., Fan, J.W.: Parsing clinical text: how good are the state-of-the-art parsers? In: ACM 8th International Workshop on Data and Text Mining in Biomedical Informatics, China, Shanghai, pp. 15–21 (2014)
13. Jie, C.Y.: Some key issues upon contemporary Chinese language word segmentation standard used for information processing. J. Chin. Inf. Process. **3**(4), 33–41 (1989)
14. Jurafsky, D., Martin, J.H.: Speech and Language Processing: An Introduction to Natural Language Processing, Computational Linguistics and Speech Recognition, 3rd edn. Tracy Dunkelberger, Upper Saddle River (2020)
15. Liu, Z.Y.: Knowledge guided natural language understanding. In: 7th China Conference on Data Mining, China, Jinan, pp. 199–206 (2018)
16. Qian, L.W., Sadouski, M.E., Li, W.Z.: Ontology method for chinese language processing. In: 10th International Scientific and Technical Conference "Open Semantic Technologies for Intelligent Systems", Belarus, Minsk, pp. 207–214 (2020)
17. Sadouski, M.E., Boriskin, A.S., Koronchik, D.N., Zhukau, I.I., Khusainov, A.F.: Ontology-based design of intelligent systems user interface. In: 7th International Scientific and Technical Conference "Open Semantic Technologies for Intelligent Systems", Belarus, Minsk, pp. 95–106 (2017)
18. Shunkevich, D.V.: Ontology-based design of knowledge processing machines. In: 7th International Scientific and Technical Conference "Open Semantic Technologies for Intelligent Systems", Belarus, Minsk Belarus, Minsk, pp. 73–94 (2017)
19. Xu, B., et al.: CN-DBpedia: a never-ending Chinese knowledge extraction system. In: Benferhat, Salem, Tabia, Karim, Ali, Moonis (eds.) IEA/AIE 2017. LNCS (LNAI), vol. 10351, pp. 428–438. Springer, Cham (2017). https://doi.org/10.1007/978-3-319-60045-1_44
20. Yu, S.W., Zhu, X.F.: Development of machine dictionary for natural language processing. Lexicographical Stud. **2**, 22–30 (2019)
21. Yu, S.W., Zhu, X.F., Wang, H.: New progress of the grammatical knowledge-base of contemporary Chinese. Chin. J. Lang. Policy Plann. **15**(1), 59–65 (2001)
22. Zong, C.Q.: Chinese language processing: achievements and problems. Chin. J. Lang. Policy Plann. **1**(5), 19–26 (2016)
23. Zong, C.Q., Cao, Y.Q., Yu, S.W.: Sixty years of Chinese information processing. Appl. Linguist. **1**(4), 53–61 (2009)

Ontological Approach for Question Generation and Knowledge Control

Wenzu Li$^{(\boxtimes)}$, Natalia Grakova , and Longwei Qian

Belarusian State University of Informatics and Radioelectronics, Minsk, Belarus
lwzzggml@gmail.com, grakova@bsuir.by, qianlw1226@gmail.com
https://www.bsuir.by/ru/kaf-iit/sostav-kafedry

Abstract. With the development of intelligent information technology, automatic generation of questions and automatic verification of answers have become one of the main functions of the intelligent tutoring systems. Although some existing approaches to automatic generation of questions and automatic verification of answers are introduced in the literature, these approaches only allow to generate very simple objective questions and verify user answers with very simple semantic structure. So, this article proposes an approach for designing a general subsystem of automatic generation of questions and automatic verification of answers in intelligent tutoring systems built using OSTIS technology. The designed subsystem allows to automatically generate various types of questions based on information from the knowledge bases and multiple question generation strategies, and the subsystem can also automatically verify the correctness and completeness of user answers in the form of semantic graphs. Compared with existing approaches, the subsystem designed using the approach proposed in this article can not only generate various complex types of questions, such as multiple-choice questions, fill in the blank questions, questions of definition interpretation, etc., but also verify user answers with complex semantic structures.

Keywords: Question generation · Answer verification · Tutoring systems · OSTIS technology · Knowledge base

1 Introduction

With the rise of artificial intelligence technologies in recent years, learning methods have moved from the multimedia training mode to the era of intelligent education. The use of advanced learning methods provided by artificial intelligence technologies in the learning process can form a new learning mode, stimulate the user's learning interest and improve the user's learning efficiency [9].

The first multimedia training system (MTS) was built according to a rigid scenario of presenting training information and dialogue with the user. Such systems, for example, include automated training systems, as well as electronic textbooks, which still play an important role in the teaching field. However, at

© Springer Nature Switzerland AG 2020
V. Golenkov et al. (Eds.): OSTIS 2020, CCIS 1282, pp. 161–175, 2020.
https://doi.org/10.1007/978-3-030-60447-9_10

the present stage, when the amount of information is rapidly increasing, MTS has been unable to meet the needs of users for new knowledge due to slow updates of new content and fixed types of test questions. Therefore, in recent years, the intelligent tutoring system (ITS) has become an important research direction, which not only allows users to view the information of interest through hyper-structure navigation, but also can ask the system various complex questions [5,6].

Compared with the MTS, the most important feature of the ITS is that ITS can use the knowledge base to automatically generate various types of questions and automatically verify the user answers. But the approaches to question generation proposed by most researchers only allow to generate very simple questions (multiple-choice questions; fill in the blank questions and judgment questions), and the correlation between the correct options and the incorrect options (disturbing options) of the generated multiple-choice questions is not high. Therefore, the questions generated using these approaches cannot compre-hensively examine the user's understanding of knowledge, and the knowledge bases of different systems have different knowledge structures, so these exist-ing approaches can only be implemented on the corresponding systems and are not universal. At present, most approaches of answer verification are based on keyword matching and probability statistics and these approaches rely heavily on the quality of the text corpus and do not consider the semantic similarity between the answers [10]. In the article [3], an approach for automatically eval-uating the quality of automatically generated image captions based on semantic scene graphs was introduced, but the semantic scene graphs introduced in this article can only represent image captions with very simple semantic structure. Because the semantic scene graph is one of the representation forms of the seman-tic graph, we unified it as a semantic graph in this article. A semantic graph is a network that represents semantic relationships between concepts. It is a directed or undirected graph consisting of vertices, which represent concepts, and edges, which represent semantic relations between concepts.

In order to solve the problems in the introduced approaches, this article proposes an approach to automatic generation of questions and automatic veri-fication of user answers based on OSTIS technology (Open Semantic Technology for Intelligent Systems) for intelligent tutoring systems. In the knowledge base built using OSTIS technology, each type of knowledge has a specific semantic structure, so this article proposes a series of question generation strategies by summarizing the semantic structure of each type of test question, and using these question generation strategies can automatically generate multiple-choice questions, fill in the blank questions, questions of definition interpretation, etc. Because OSTIS technology has strong knowledge expression ability, the pro-posed approach allows to generate very complex questions. The core idea of the answer verification approach proposed in this article is to decompose the stan-dard answers and user answers expressed in the form of semantic graphs into substructures according to the knowledge representation rules, and then calcu-late the similarity between them based on the number of matched substructures

[1,7,8]. Because OSTIS technology has a unified knowledge representation language, the approach proposed in this article allows to calculate the similarity between answers with complex semantic structures. Because discrete mathematics is a very important course in the computer field, we decided to choose the discrete mathematics tutoring system developed by OSTIS technology as the demonstration system of subsystem of automatic generation of questions and automatic verification of answers.

The article is based on the article [10]. This article describes in detail the approach to automatically generating questions and automatically verifying user answers in the intelligent tutoring systems. Compared with the original article, the biggest difference of this article includes the following parts:

- some question generation strategies are optimized and the detailed process of generating questions using each strategy is introduced;
- taking the judgment question as an example, the semantic structure and the classification model of the judgment question are described in detail;
- the semantic model of knowledge base structure for storing automatically generated questions is redesigned.

2   Existing Approaches and Problems

2.1   Automatic Question Generation

Automatic question generation method (AQGM) studies how to automatically generate test questions from electronic documents, text corpus or knowledge bases through computer technologies. Compared with the traditional approach of using database to extract questions, AQGM is a knowledge-based question generation method, so the generated questions are more flexible [4,9,10].

Approaches for automatic generation of questions can be divided into the following categories:

- based on electronic documents;
- based on text corpus;
- based on knowledge base.

Compared with the other two knowledge sources, the knowledge base is developed after the domain experts analyze the knowledge, this knowledge is filtered and has a certain structure, so the questions automatically generated using the knowledge base are more flexible and diverse [12]. With the development of semantic network technology, the use of knowledge base to automatically generate questions has become one of the main research directions of automatic generation of questions. At present, many researchers have conducted in-depth research on the automatic generation of test questions using the knowledge base, here are some research results:

- The system for automatic generation of multiple-choice questions developed by Andreas Papasalouros mainly uses the relation between parent class and subclass, class and element, element and attribute in OWL ontology to automatically generate multiple-choice questions [2,13];

- Based on the above approach, Li Hui used Protégé to create an ontology in the field of computer science, using various relations between parent class and subclass, element and attribute in the ontology to automatically generate multiple-choice questions, fill in the blank questions and judgment questions, where incorrect options (disturbing) of multiple-choice questions are also automatically generated through these relations [2,9].

Although these approaches discussed above have many advantages, there are also many problems:

- the approach of automatically generating questions using electronic documents and sentence templates requires a large number of sentence templates, and the types of questions generated are fixed and of low quality;
- the scope and quality of the automatically generated questions using the text corpus depend on the size and quality of the text corpus, and the correlation between the incorrect options (disturbing options) and correct options of the generated multiple-choice questions is not high;
- at present, there is no unified standard for the development of most knowledge bases, so different knowledge bases have different knowledge structures and they are not compatible with each other. Because the knowledge bases are not compatible with each other, the approach of using the knowledge base to automatically generate questions can only be used in the corresponding knowledge base, and for the knowledge base developed by other approaches, only new question generation approaches can be developed;
- the approaches introduced above allow to automatically generate only the simplest objective questions (refers to a type of question that has a unique standard answer).

Based on existing approaches and OSTIS technology [7,8], this article proposes an approach of using the knowledge base to automatically generate subjective and objective questions for ITS. Objective questions are those that require a specific answer. An objective question usually has only one potential correct answer, and they leave no room for opinion. Objective questions in this article include: multiple-choice questions, judgment questions and fill in the blank questions. Objective questions differ from subjective questions, which have more than one potential correct answer and sometimes have room for a justified opinion. Subjective questions in this article include: definition explanation questions, proof questions and theorem interpretation questions.

2.2   Automatic Verification of Answers

Answer verification is divided into answer verification of subjective question and answer verification of objective question. Because the objective question has a specific standard answer, the answer verification of the objective question only needs to compare whether the user answer and the standard answer are the same [11]. Subjective questions do not have a specific standard answer, so in order to verify the answers of subjective questions, it is necessary to compare the similarity between the standard answer and the user answer [10,15]. If the similarity is higher, the user answer is closer to the standard answer, and the score the user gets is higher. The essence of similarity comparison of subjective questions is text similarity comparison. Text similarity comparison is currently divided into two directions:

- comparison of text similarity based on natural language;
- comparison of text similarity based on semantic graph.

Approach for comparing text similarity based on natural language:

1. Based on keywords and keyword combinations:
   - N-gram similarity
     The N-gram approach decomposes texts or sentences according to N-tuples, and then calculates the similarity between the texts or sentences;
   - Jaccard similarity
     The Jaccard approach uses the idea of set theory to determine the similarity between texts or sentences based on the ratio of the number of identical words or word groups to the number of all non-repeating words or word groups between texts or sentences [15].
2. Based on vector space model (VSM):
   The core idea of VSM is to first convert the text into a vector in space by mathematical modeling, and then calculate the similarity value between the spatial vectors through cosine similarity, Euclidean distance, etc. [16,17]. VSM includes the following approaches:
   - TF-IDF
   - Word2vec
   - Doc2Vec
3. Based on deep learning:
   In recent years, many researchers have begun to use deep learning for natural language processing. This approach mainly uses DSSM, ConvNet, Tree-LSTM, Siamese LSTM and other multi-layer neural networks to model words or sentences to obtain word vectors or sentence vectors, and then calculate the text similarity [11,17].

Similarity comparison approach based on semantic graph
The core idea of the text similarity comparison approach based on semantic graphs is to first convert natural language text into semantic graphs through tools such as syntactic dependency trees or natural language interfaces, and then calculate the text similarity by comparing the similarities between semantic graphs.

SPICE (Semantic Propositional Image Caption Evaluation) approach is mainly used to evaluate the quality of automatically generated image caption. The main working principle of this approach is to compare the similarity between the automatically generated image caption (candidate caption) and the image caption (reference caption) manually labeled by the staff. The main feature of SPICE is the comparison of similarities through semantic content [3,10].

Although the approaches discussed above can compare text similarity to some extent, these approaches also have many shortcomings:

- the text similarity comparison approach based on keywords only compares the similarity between texts by words or word groups, and cannot distinguish the synonymy and polysemy of words or word groups;
- TF-IDF approach assumes that each feature word in the text exists independently, and does not consider the relation between words and their positions in the sentence. When the corpus is large, this method will generate a high-dimensional sparse matrix, resulting in increased computational complexity;
- although the approach based on deep learning has greatly improved the accuracy compared with other approaches, it is also a main research direction now, but this approach relies heavily on the quality of corpus, and when the corpus changes and updates, it needs to retrain the neural network model;
- although the SPICE approach compares text similarity from the semantic level, this approach only supports the description of simple semantic relations;
- these approaches depend on the corresponding natural language.

Based on the SPICE approach, this article proposes an approach for comparing text similarity using OSTIS technology and a unified knowledge representation language SC-code (as a basis for knowledge representation in the framework of OSTIS Technology, a unified version of coding information of any kind based on semantic networks is used, named SC-code) [3,7]. The main idea of the text similarity calculation is to first decompose the semantic graph of the standard answer and the semantic graph of the user answer into substructures according to the knowledge representation structure, and then calculate the similarity between the standard answer and the user answer according to the same number of substructures. The user answer in natural languages (English, Chinese, Russian, etc.) is converted to SC-code using the natural language interface. In article [14], the approach of using OSTIS technology to design Chinese natural language interface is introduced in detail.

3   Proposed Approach

The main task of this article is to introduce the design approach to subsystem of automatic generation of questions and automatic verification of user answers for ITS. Because the subsystem needs to complete two basic functions, so it can be divided into two parts: automatic generation of questions and automatic verification of answers. Next, we will introduce the implementation process of these two parts in detail.

3.1   Proposed Question Generation Approach

Combining the previously discussed approaches for automatic generation of questions and the structural characteristics of the OSTIS tutoring system knowledge base, this article proposes an approach for automatically generating various types of questions for the ITS. Using the approaches for automatic generation of questions and the OSTIS technology, subjective and objective questions can be automatically generated from knowledge base [7,10–12]. The automatically generated questions are stored in the subsystem knowledge base in the form of SC-code. Using natural language interface can convert these generated questions into corresponding natural questions, which is not the task of this work.

Consider in more detail the strategies for generating questions:

1. Question generation strategy based on classes
   This strategy uses various relations satisfied between the classes to automatically generate objective questions.
   – Based on "inclusion*" relation
     In the knowledge base of the OSTIS tutoring systems, many classes satisfy the inclusion relation, and some classes contain many subclasses, so the inclusion relation between classes can be used to automatically generate objective questions. The set theory expression form of inclusion relation between classes is as follows: $S_i \subseteq C (i \geq 1)$, ($S$-subclass, i-subclass number, C-parent class). Taking the generated judgment questions as an example, its set theory expression is: $S_i \subseteq C$ is "TRUE" or $S_i \subseteq C$ is "FALSE". Figure 1 shows an example of the semantic structure of a judgment question that is automatically generated using this strategy in SCg-code (SCg-code is a graphical version for the external visual representation of SC-code) [7,10].

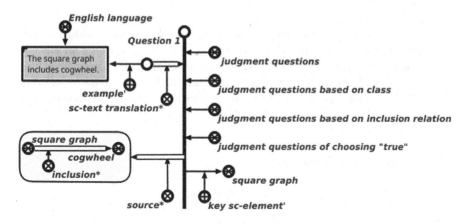

Fig. 1. The semantic structure of judgment question.

The user needs to judge whether the generated judgment question is "TRUE" or "FALSE". The natural language description form of this example is as follows:
≪The square graph includes cogwheel.≫
   ○ "TRUE"   ○ "FALSE"
   – Based on "subdividing*" relation Subdividing relation is a quasi-binary oriented relation (quasi-binary relation is a set of oriented pairs whose first components are sheaves) whose domain of definition is a family of

all possible sets. The result of set subdivision is to get pairs of disjoint sets, and the union of these disjoint sets is the original set [1]. There are also many classes in the knowledge base that satisfy the subdivision relation, so this relation can be used to automatically generate various types of objective questions. The expression form of set theory of subdividing relation between classes is as follows: $S_1 \cup S_2 \cup S_3 ... \cup S_i = U$ $(i > 1, S_i \cap S_j = \phi)$. Taking the generated fill in the blank questions as an example, its set theory expression is: Set U is subdivided into S_1, S_2, ____ and S_i.

– Based on "strict inclusion*" relation

Strict inclusion relation is a special form of inclusion relation, it is also a very important relation in knowledge base. Using strict inclusion relation to automatically generate objective questions is similar to using inclusion relation. The expression form of set theory of strict inclusion relation between classes is as follows: $S_i \subset C(i \geq 1)$, (S-subclass, i-subclass number, C-parent class). Taking the generated multiple-choice questions as an example, its set theory expression is: Set C strictly contains____? The correct options of multiple-choice questions are the subclasses strictly contained in set C, and the incorrect options (disturbing) are the disjoint sibling and parent classes of set C [10].

2. Question generation strategy based on elements
   – Based on role relation
   – Based on binary relation

   Role relation (a relation that specifies the role of elements within a certain set) and binary relation (binary relation is a set of relations on a set M that are a subset of the Cartesian product of the set M with itself) are the types of relations often used when building knowledge bases based on OSTIS technology [1]. The following shows a fragment of knowledge base using the binary relation "author*" in SCn-code (one of SC-code external display languages):

   Conditional convergence
   $\Rightarrow$ *author**:
      Johann Peter Gustav Lejeune Dirichlet

   Taking the generated fill in the blank question as an example, which can be described as this form: ≪The author of the concept of conditional convergence is ____≫. Therefore these relations between elements can be used to automatically generate objective questions.

3. Question generation strategy based on identifiers

   Usually some sets and relations in the knowledge base have multiple identifiers (identifier is a file that can be used to denote (name) an entity in the framework of external language) [1]. For example, ≪in discrete mathematics oriented set is also called tuple, vector and ordered sequence;≫. So multiple identifiers of sets and relations can be used to automatically generate objective questions.

4. Question generation strategy based on axioms

   Many axioms and their mathematical expressions are stored in the discrete mathematical knowledge base. For example, the union axiom and its corresponding mathematical expression in the knowledge base are formally expressed: $\forall a \exists d \forall c(c \in d \sim \exists b(b \in a \wedge c \in b))$. So these axioms and their mathematical expressions can be used to generate objective questions automatically.

5. Question generation strategy based on relation attributes

   Many relations in the knowledge base satisfy the attributes of reflexivity, symmetry and transmission. The following is a fragment in the knowledge base that satisfies this type of relation in SCn-code:

   strict inclusion*
   $\in$ *antireflexive relation*
   $\in$ *transitive relation*

   Taking the judgment question generated using this strategy as an example, it can be described as follows: ≪If set A strictly contains set B and set B strictly contains set C, then set A strictly contains set C?≫. Therefore, these relations and their properties can be used to generate objective questions.

6. Question generation strategy based on image examples

   This approach uses some concepts, relations and theorems in the knowledge base and their explanatory image examples to automatically generate some objective questions.

7. Subjective question generation strategy

   The definition of the concepts and the proof of the theorems are stored in the knowledge base according to the rules of knowledge representation, so the process of generating subjective questions can be divided into the following steps:

   - using logical formula templates to search for definitions of certain concepts and proofs of certain theorems in the knowledge base;
   - store the found knowledge base fragments in the corresponding domain of the subsystem knowledge base according to the fragment type (definition or proof);
   - finally, using manual or automatic approaches to describe the definition of each specific concept and the proof process of each specific theorem in SCg-code or SCL-code (a special sub-language of the SC language intended for formalizing logical formulas) in accordance with the rules of knowledge representation and use the "correct answer*" relation to connect them to the corresponding semantic fragments.

   Figure 2 shows the semantic structure of the definition of the inclusion relation $(\forall A \forall B(A \subseteq B) \Longleftrightarrow (\forall a(a \in A \rightarrow a \in B)))$ in SCg-code.

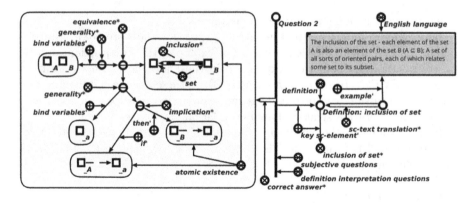

Fig. 2. The semantic structure of definition interpretation question.

The questions automatically generated using the above strategies may contain duplicate and incorrect questions, so in order to ensure the quality of the generated questions, first save these generated questions to the subsystem knowledge base, and then use manual or automatic approaches (comparing similarities between questions) to filter out duplicate and incorrect questions. The basis of any OSTIS system knowledge base is the hierarchical system of the subject domain and its corresponding ontology (ontology is a type of knowledge, each of which is a specification of the corresponding subject domain, focused on describing the properties and relations of concepts that are part of the specified subject domain) [7]. Figure 3 shows the hierarchy of the subject domain of questions in the subsystem knowledge base, which is used to store the generated questions in SCg-code.

Among them, objective type of questions can be decomposed into more specific types according to the question generation strategies and the characteristics of each type of questions (for example, judgment questions include: judgment questions of choosing true and judgment questions of choosing false). Let's consider the semantic segment of judgment question classification in the subject domain of judgment questions in SCn-code:

judgment questions
⇐ *subdividing*:
 {
 • *judgment questions based on relation attributes*
 • *judgment questions based on axioms*
 • *judgment questions based on image examples*
 • *judgment questions based on identifiers*
 • *judgment questions based on elements*
  ⇐ *subdividing*:
  {
  • *judgment questions based on role relation*
  • *judgment questions based on binary relation*

}
- *judgment questions based on classes*
    ⇐ *subdividing*:*
        {
        - *judgment questions based on subdividing relation*
        - *judgment questions based on inclusion relation*
        - *judgment questions based on strict inclusion relation*
        }
}
⇐ *subdividing*:*
    {
    - *judgment questions of choosing true*
    - *judgment questions of choosing false*
    }

Judgment questions automatically generated using the knowledge base will be stored in the corresponding sections of the subsystem knowledge base according to the above classification criteria. Since the generated questions are stored in the subsystem knowledge base according to the type of question, when testing users, specific types of questions can be extracted according to the user's requirement, which not only ensures the quality of the test questions, but also greatly improves the efficiency of the extraction questions.

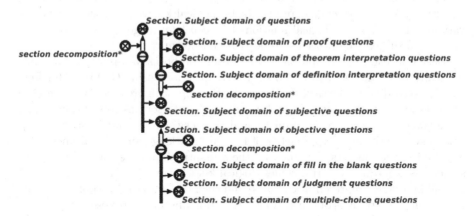

Fig. 3. Hierarchy of the subject domain of questions.

The approach for automatic generation of questions and the approach of using ontology to storage the generated questions, which proposed in this article have the following advantages:

- because the knowledge bases developed using OSTIS technology have the same knowledge storage structure, so only a simple modification of the approach to automatic generation of questions proposed in this article can be used in other OSTIS systems;

- the generated questions are expressed using a unified knowledge representation language SC-code, so they do not depend on natural language;
- the generated questions are stored in the subsystem knowledge base according to the types of the questions and the generation strategies, so the efficiency of question extraction can be greatly improved;
- using the approach proposed in this article it is possible not only to generate subjective and objective questions, but also to reach a very high quality of the generated statements.

3.2 Proposed Answer Verification Approach

In this article, the answer verification is divided into subjective question answer verification and objective question answer verification. Because objective questions have definite standard answers, it is only needed to directly compare standard answers with user answers. There is no definite standard answer for subjective questions, so it is necessary to compare the similarity between the standard answers and the user answers [10]. According to the types of knowledge, subjective question answer verification can be divided into:

- factual knowledge answer verification;
- logical knowledge answer verification.

Factual knowledge refers to knowledge that does not contain variable types, and this type of knowledge expresses facts. Logical knowledge usually contains variables, and there are logical relations between knowledge [7,10]. Most of the answers to subjective questions are logical knowledge.

Based on the SPICE approach, this article proposes an approach for automatically verifying the answers to subjective questions using OSTIS technology [3,7,8]. According to the task requirements, the approach proposed in this article needs to verify the correctness and completeness of user answers (for example, the answer is correct but incomplete, and the answer is partially correct, etc.). The answer verification approaches of factual knowledge and logical knowledge are similar, the answers described by the semantic graph are divided into substructures according to certain rules (logical knowledge representation rules and factual knowledge representation rules) and then the similarity is compared. The implementation process of the answer verification approach proposed in this article is as follows:

- first, we use s to represent standard answers in the form of semantic graphs in the subsystem knowledge base;
- then the standard answers s and user answers u expressed using SCg-code/ SCL-code are decomposed into substructures according to the rules of knowledge representation. u refers to the expression form after the natural language users answers are transformed to SC-code through the natural language interface [14]. The set $T_{sc}(s)$ represents all the substructures after the decomposition of the standard answers s, and the set $T_{sc}(u)$ represents all the substructures after the decomposition of the user answers u [10];

- finally, the similarity is calculated by comparing the ratio between the number of identical substructures and the total number of substructures between the standard answer and the user answer. The main calculation parameters include: precision P_{sc}, recall R_{sc}, and similarity F_{sc}. Their specific calculation process is shown in formulas (1), (2), (3).

$$P_{sc}(u, s) = \frac{|T_{sc}(u) \otimes T_{sc}(s)|}{|T_{sc}(u)|} \tag{1}$$

$$R_{sc}(u, s) = \frac{|T_{sc}(u) \otimes T_{sc}(s)|}{|T_{sc}(s)|} \tag{2}$$

$$F_{sc}(u, s) = \frac{2 \cdot P_{sc}(u, s) \cdot R_{sc}(u, s)}{P_{sc}(u, s) + R_{sc}(u, s)} \tag{3}$$

Figure 4 shows an example of similarity calculation of knowledge of factual types in SCg-code.

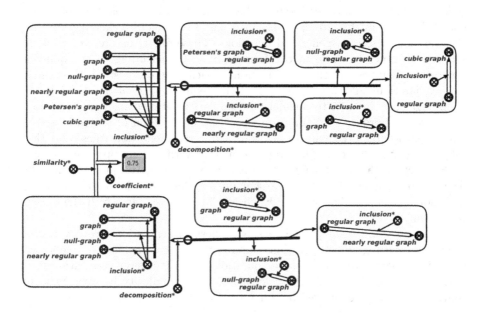

Fig. 4. An example of similarity calculation of knowledge of factual types.

Compared with existing answer verification approaches, the approach proposed in this article has many advantages:

- it uses semantics to compare the similarity between answers;
- the OSTIS technology has a unified model of knowledge representation, so our approach can calculate the similarity between texts with more complex content than the SPICE approach;

- compared with the approach of deep learning, our approach can judge the completeness and find the incorrect parts of the user answers through the substructures;
- it uses a unified knowledge representation language SC-code, so can be used in other OSTIS systems only by modifying a few rules.

4   Conclusion and Further Work

In this article, an approach for automatic generation of test questions and automatic verification of answers in ITS built using OSTIS technology has been proposed. In the knowledge base built using OSTIS technology, based on the representation rules of each type of knowledge and the semantic structure of each type of test question, a series of question generation strategies are summarized in this article. Based on these question generation strategies, the proposed approach to automatic generation of questions allows various types of questions to be generated, not only simple multiple-choice questions, but also more complex types of questions. In order to store these generated questions, the subsystem knowledge base in this article is designed based on OSTIS technology and the classification criteria of generated questions. These questions are stored in the subsystem knowledge base in the form of SC-code according to the question generation strategy and the classification of each type of question, this way of storing questions allows to quickly find the required type of questions in the knowledge base. In order to calculate the similarity between answers, this article proposes an approach of decomposing answers in the form of semantic graphs into substructures according to the knowledge representation rules, and then calculating the similarity. The proposed answer verification approach not only allows to check the correctness of the answer to the objective question, but also to the subjective question, while the semantics of the answer is considered, which does not depend on the form (in English; Chinese; etc.), in which the answer was given.

In future work, we hope that a single question generation strategy can be combined by using union operations, intersection operations, and simple logical reasoning to generate more complex questions. For the answer verification part, we hope that in the future, the calculation of the similarity between logically equivalent formulas expressed by semantic graphs can be realized.

Acknowledgments. The work in this article was done with the support of research teams of the Department of Intelligent Information Technologies of Belarusian State University of Informatics and Radioelectronics. Authors would like to thank every researcher in the Department of Intelligent Information Technologies.

References

1. IMS.ostis Metasystem. https://ims.ostis.net. Accessed 15 Jun 2020
2. Protégé. http://protege.stanford.edu. Accessed 17 Jun 2020
3. Anderson, P., Fernando, B., Johnson, M., Gould, S.: SPICE: semantic propositional image caption evaluation. In: Leibe, B., Matas, J., Sebe, N., Welling, M. (eds.) ECCV 2016. LNCS, vol. 9909, pp. 382–398. Springer, Cham (2016). https://doi.org/10.1007/978-3-319-46454-1_24
4. Ding, X., Gu, H.: Research on automatic generation of Chinese multiple choice questions based on ontology. Comput. Eng. Design **31**(6), 1397–1400 (2010)
5. Fargieva, Z.S., Daurbekova, A.M., Ausheva, M.A., Belkharoeva, E.: Computer training programs. Problems of educational process organization. Probl. Pedagogy **7**(18), 48–51 (2016)
6. Golenkov, V.V., Tarasov, V.B., Eliseeva, O.E.: Intellectual training systems and virtual training organizations. In: Distance Learning - Educational Tools of the XXI Century, Belarus Minsk, pp. 21–26 (2001)
7. Golenkov, V.V., Gulyakina, N.A.: Project of open semantic technology for component design of intelligent systems. Ontol. Des. **1**(11), 42–64 (2014)
8. Golovko, V.A., et al.: Integration of artificial neural networks and knowledge bases. Ontol. Des. **29**, 366–386 (2018)
9. Li, H.: Research on item automatic generation based on dl and domain ontology. J. Changchun Univ. Technol. (Nat. Sci. Ed.) **33**(4), 460–464 (2012)
10. Li, W., Grakova, N.V., Qian, L.: Ontological approach to automating the processes of question generation and knowledge control in intelligent learning systems. In: 10th International Scientific and Technical Conference "Open Semantic Technologies for Intelligent Systems", Belarus Minsk, pp. 215–224 (2020)
11. Li, X.: Realization of automatic scoring algorithm for subjective questions based on artificial intelligence. J. Jiangnan Univ. (Nat. Sci. Ed.) **8**(3), 292–295 (2009)
12. Mitkov, R., Le, A.H., Karamanis, N.: A computer-aided environment for generating multiple-choice test items. Nat. Lang. Eng. **12**(2), 177–194 (2006)
13. Papasalouros, A., Kanaris, K., Kotis, K.: Automatic generation of multiple choice questions from domain ontologies. In: IADIS International Conference e-Learning, pp. 427–434. Citeseer (2008)
14. Qian, L., Sadouski, M.E., Li, W.: Ontology method for Chinese language processing. In: 10th International Scientific and Technical Conference "Open Semantic Technologies for Intelligent Systems", pp. 207–214, Belarus Minsk (2020)
15. Qin, C., Zhu, T., Zhao, P., Zhang, Y.: Research progress in semantic analysis of natural language. Library Inf. Work **58**(22), 130–137 (2014)
16. Ramos, J.: Using TF-IDF to determine word relevance in document queries. In: Proceedings of the First Instructional Conference on Machine Learning, New Jersey, USA, pp. 133–142 (2003)
17. Yang, M., Li, P., Zhu, Q.: Sentence similarity calculation method based on tree-LSTM. J. Peking Univ. (Nat. Sci. Ed.) **54**(3), 481–486 (2018)

Plagiarism Problem Solving Based on Combinatory Semantics

Aliaksandr Hardzei(✉)

Minsk State Linguistic University, Minsk, Belarus
alieks2001@yahoo.com

Abstract. The paper is presenting an updated edition of the second version of Theory for Automatic Generation of Knowledge Architecture (TAPAZ-2) and proposes a new approach to solving the problem of automatically identifying the semantic equivalence of text documents and borrowing scientific ideas in order to curb the spread of plagiarism and prevent clogging the information space under the conditions of its globalization.

Keywords: Semantic classifier · Knowledge graph · Role list of individs · Subject · Object · Action · Macroprocess · Specialized process · Subject domain · World model · TAPAZ-algebra

1 Introduction

At the boundary of XX – XXI centuries, the problem with development of large knowledge bases on a foundation of universal semantic classifiers, despite all attempts to avoid it or reduce the disadvantages of hardware, has become central in research on computer modeling of intellectual activities.

D. Lenat, the author of the CYC project, concerning the problem wrote: "Entering knowledge into CYC means that we must represent the knowledge in such a form that the program can find and use it when appropriate. For this reason, simply having an online version of an encyclopedia would be of little use, as there is practically nothing that current AI technology could draw from the raw text. Rather, we must carefully re-represent the encyclopedia's knowledge – by hand – into some more structured form" [39, p. 75].

This understandable and solvable problem on the appropriate level of hardware evolution is related to another one, difficult and unknown to software developers but long-known to mathematicians, logicians, philosophers and linguists and which was drawing attention of researchers on the dawn of evolution of AI and this is a problem of embedding semantics in formal representation. "What has not been attempted in order to avoid, ignore, or expel meaning? It has been useless; this Medusa's head is always there at the center of language, fascinating those who contemplate it" [5, p. 106–107].

We underline only several dramatic episodes. H. G. Gadamer wrote "The merit of semantic analysis, it seems to me, is that it has brought the structural

© Springer Nature Switzerland AG 2020
V. Golenkov et al. (Eds.): OSTIS 2020, CCIS 1282, pp. 176–197, 2020.
https://doi.org/10.1007/978-3-030-60447-9_11

totality of language to our attention and thereby has pointed out the limitations of the false ideal of unambiguous signs or symbols and of the potential of language for logical formalization" [15, p. 83].

However, in the late '60s of XX century S. Amarel concluded that the efficiency of problem solving depends on the form of its representation [4], i.e., implicitly he suggested that the correct representation of the problem is, in fact, its solution.

The conclusion had resonance and was consistent with the common scientific understanding of a proof; the process of reducing complex statements (theorems) to simple statements (axioms)[1], i.e. the conversion of hidden tautologies to explicit tautologies [8].

In particular, M. Minsky took the idea of replacing heuristics with algorithmic representation of knowledge "as moving away from the traditional attempts both by behavioristic psychologists and by logic-oriented students of Artificial Intelligence in trying to represent knowledge as collections of separate, simple fragments" [49, p. 111].

Nevertheless, T. Winograd, the student of M. Minsky, despite all desperate efforts to make progress in this direction, was forced to admit: nobody yet operates with systems that would not be reduced to isolated examples [63] and in continuation "Current systems, even the best ones, often resemble a house of cards. <...> The result is an extremely fragile structure, which may reach impressive heights, but collapses immediately if swayed in the slightest from the specific domain (often even the specific examples) for which it was built" [6, p. 4].

The Russell's paradox inevitably arises because of an object and an instrument of research overlapping[2] in the absence of a formal semantic metatheory[3] and that is clearly following from the statement of T. Winograd: "Language is a process of communication between people, and is inextricably enmeshed in the knowledge that those people have about the world. That knowledge is not a neat collection of definitions and axioms, complete, concise and consistent. Rather it is a collection of concepts designed to manipulate ideas. It is in fact incomplete, highly redundant, and often inconsistent. There is no self-contained set of

---

[1] "The philosophers of all ages have regarded it as their highest aim to prove their conclusions "by the geometrical method"" [53, p. 1].

[2] On this problem in linguistic analysis has repeatedly pointed out L. Hjelmslev [32] and U. Weinreih [60,61].

[3] "To exclude such contradictions from an axiomatic theory, it is necessary to describe its language precisely, i.e. the set of sentences of the theory and the set of signs used to build these sentences. In this way we avoid contradictions caused by a collision between the theory and its metatheory, that is, by including metatheoretical statements in the theory. This inclines us to introduce still greater precision in the construction of mathematical theories and leads to the concept of formalized theories, in which not only the properties of the primitive notions are given in an exact way by means of a set of axioms, but also the language of the theory is precisely defined" [52, p. 146–147].

"primitives" from which everything else can be defined. Definitions are circular, with the meaning of each concept depending on the other concepts" [62, p. 26].

T. Winograd understood what is required from semantics "a transducer that can work with a syntactic analyzer, and produce data which is acceptable to a logical deductive system. Given a syntactic parser with a grammar of English, and a deductive system with a base of knowledge about particular subjects, the role of semantics is to fill the gap between them" [62, p. 28].

But how to achieve that with help of mathematics where an object and an instrument of research are overlapping as well, no one knew.

Such a logical paradox was detected by Bertrand Russell in 1902 in foundations of arithmetic by G. Frege and this almost provoked the author of predicative second-order logic and founder of logical semantics to suicide.

During the whole XX century mathematics through the formalization of the meta-language tried to eliminate contradictions in its foundations.

Neither predicate calculus [13] nor Boolean algebra [56] nor pseudo-physical and modal logic [35], nor Cantor's theory of sets [9] have been able to formalize the language semantics: mathematics still did not have its own means of transformation of expressions and logic did not have its own means of representation.

To the credit of the Belarusian science, essential progress in this area was reached by V. V. Martynov in creating a semantic coding approach [40].

The creator of Universal Semantic Code (USC) wrote about the approach: "This is a system that can generate new concepts and build hypotheses about causes and effects. It is implemented as a result of formal transformation of semantic strings. Thus, languages like USC are deductive systems where semantics is not defined but calculated. As a result, USC has its own means of representation and transformation of semantics" [48, p. 62]. The first version of USC was published at 1974 [41], 1977 – the second [42], 1984 – the third [43], 1988 – the fourth [44], 1995 – the fifth [45], 2001 – the sixth [47].

From version to version the algebraic apparatus and the list of "non-existent", according to T. Winograd, semantic primitives were improving. Thus, the list of tasks to equip computer with encyclopedic knowledge bases was narrowed, and finally the list consists of five components:

"1. To calculate semantic primitives, i.e. semantically irreducible kernel words and define rules of their combinatorics.
2. To define the necessary and sufficient set of formal characteristics constituting 'dictionary entry'.
3. **To define a set of semantic operations for calculating a subject domain of any kind.**
4. To propose heuristic teaching rules to work with the system.
5. To build a system of mutual references based on semantics" [47, p. 42].

In 1993 achievements in the approach allowed the researchers of the center "Semantics" of Minsk Linguistic State University, headed by V. V. Martynov, to begin an intensive research of ways to expand the basic semantic classifier to the encyclopedic knowledge base.

It occurred that the multiplicity of complex USC strings does not provide input into the subject domain, because the depth is greater than the threshold of Yngve [67]: for the threshold more than eight strings were not readable or understandable [18].

In 1994, the first procedure of calculating the subject domains in the form of a directed graph of complex strings was proposed by A. Hardzei [17].

Use of the procedure has required the establishment of a one-to-one (vector) transition between actions in basic semantic classifier and has led to the creation of the automatic generation of knowledge architecture theory (TAPAZ) which was founded on: the formal theory; the semantic counterpart; the set of macroprocesses (actions) as semantic primitives; the algorithm defining roles of individs, and the graph for searching processes through macroprocesses (knowledge graph) [19,20].

Concerning what V. V. Martynov wrote: "Solving the problem of 'semantic calculus', Hardzei refused knowledge representation based on inference such as 'if..., then...' (cause – effect) and instead started to build organized tuples of components (different terminology may be used, which in any case refers to the undefined concepts).

In fact, it limits the semantic constructs with simple extended strings (in the sense of USC) without transforming them into complex strings <...> Besides, defined in USC operations of superposition (*) and complement ($^-$), he introduces the operation of 'taking the inside' ($\sim$) <...> Hardzei calculates simple extended strings on the basis of so-called transpositional transformation of strings according to S. N. Furs [14].

Herewith Hardzei embedded semantics in such transformations based on the World Model built by him <...> Hardzei's main achievement as the author of a new version of the theory of semantic coding is in its application for calculating the semantic domains.

This is still a project, but in the case of its implementation, we will have an extremely useful tool for artificial intelligence systems" [46].

TAPAZ-2 as the new version of the Theory for Automatic Generation of Knowledge Architecture differs from the previous version [19,20] in several ways: simplified algebraic apparatus, increased number of rules for interpretation of the standard superposition of individs, and minimized semantic calculus.

The number of operations with the strings of semantic code are reduced to two and it is now the algebra type:

$$A = \langle M, *, {}^- \rangle$$

where: M is a set of elements, '*' is operation of superposition, '$^-$' is operation of extension[4].

In the previous version the operation of 'taking the inside' (denoted by '$\sim$') was used to distinguish physical and informational actions, since on the highest abstract semantic level the physical action was considered as an influence of one

---

[4] For a detailed description of the new version of TAPAZ-algebra, see: [27].

individ onto another through its shell, and the informational action – through its surroundings [22].

At the same time, the superposition of the individ with its surroundings has been interpreted as its annihilating [19], so we had to distinguish external and internal environment of the individ for superposition the individ with its external surroundings to be interpreted as annihilating, but superposition with its internal surroundings – as the transition of the physical action into the informational [20].

Such a formal method has established parallelism and symmetry of the physical and information actions.

Indeed, to transmit information a material carrier is needed. The carrier physically effects the object, and according to changes in the object after their physical interaction, we can evaluate the nature of the interaction.

For example, while teaching (informational action) a teacher uses the vocal cords; straining them, which increases the amplitude of the sound waves (material carrier) and can stun the students, i.e. have a physical effect on them.

Another example, the clashing of metal balls while thrown is a physical action but by examining the dents on the balls you can find information about the strength of their clash.

In other words, it depends on the view point of an observer and which component (physical or informational) he prioritizes. Similar to perceiving the corner of a cube in three-dimensional space and observing it in the form of *a fork* or *an arrow* [64].

Taking into consideration the requirement of one-to-one correspondence between presentation and content[5], the expressions with the operator 'taking the inside' of the first individ are presenting the informational action and expressions, and those without the operator 'taking the inside' are presenting the physical action.

At the same time, all expressions with the operator 'taking the inside' and those without it, while possessing the same set of arguments were algebraically and geometrically equivalent: the superposition of individs assumed to juxtapose their boundaries and cores, as well as the superposition of the cores of individs assumed to juxtapose their borders.

Further research revealed that the superposition of the individ with its environment during continuation of the action can be considered as transition of the physical action into informational[6].

---

[5] One, and only one sense must correspond to each string (the combination of elementary symbols) [46].

[6] Such a transition for G. H. von Wright seemed inconceivable: "Suppose someone asked how I turned the handle, and I answer that I seized it with my right hand and turned the hand clockwise. Here again it would be correct to say that I brought about the turning of the handle by performing those actions. But if someone were to ask how I turned my hand, it would not be correct to say that I brought this about by contracting and relaxing a particular group of muscles. For, unless I happen to have a special knowledge of anatomy, I do not know which muscles these are nor how to contract them - except by turning my hand" [66, p. 67].

TAPAZ-2 is a tool for generating a world model in a form suitable for Natural Language Processing in systems of Artificial Intelligence. The Intellectual Knowledge Base built in a computer combines the Semantic Classifier – a final ordered (vector) set of semantic primitives (actions and roles of individs) and the Semantic Ontology – an algorithm for generating new sense units based on the original set of primitives, presented in the form of the Semantic Classifier Graph or **TAPAZ Knowledge Graph** [27].

An Intelligent (Expert) Search System based on the TAPAZ-2 Semantic Classifier may consist of an intelligent search engine that selects and reviews content on a given topic from the Internet, and a dialog user interface that allows the system to process user requests and transform them in the canonized text corresponding to the machine-readable World Model, and the user will confirm whether this conversion was performed correctly, and if not, then offer his own decoding through the Semantic Classifier.

This Intelligent Search System can be used to solve various problems, including the task of automatic identification of semantically equivalent fragments of text documents, which will be discussed below.

The main components of this Intelligent Search System are: an online content monitoring module with adequate crawler and stapler; automatic lexical analysis module with a tagger on a semantic (Parts of Language), not on a morphological (Parts of Speech) basis; dynamic syntactic analysis module with a recursive reconstruction algorithm (parser) for sentence string elaborated in combinatory semantics technology; a module for direct and reverse conversion of syntactic expressions into TAPAZ-2 algebraic formulas, as well as the Intellectual Knowledge Base (IKB) consisting of TAPAZ-units (IKB-taxonomy) assembled in the order indicated by the Knowledge Graph of the Semantic Classifier (IKB-ontology). The knowledge base taxonomy also serves as a corresponding subject domain semantic dictionary during automatic lexical analysis.

2   Definitions of Initial Semantic Notions

Combinatory semantics studies the linguistic mapping of the dynamics of individs' roles in an event. Its founder, as we consider, is Z. Harris, who put forward the nuclear semantic string *subject – action – object* as a starting point of formalizing sentences [31]. Research in this direction was continued at Minsk Semantic School under the guidance of V. V. Martynov and A. Hardzei. Combinatory semantics should not be confused with combinatorial semantics, which studies co-occurrence of signs using statistical methods, the founder of which is also Z. Harris [30]. Now combinatory semantics operates the following initial notions.

The World – everything that surrounds us, without restrictions in space and time.

The Copy of the World – a reflection of the World by the sense organs.

Internal encoding – automatic implementation of the innate ability of intelligence to code on a subconscious level by means of some internal code.

The pattern – an encoded by intellect recurring element in a copy of the World. For example, in a visual image of a table and a chair the same part serving as a support and bearing a surface is repeated. Recognition of this part creates the pattern of the 'leg'. Comparing patterns and deducing from others, intellect gradually builds a Model of the World. Using which, solves a variety of problems on a subconscious level. For instance, when a person crosses a street, his mind in a split of a second determines the distance to the car depending on its speed, thus forcing the musculoskeletal system to slow down or speed up the pace [22].

The World Model (hidden knowledge) – architecture of patterns, i.e. the ordered set of patterns and the ordered set of transformations of some patterns in others.

The subject domain *(domain knowledge or field knowledge)* – a separate part of the World Model.

The event – a highlighted fragment in a separate part of the World Model.

The semantic counterpart – coupled with a mathematical formalism a highlighted fragment of the World Model. In a narrow sense, the term 'semantic counterpart' means a formal world model coupled with the geometric model and consisting of patterns generated by TAPAZ formalisms. The term 'semantic counterpart' is borrowed from: [65].

The individ – a kind of the pattern as a separate entity in the selected fragment of the World Model. It consists of three elements: the core, the shell, and the surroundings. *The element* is the individ without parts – ultimate individ. *The core* is the element enclosed in the shell and placed in the surroundings. *The shell* is the permanent closest environs of the element. *The surroundings* is variable closest environs of the element.

The attribute of the individ – a kind of the pattern as the property of a separate entity in the selected fragment of the World Model or of the action (process) in which the entity is involved.

The action – an influence of one individ onto another.

The process – an influence (action) of one individ onto another within the highlighted subject domain. It includes active and passive phases (impact and state).

The macroprocess – an invariant of processes (actions) in superposition to other invariants.

The specified process – a process (action) associated with a macroprocess. Roles of the individs:

subject – the originator of the action; varieties of the subject: *initiator* – initiates the action, *spreader* – spreads the action, *inspirer* – involves into the action, *creator* – completes the action by creating a product from the object.

object – the recipient of the action;

instrument – a performer of the action, the closest individ to the subject; varieties of the instrument: *activator* – directly affects the mediator, *suppressor* – suppresses the resistance of the mediator, *enhancer* – increases the effect on the mediator, *converter* – converts the mediator into an instrument.

mediator, i.e. mediator of the action – the closest individ to the object; varieties of the mediator: *landmark* – orientates the impact on the object, *locus* – the closest environs of the object partially or completely surrounding the object and thereby containing (enclosing) it, *carrier* – carries the object, *adapter* – adapts the instrument to affect the object, *material* – a raw for a product creation, *prototype* – a physical model for creating a product from the object, *resource* – feeds the instrument, *source* – serves as initial data (information model) for creating a product from the object, *chronotope* – indicates time of exposure to the object, and *fund* – provides information into the instrument.

Depending on which ultimate individ acts as the instrument: the shell of the subject or its surroundings, the action is classified as *physical* or *informational*.

The semantic field of a macroprocess (general field of TAPAZ) – a typical role of an individ involved in a macroprocess.

The semantic field of a process (subject field of TAPAZ) – a role of an individ involved in a process within the highlighted subject domain.

The TAPAZ Semantic Classifier – a final ordered (vector) set of semantic primitives (macroprocesses and roles of individs).

Semantics (from the Greek. Sēmantikós – *signifying*) – linguistic discipline that studies the relation of Language to the World Model, unlike philosophy, designed to study the relation of the World Model to the World. Also, semantics refers to the *content* of patterns, *meaning* of signs, and *sense* of sentences.

The Linguistic Image of the World (open knowledge) – a part of the World Model decoded by means of language for the conscious control of intellectual activity, i.e. a partially ordered set of patterns and a partially ordered set of transformations of some patterns in others.

Parts of Language – subsets of a language system whose elements are signs with a common extremely abstract meaning. They are divided into *substantives* denoting individs, for example: 'a book', 'a table', 'eight', 'we', and *predicatives* denoting attributes of individs, for example: 'to run', 'brown', 'bold', 'very'. Substantives and predicatives are divided into *constants* and *variables,* depending on whether they denote the sets of homogeneous individs *i-const,* for example: 'idea', 'horse' *(constant substantives)* or the sets of heterogeneous individs *i-var,* for example: 'it', 'this' *(variable substantives)*, whether they denote the set of properties of individs $p(i)$: 'mental', 'gray' *(constant predicative)* or the sets of functions of individs $f(i)$, i.e., the processes in which individs are involved: 'to think', 'to gallop' *(variable predicative).*

Signs of Syntax Alphabet – auxiliary means of syntax *(prepositions, postpositions, conjunctions, particles,* etc.) that serve to connect the components of linguistic structures. The Signs of Syntax Alphabet do not belong to the Language, but to a Metalanguage (a language that is interpreted by another language), because they are not the facts of the World Model but the facts of the Language. For example, the preposition 'on' is used to construct locatives as 'on the table', but not to designate the individs playing the role of locus in the World Model. The preposition 'on' disappears if the structure of the sentence is brought into line with the structure of the World Model, for example, 'the surface of the table holds the book' instead of 'the book lies on the table'.

The Signs of Syntax Alphabet do not play independent roles in the sentence and are not parts of the sentence.

The sentence – an actional (semantically non-commutative) sequence of combinatorial variants of signs, compare: 'The door has a lock' and *'The lock has a door', 'I eat soup' and *'Soup eats me'. Sentences are divided into:

- narrative and interrogative (according the form);
- affirmative and directive (according the purpose);
- positive and negative (according the estimation);
- neutral and exclamatory (according the expression).

Parts of the Sentence – the roles of Parts of Language in the sentence: *the grammatical subject* is the starting point of the event description selected by the observer, *the grammatical direct object* is the final point of the event description selected by the observer, *the grammatical predicate* is the mapping by the observer of the starting point of the event description to the final point. The grammatical subject, grammatical predicate and grammatical direct object, both in terms of semantics and syntax, are the three principal parts of the sentence. Secondary parts are generated from the principal ones by recursion, when the observer perceives the event in more detail, that, accordingly, complicates its description [26].

Metalinguistic operation (predication) – the establishment of a one-to-one correspondence between syntax and semantics, in which each role of a part of a language in a sentence is mapped to each role of an individ in the highlighted fragment of the World Model.

3   TAPAZ Semantic Classifier

3.1   Set of Semantic Primitives or Paradigm of Macroprocesses (Actions)

The paradigm consists of informational and physical macroprocesses ordered by TAPAZ-algebra. The physical macroprocesses are shaded (see Fig. 1).

The table uses the following notation:

A – activation group, B – exploitation group, C – transformation group, D – normalization group; a – surroundings-shell subgroup, b – shell-core subgroup, c – core-shell subgroup, d – shell-surroundings subgroup; I – initiation raw, II – accumulation raw, III – amplification raw, IV – generation raw.

3.2   Role List of Individs

The Role List of Individs ordered by TAPAZ-algebra is as follows:

subject (initiator → spreader → inspirer → creator) → instrument (activator → suppressor → enhancer → converter) → mediator (landmark →locus → carrier → adapter → material →prototype →resource →source → chronotope → fund) → object → product.

		I	II	III	IV
A	a	1 perceive / attract 57	2 reflect / cumulate 58	3 comprehend / constrict 59	4 understand / attain 60
	b	5 adopt / absorb 61	6 memorize / accumulate 62	7 contemplate / center 63	8 learn / assimilate 64
	c	9 feel / over absorb 65	10 behold / concentrate 66	11 feel profoundly / centrifuge 67	12 experience / dissimilate 68
	d	13 reject / expel 69	14 erase / decompress 70	15 rethink / force off 71	16 overcome / disassociate 72
B	a	17 notify / approach 73	18 advertise / joint 74	19 instill / press down 75	20 state / connect 76
	b	21 explain / insert 77	22 propagandize / pump 78	23 prove / press in 79	24 certify / link 80
	c	25 reveal / conduct 81	26 prophesize / spread 82	27 enlighten / squeeze out 83	28 divine / disconnect 84
	d	29 darken / take out 85	30 encode / pull up 86	31 discredit / push out 87	32 disavow / unlink 88
C	a	33 inform / touch on 89	34 interest / envelope 90	35 assure / squeeze 91	36 predispose / mold 92
	b	37 admonish / rip up 93	38 teach / fill up 94	39 convince / press 95	40 nurture / form 96
	c	41 pierce / penetrate 97	42 intend / overflow 98	43 transfigure / unclamp 99	44 reincarnate / eviscerate 100
	d	45 pester / punch 101	46 mesmerize / uplift 102	47 lose conscious / disband 103	48 go mad / annihilate 104
D	a	49 recollect / recrystallize 105	50 recreate / reintegrate 106	51 restart / regenerate 107	52 render / restore 108
	b	53 reproduce / recuperate 109	54 reclaim / rehabilitate 110	55 renew / reactivate 111	56 revive / reanimate 112

Fig. 1. Paradigm of macroprocesses (actions).

We note that the power of the TAPAZ semantic markup, only in terms of the typical roles of individs, not even talking about the TAPAZ-algebra and generated by it Paradigm of Actions and the Knowledge Graph, almost 5 times exceeds the power of the closest analogue – the technology of Active Vocabulary, standardized and adopted by W3C Consortium in 2017 [2] within the framework of Semantic Web project [55] and then Schema.org [54]. This technology is predominantly based on the theory of semantic cases of C. Fillmore [12] and Jackendoff's early work [33,34], the inventory of which is:

agent – the initiator of some action, capable of acting with volition, and *actor* – supertype of agent which performs, affects, instigates, or controls the situation denoted by the predicate;

patient – the entity undergoing the effect of some action, often undergoing some change of state;

theme – the entity which is moved by an action, or whose location is described;

beneficiary – the entity for whose benefit the action was performed;

experiencer – the entity which is aware of the action or state described by the predicate but which is not in control of the action or state;

percept or *stimulus* – the entity which is perceived or experienced;

instrument – the means by which an action is performed or something comes about;

source – the entity from which something moves, either literally or metaphorically;

goal – the entity towards which something moves, either literally or metaphorically, and *recipient* – subtype of goal involved in actions describing changes of possession;

location – the place in which something is situated or takes place [1, p. 94–95].

It is not difficult to see that *experiencer, source, goal* and *recipient*, in fact, represent the same typical role of *landmark* in TAPAZ-2; *patient* and *theme* – the role of *object; agent* and *actor* – the roles of *subject* and *creator; beneficiary* – the role of *mediator; percept* or *stimulus* – the role of *source; location* – the role of *locus;* the role of *instrument* in both theories is the same. There is no any algebra in the substantiation of Fillmore's "case frames" or Stowell's "theta-grids" [59], all these semantic categories were empirically distinguished, so it is impossible to establish their consistency, independence and completeness, thereby avoid the Russell's paradox, which inevitably arises from a mixture of theory and metatheory, language and metalanguage, semantics and metasemantics.

3.3   TAPAZ Knowledge Graph

The Graph describes the relations of active and clarifying macroprocesses (see Fig. 2):

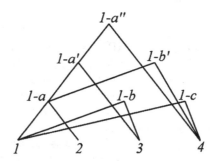

Fig. 2. TAPAZ knowledge graph (the semantic classifier graph).

where: *1* – active macroprocess; *2, 3, 4* – clarifying macroprocesses; *1-a, 1-b, 1-c* – derivative processes with *1-a* as the active derivative process; *1-a'* and *1-b'* – derivative processes of the second level with *1-a'* as the active derivative process of the second level *1-a"* – the active derivative process of the third level.

For example, the macroprocess *'restore'* may be considered as a set and the processes *'treat', 'repair', 'adjust'* as its subsets. Such subsets represent isomorphism of subject domains and create a knowledge structure where subsets of processes fill cells of the knowledge structure with a concrete content [27].

Let n be the number of actions in the initial generating list (the number of the first degree vertices) of the Paradigm of Actions. *The degree of the vertex S* will be called the number of vertices of the initial generating list directly or indirectly participating in the generation of this vertex. There can be several ways to generate an intermediate vertex from the same set of vertices of the first degree. The subgraph that specifies one of the possible ways to generate a vertex is a binary tree, since exactly two ancestor vertices participate in the generation of each child vertex. Thus, the number of ways to generate an intermediate vertex of degree k is expressed by the number of binary trees with the number of leaves equal to k (the Catalan number) [58]. For $k = 4$, the number of such trees is 5, all possible configurations are shown in Fig. 3 [29].

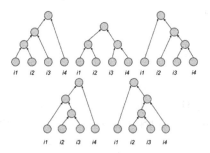

Fig. 3. All possible configurations of binary trees for $k = 4$.

The number of k degree vertices is determined by the formula (1):

$$N_k = A_n^k \times C_k \tag{1}$$

where A_n^k – is the number of allocations from n vertices with respect to k [57] (that is, the set of all the vertices of the initial list participating in generation of a vertex) and – is the Catalan number, which is calculated by the formula (2) or (3):

$$C(n+1) = \frac{(2n)!}{n!(n+1)!} \tag{2}$$

$$C_n = \frac{(2(n-1))!}{((n-1)!n!)} \tag{3}$$

where n is the number of leaves of a binary tree [57,58].
The maximum degree of a vertex in the Semantic Classifier Graph is equal to the number of vertices in the initial set (all vertices of the initial set participate in generating a vertex of degree n). Thus, in order to obtain the number of vertices in the Graph, it is necessary to sum up the number of vertices of all degrees from *1* to *n:*

$$S_n = \sum_{k=1}^{n} A_n^k \times C_k = \sum_{k=1}^{n} \frac{n!}{(n-k)!} \times \frac{(2(k-1))!}{(k-1)k!} \tag{4}$$

Python program code, calculating the function $S(n)$ by the formula (4):

```
from math import factorial as fact

def S(n):
    sum=0
    for k in xrange(1, n+1):
        A=fact(n)/fact(n-k)
        C=fact(2*(k-1))/(fact(k-1)*fact(k))
        sum+=A*C
    return sum


print "%e" % S(112)
```

The Paradigm of Actions, which is used to build the Semantic Classifier Graph, contains 112 macroprocesses. Substituting this number into formula (4) as n, we get:

$$S_n \approx 8,2 \times 10^{245}$$

At present, there are no devices whose computational capacities are capable of processing and storing a similar amount of information, therefore it is necessary to select the most significant part of the Graph in order to sequentially generate, process and store this graph using computer technology. Reducing the number of vertices is achieved in three ways:

- restrictions on the generation of vertices;
- division of the complete graph into two separate subgraphs;
- limiting the depth of actions' detailing.

The combination of all three methods allows you to adjust the number of processed vertices. For example, we can find the k degree at which the depth of detailing of the new actions is sufficient to achieve the required semantic power, but the number of vertices in the graph remains within the limits allowing it to be processed and stored by modern computing means.

Let us investigate the number of vertices in the Semantic Classifier Graph and in the graph constructed by the method of sequential detail (Table 1). Already at the level of $k_{max} = 3$ detailing, the number of generated vertices, multiplied by the number of $k = 31$ roles of individs, exceeds 85 million, despite the fact that the Dictionary of the modern Russian literary language in 17 volumes contains 120,480 words, the declared volume of the Large Academic Dictionary of the Russian language is 150,000 words, and the available electronic resources of the Institute of Linguistic Studies of the Russian Academy of Sciences for 1.4

Table 1. The dimension of graphs with limited depth of detailing.

Depth of detailing k_{max}	Semantic classifier graph		Graph of the standard form	
	S_n	$S_n \times 31$	S_n	$S_n \times 31$
2	12544	388864	12544	388864
3	2747584	85175104	2747584	85175104
4	748045984	2318925504	598986304	18568575424

billion of word usage contain about 5 million Russian words of the XVIII – XXI centuries [38].

At the level of $k_{max} = 4$ detailing, the number of vertices of the Semantic Classifier Graph, multiplied by the number of roles of individs, exceeds 23 billion. Since the generation of separate graphs for physical and informational actions significantly reduces the number of values obtained, this method of calculation will increase the possible depth of detailing. These results are presented in Table 2, similar Table 1, only for a graph built on a set of 56 vertices of the first degree:

Table 2. The dimension of the graphs of physical and information processes with limited depth of detailing.

Depth of detailing k_{max}	Semantic classifier graph		Graph of the standard form	
	S_n	$S_n \times 31$	S_n	$S_n \times 31$
2	3136	97216	3136	97216
3	335776	10409056	335776	10409056
4	44410576	1376727856	35595616	1103464096
5	6461701456	200312745136	3702618976	114781188256

At the depth of $k_{max} = 4$ detailing, the number of vertices in the Semantic Classifier Graph, multiplied by the number·of roles of individs, does not exceed two billion. Thus, we get an additional level of detailing that improves the accuracy of calculating subject domains [29].

3.4   TAPAZ Semantic Dictionary

There must be a one-to-one correspondence not only between noun phrases and thematic roles, as N. Chomsky mentioned [10], but a one-to-one correspondence between roles of individs in the event, parts of the sentence, mapping this event[7],

---

[7] Syntactical rules for dynamic syntactic analysis module with a recursive reconstruction algorithm (parser) for sentence string is described in: [24,26].

and parts of the language[8], playing relevant roles in this sentence, otherwise, we will not be able to implement machine learning algorithms, such as, for example, an artificial neural network or a random forest and thereby provide automatic semantic markup of texts collected in the Knowledge Base.

TAPAZ Semantic Dictionary consists of subject domains' TAPAZ-units assembled in the order indicated by TAPAZ Knowledge Graph. TAPAZ-units simultaneously form the taxonomy of the Intellectual Knowledge Base. Initially, TAPAZ-units are manually assembled by experts until the training data is sufficient to implement machine learning algorithms. Now TAPAZ technology is used as linguistic support for the event's Internet monitoring subsystem 5[1] "Development of an Intelligent Web-Based System for Searching and Processing Content in English and Russian Using the Semantic Coding Method for Information Support for Solving Managerial, Design-and-Search and Expert Tasks in the Field of Remote Sensing of the Earth (ERS)", Sect. 1 "Development of the Belarusian Space System for Remote Sensing of the Earth", sub-programme 7 "Research and Peaceful Use of Outer Space" of the State program "High Technology and Technics" for 2016–2020, and we are developing TAPAZ Intellectual Knowledge Base to operate in Chinese, English and Russian sectors of IT-Industry. The algorithm for extracting specialized Russian terminology from ERS-content by an expert to fill the Knowledge Base involves the software ExpertTool version 2.3.4.7, developed by A. A. Matsko (see Fig. 4, Fig. 5).

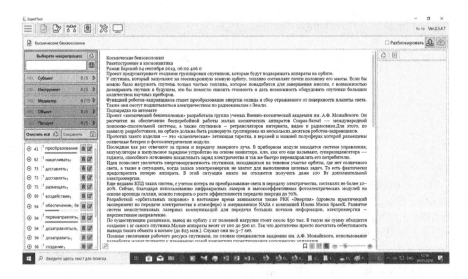

Fig. 4. The working window of the software tool.

---

[8] For definitions of Parts of Language, their paradigm, and semantic delineation procedures, see: [21, 23].

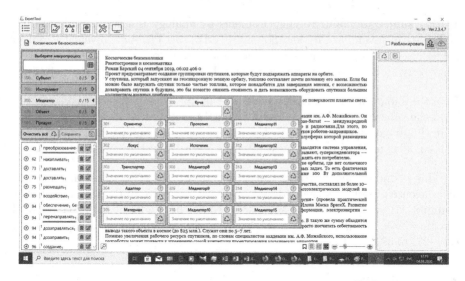

Fig. 5. The working window of a software tool with an expanded tab.

The algorithm for extracting specialized terminology from ERS-content by an expert and filling in the TAPAZ semantic fields (the role list of individs in the ERS-domain) is similar to the TAPAZ Role List of Individs: *subject (initiator → spreader→inspirer → creator) → instrument (activator → suppressor → enhancer → converter) → mediator (landmark → locus → carrier → adapter → material → prototype → resource → source → chronotope → fund) → object → product.*

Interactive filling the semantic fields for each specified process of any subject domain requires answers to typical questions:

Who? With which tool? In relation to whom/what? In what place? Arriving on what? Adjusting with what? Making of what? Following what example? Spending what? Knowing what? In what period? Due to whose prompt? Affecting who/what? Produces whom/what?

TAPAZ Semantic Dictionary plays a key role in identifying the semantic equivalence of text documents and borrowing scientific ideas:

– if, as a result of automatic semantic markup of two texts belonging to the same subject domain, the fact of the coincidence of one, two or three TAPAZ-units is detected, then the semantic equivalence of these texts is evaluated, respectively, as weak, medium and strong;
– if, as a result of automatic semantic markup of two texts belonging to different subject domains, the fact of the coincidence of one, two or three TAPAZ-units is detected, then the borrowing of the idea is evaluated, respectively, as weak, medium and strong.

The borrowing of an idea should not always be qualified as plagiarism, since considerable intellectual efforts are often required to adapt the borrowed idea to another subject domain. Solving problems by analogy is a standard procedure in Theory of Inventive Problem Solving (TRIZ) [3]. TAPAZ Universal Problem Solver also allows you to make some decisions by analogy, for example, the ordinary everyday task, such as removing the shallow of an egg has three solutions:

1. in the subgroup *surroundings-shell*—break up;
2. in the subgroup *shell-core*—insert a splitting reagent;
3. in the subgroup core-shell—unclench from inside expanding the volume of the core. This method is used most often by birds when they incubate chicks.

This is one of many ordinary everyday tasks, but all semantically isomorphic inventive problems that are not ordinary, are solved in a similar way. For example: "How to remove the snow adhered to the blades of the snow-removal machine?" Or "How to remove the ice from the submarine or aircraft hull?", Etc. [27, p. 39].

4   Conclusion

Thus, the system core (World Model) based on TAPAZ is a combination of 112 macroprocesses (actions) of the TAPAZ Semantic Classifier with a series of specialized processes of the highlighted subject domain, for example, Remote Sensing of the Earth (ERS). Each process has 18 semantic fields in accordance with TAPAZ Role List of Individs. The semantic weight of ERS-process in a synonymous series is determined by the completeness of the fields, the frequency index and the height of TAPAZ Knowledge Graph as its vertices are filled.

The construction of the system core is carried out in manual, semi-automatic and automatic modes. At the first stage, the formation of the Intellectual Knowledge Base by prescribing ontological relationships between the independent taxonomy of ERS-individs and the dependent taxonomy of ERS-processes is allowed.

The Specialized Intellectual Knowledge Base (SIKB) of actual space research and technology in the field of ERS combines the TAPAZ-based system core with the periphery generated by TAPAZ Knowledge Graph, complemented by stepwise recursion [27, p. 41] and expanded by TAPAZ Role List of Individs.

The rules for constructing, restricting, reducing and transforming algebraic formulas, the rules for semantic reading of algebraic formulas and interpreting typical combinations of individs, the rules for constructing TAPAZ Knowledge Graph, the procedure for semantic coding and decoding of its vertices, the groups and rows of TAPAZ Paradigm of Actions, TAPAZ Role List of Individs and step recursion form the TAPAZ Universal Problem Solver directly interacts with Web Interface.

All search engines currently operating in the world search either by keywords or by tuples of keywords (keywords in noun and/or verb groups) using standard software tools for content preprocessing and automatic lexical (tagger) and syntax (parser) markup.

The main drawback of both types of search is its inaccuracy and, as a consequence, the immensity for the user of the huge number of URL (Uniform Resource Locator) found by the search engine, forcing search engine developers to limit the search area on the Internet to the region of the query place, which leads to the knowingly incomplete search results. Attempts to supplement the search for keywords and/or their tuples with contextual synonyms based on empirical ontologies that are incorrectly called "semantic"[9] only increase the inaccuracy and incompleteness of the search, overloading the search page with information clog and causing the user to feel the precariousness of the received samples.

The TAPAZ technology offers a search by event fragments or technological cycles, which are described by special TAPAZ-units, which are macroprocesses[10] in the assembly, when specialized ERS-processes are algorithmically correspond to TAPAZ macroprocesses and the roles of all participants in the events are algorithmically calculated[11].

This approach provides maximum accuracy and speed of search, relevance of search results. In addition, it allows you to find similar technological cycles in close (adjacent) and distant subject domains, thereby providing support to the user in analytical activities, which greatly expands the functionality of the search engine, shifting it towards inventive level.

Within the framework of the "Fractal" Development Work, the software ExpertTool 2.3.4.2 was created, which allows manual semantic markup of content using the TAPAZ technology. A manual of the semantic pre-processing of ERS-content has been prepared for experts in order to unify manual conjugation of specialized ERS-processes with TAPAZ macroprocesses. The following were developed: 1) the algorithm for formation of TAPAZ-units; 2) the algorithm for an expert to extract specialized terminology from thematic ERS-content and replenish the Knowledge Base; 3) the algorithm for updating the user request to the system at the request of the system. The properties of the TAPAZ Knowledge Graph as a constructor of the Knowledge Base Architecture of an Intelligent WEB-system and ways to reduce the number of its vertices for sequential generation, processing and storage of the Graph taking into account the capabilities of modern computing technology are determined. The prototype of the TAPAZ-2 dictionary was prepared in the form of an Excel spreadsheet, including 516 of the most commonly used specialized Remote Sensing predicates in combination with 112 macroprocesses of the TAPAZ Semantic Classifier. The semantic structure and semantic functionality of the System were proposed and justified, the algebraic formulas of 18 typical roles of individuals were decoded.

---

[9] "Functional notions like "Subject," "Predicate" are to be sharply distinguished from categorial notions such as "Noun Phrase," "Verb," a distinction that is not to be obscured by the occasional use of the same term for notions of both kinds" [11, p. 68].

[10] We emphasize that macroprocess is one of 112 extremely abstract processes that are isomorphic to any subject domain and are calculated and encoded by the TAPAZ-algebra.

[11] "There exist such terms as "the agent", "the instrument", "the result" < ... > And yet these are different categories, apparently ontological, but in fact semantic" [37, p. 11].

The ultimate goal is automatic semantic markup of ERS-content in the TAPAZ technology, which allows to achieve maximum efficiency (accuracy, speed and completeness) of the search engine, as well as the automatic assembly of TAPAZ-units in the Intellectual Knowledge Base for the analytical support of management, design-and-search and expert solutions remote sensing tasks. This approach simultaneously solves the problem of automatically identifying the semantic equivalence of text documents and borrowing scientific ideas in order to curb the spread of plagiarism and prevent clogging the information space under the conditions of its globalization.

Given the trends in the development of Artificial Intelligence, now we are joining our efforts together with prof. V. V. Golenkov, who proposed the Open Semantic Technology for Intelligent Systems Design (OSTIS Technology) [16], which is focused on the development of a hybrid intelligent systems. Examples of the OSTIS knowledge base, describing lexical, syntactic, and semantic categories in terms of TAPAZ, are available for implementation in algorithms of Natural Language Processing and Natural Language Understanding [28].

We conclude the article with the words of Kenneth Boulding, who made a significant contribution to the development of the General Systems Theory: "Specialization has outrun Trade, communication between the disciples becomes increasingly difficult, and the Republic of Learning is breaking up into isolated subcultures with only tenuous lines of communication between them <...> The reason for this breakup in the body of knowledge is that in the course of specialization the receptors of information themselves become specialized. Hence physicists only talk to physicists, economists to economists − worse still, nuclear physicists only talk to nuclear physicists and econometricians to econometricians. One wonders sometimes if science will not grind to a stop in an assemblage of walled-in hermits, each mumbling to himself words in a private language that only he can understand <...> The spread of specialized deafness means that someone who ought to know something that someone else knows isn't able to find it out for lack of generalized ears. <...> Thus the economist who realizes the strong formal similarity between utility theory in economics and field theory in physics[12] is probably in a better position to learn from the physicists than one who does not" [7, p. 198–199].

References

1. Aarts, B.: English Syntax and Argumentation, 2nd edn. Palgrave (Macmillan), Basingstoke (2001)
2. Activity Vocabulary. W3C Recommendation. https://www.w3.org/TR/activitystreams-vocabulary/#dfn-activity. Accessed 06 July 2020
3. Altshuller, H.: The Art of Inventing (And Suddenly the Inventor Appeared). Technical Innovation Center, Worcester, MA (1994)
4. Amarel, S.: On representations of problems of reasoning about actions. In: Machine Intelligence, vol. 3 (1968)

---

[12] See: Pikler, A.G.: Utility Theories in Field Physics and Mathematical Economics. British Journal for the Philosophy of Science, vol. 5, pp. 47, 303 (1955).

5. Benveniste, E.: Problems in General Linguistics. University of Miami Press, Coral Gables (1971). Translated by Mary Elizabeth Meek
6. Bobrow, D., Winograd, T.: An overview of KRL, a knowledge representation language. Cogn. Sci. **1**, 3–46 (1977)
7. Boulding, K.: General systems theory – the skeleton of science. Manage. Sci. **2**, 197–208 (1956)
8. Bourbaki, N.: Elements of the History of Mathematics. Springer, Heidelberg (1994). https://doi.org/10.1007/978-3-642-61693-8
9. Cantor, G.: Foundations of a general theory of manifolds: a mathematico-philosophical investigation into the theory of the infinite. In: Ewald, W.B. (ed.) From Kant to Hilbert: A Source Book in the Foundations of Mathematics, pp. 878–920. Oxford University Press, Oxford (1996)
10. Chomsky, N.: Lectures on Government and Binding: The Pisa Lectures. ForisPublications, Dordrecht and Cinnaminson, New Jersey (1981)
11. Chomsky, N.: Aspects of the Theory of Syntax, pp. 119–152. MIT Press, Cambridge (1965). In: Journal of Linguistics
12. Fillmore, C.J.: The case for case. In: Bach, E., Harms, R. (eds.) Universals in Linguistic Theory, pp. 1–88. Holt, Rinehart and Winston, New York (1968)
13. Frege, G.: Begriffsschrift, a formula language, modeled upon that of arithmetic, for pure thought. In: Heijenoort, J. (ed.) From Frege to Gödel: A Source Book in Mathematical Logic, pp. 1–82. Harvard University Press, Harvard (1967)
14. Furs, S.N.: An introduction to action analytics. In: Belarussian Science. Minsk (1999)
15. Gadamer, H.G.: Semantics and Hermeneutics. Philosophical Hermeneutics, pp. 82–94 (1976)
16. Golenkov, V.V., et al.: From training intelligent systems to training their development tools. In: Open Semantic Technologies for Intelligent Systems, pp. 81–98, no. 2. BSUIR, Minsk (2018)
17. Hardzei, A.: Procedural semantics and calculus of subject domains. In: Leschenko, M. (ed.) CONFERENCE 1994, Language: Semantics, Syntactics, Pragmatics, pt. 1, pp. 16–17. Minsk State Linguistic University, Minsk (1994)
18. Hardzei, A.: Cognitive approach to teaching of signs. In: Gabis, A.A., Detskina, R.V., Zubov, A.V., Karpilivich, T.P., Mihnevich, A.E., Piotrovsky, R.G. (eds.) CONFERENCE 1995, Computer Programs in Teaching Byelorussian and Foreign Languages, pp. 18–20. Minsk State Linguistic University Publ, Minsk (1995)
19. Hardzei, A.: The Deductive Theory of Language. Belarus Science, Minsk (1998)
20. Hardzei, A.: The Principles of Calculating the Semantics of Subject Domains. Belarusian State University, Minsk (1998)
21. Hardzei, A.: The paradigm of parts of language. In: Emelyanova, S., Rychkova, L., Nikitevich, A. (eds.) CONFERENCE 2003, Word Formation and Nominative Derivation in Slavic Languages, pp. 173–179. Grodno State University Publ, Grodno (2003)
22. Hardzei, A.: The foundations of combinatory semantics. In: Rychkova, L.V., Voronovich, V.L., Emelyanova, S.A. (eds.) Word and Vocabulary = Vocabulum et vocabularium, pp. 32–35. Grodno State University, Grodno (2005)
23. Hardzei, A.: Parts of language and the procedures of its delineation. In: Hardzei, A., Hongbin, W. (eds.) The Paths of the Middle Kingdom, pp. 69–75, no. 1, pt. 1. Belarusian State University Publ., Minsk (2006)
24. Hardzei, A.: Virtual string as a syntactic code of a sentence (on the exampleof the Chinese language). In: Language, Society and Problems of Intercultural Communication, pp. 349–358. Grodno State University, Grodno(2007)

25. Hardzei, A.: Theory for automatic generation of knowledge architecture (TAPAZ-2) and further minimization of semantic calculus. In: Open Semantic Technologies for Intelligent Systems, pp. 49–64. BSUIR, Minsk (2014)

26. Hardzei, A.: Dynamic syntax: a semantic view. Foreign Lang. Tert. Educ. **4**, 26–34 (2017)

27. Hardzei, A.: Theory for Automatic Generation of Knowledge Architecture: TAPAZ-2. National Institute for Higher Education, Minsk (2017)

28. Hardzei, A., Krapivin, Y.: Perspective approaches to semantic knowledge representation and their applications in the context of the task of automatic identification of the semantically equivalent fragments of the text documents. In: Open Semantic Technologies for Intelligent Systems, pp. 183–188, no. 4. BSUIR, Minsk (2020)

29. Hardzei, A., Udovichenko, A.: Graph of TAPAZ'2 semantic classifier. In: Open Semantic Technologies for Intelligent Systems, pp. 281–284, no. 3. BSUIR, Minsk (2019)

30. Harris, Z.: Co-occurrence and transformation in linguistic structure. Language **33**, 283–340 (1957)

31. Harris, Z.: String Analysis of Sentence Structure. The Hague: Mouton (1962)

32. Hjelmslev, L.: Prolegomena to a Theory of Language. University of Wisconsin, Madison (1961)

33. Jackendoff, R.: X-bar syntax: a study of phrase structure. In: Linguistic Inquiry Monographs. MIT Press, Cambridge (1977)

34. Jackendoff, R.S.: Semantic Interpretation in Generative Grammar. MIT Press, Cambridge (1972)

35. Kandrashina, E.U., Litvintseva, L.V., Pospelov, D.A.: Knowledge Representation about Time and Space in Intelligent Systems. Science, Moscow (1989)

36. Kornai, A., Pullum, G.: The x-bar theory of phrase structure. Language **66** (1997). https://doi.org/10.1353/lan.1990.0015

37. Kotarbinski, T.: Praxiology: An Introduction to the Sciences of Efficient Action. Pergamon Press, Oxford (1965)

38. Kruglikova, L.E.: "The Big Academic Dictionary of the Russian Language" as a follower of the traditions of Russian academic lexicography. Cuadernos de Rusística Española **8**, 177–198 (2012). https://revistaseug.ugr.es/index.php/cre/article/view/68/67. Accessed 12 July 2020

39. Lenat, D.B., Prakash, M., Shepherd, M.: CYC: using common sense knowledge to overcome brittleness and knowledge acquisition bottlenecks. AI Mag. **6**, 65–85 (1986)

40. Martynov, V.V.: Cybernetics. Semiotics. Linguistics. Science and Technics, Minsk (1966)

41. Martynov, V.V.: Semiology foundations of informatics. Science and technics,Minsk (1974)

42. Martynov, V.V.: Universal Semantic Code: Grammar. Dictionary. Texts. Science and Technics, Minsk (1977)

43. Martynov, V.V.: Universal Semantic Code: USC'3. Science and Technics, Minsk (1984)

44. Martynov, V.V.: Universal Semantic Code: USC'4. Science and Technics, Minsk: Institute of Linguistics of Academy of Science of BSSR (1988). (Preprint/Institute of Linguistics of Academy of Science of BSSR; No 2)

45. Martynov, V.V.: Universal Semantic Code: USC'5. Minsk State Linguistic University, Minsk: Minsk State Linguistic University (1995). (Preprint/Minsk State Linguistic University; No 4)

46. Martynov, V.V.: On the Book of A. Hardzei, "The Deductive Theory of Language". Byelorussian Science, pp. 3–5 (1998)
47. Martynov, V.V.: Foundations of Semantic Coding. Experience of Knowledge Representation and Conversion. European Humanitarian University, Minsk (2001)
48. Martynov, V.V.: In the Center of Human Conscious. Belarusian State University, Minsk (2009)
49. Minsky, M.: A framework for representing knowledge. In: Haugeland, J. (ed.) Mind Design II. Philosophy, Psychology, Artificial Intelligence, pp. 111–142. The MIT Press, Cambridge (1997)
50. Pikler, A.G.: Utility theories in field physics and mathematical economics. Part 1. Br. J. Philos. Sci. **5**, 47–58 (1954)
51. Pikler, A.G.: Utility theories in field physics and mathematical economics. Part 2. Br. J. Philos. Sci. **5**, 303–318 (1955)
52. Rasiowa, H., Sikorski, R.: The Mathematics of Metamathematics, 2nd edn. Polish Scientific Publishers, Waszawa (1963)
53. Reichenbach, H.: The Philosophy of Space and Time. Dover, New York (1958)
54. Schema.org Vocabulary, version 8.0. https://schema.org. Accessed 06 July 2020
55. Semantic Web. https://www.w3.org/standards/semanticweb. Accessed 06 July 2020
56. Sikorski, R.: Boolean Algebras. Springer, Heidelberg (1969). https://doi.org/10.1007/978-3-642-85820-8
57. Stanley, R.P.: Enumerative Combinatorics, vol. 1. Cambridge University Press, Cambridge (1997)
58. Stanley, R.P.: Enumerative Combinatorics, vol. 2. Cambridge University Press, Cambridge (1999). http://www-math.mit.edu/~rstan/ec/catadd.pdf. Accessed 06 July 2020
59. Stowell, T.: Origins Of phrase structure. Ph.D. thesis, Massachusetts Institute of Technology, Department of Linguistics and Philosophy, Cambridge, MA (1981)
60. Weinreich, U.: On the semantic structure of language. In: Greenberg, J. (ed.) Universals of Language, pp. 114–171. MIT Press, Cambridge (1963)
61. Weinreih, U.: Explorations in semantic theory. Curr. Trends Linguist. **3**, 395–477 (1966)
62. Winograd, T.: Understanding natural language. Cogn. Psychol. **3**, 1–191 (1972)
63. Winograd, T.: Extended inference models in reasoning by computers systems. Artif. Intell. **13**, 5–26 (1980)
64. Winston, P.H.: Artificial Intelligence. Addison-Wesley, Reading, MA (1992)
65. Wolniewicz, B.: A formal ontology of situations. Studia Logica **41**, 381–413 (1982)
66. von Wright, G.H.: Explanation and Understanding. Contemporary Philosophy, Cornell University, Ithaca (1971)
67. Yngve, V.H.: A model and a hypothesis for language structure. Proc. Am. Philos. Soc. **104**, 444–466 (1960)

User Profile Ontological Modelling by Wiki-Based Semantic Similarity

Julia Rogushina$^{(\boxtimes)}$ (iD)

Institute of Software Systems of National Academy of Sciences of Ukraine,
Glushkova Avenue, 40, Kyiv, Ukraine
ladamandraka2010@gmail.com
http://www.isofts.kiev.ua

Abstract. We consider the use of ontological knowledge from user profile (domain of interests, current tasks, experience and competences etc.) for semantic retrieval. Domain ontologies, Wiki resources and task thesauri used in general technological chain of user-oriented semantic retrieval can be generated independently by different applications and are integrated with the help of the Semantic Web standards. Open information environment is considered as an external data base with great volumes of heterogeneous and semi-structured information that can be transformed into ontologies. Semantic Wiki resources provide generation of ontology for selected set of Wiki pages that formalizes their knowledge structure and explicitly represents its main features. Semantic similarity evaluations and knowledge about typical information objects of resources are used for selection of Wiki pages pertinent to user task. Such Wiki-ontology elements as classes, property values of class instances and relations between them are used as parameters for the quantitative assessment of semantic similarity. Task thesaurus that represents current task is generated on base of domain ontology and task description. The semantic retrieval system based on ontological representation of user needs is described. The set of domain concepts that are semantically similar to currents Wiki page can be used as a base for task thesaurus.

Keywords: Semantic search · Domain ontology · User profile · Semantic Wiki

1 Introduction

Information technologies, as most digital technologies, now have become ubiquitous. Their development shows the tendencies to transition from traditional data processing to analysis of information on semantic level oriented on specifics of the open environment and great data volumes. It causes the need for integration of the traditional approaches with benefits of artificial intelligence (AI) that raise numerous challenges. The growth of the Web use increases in the number of interconnections among information systems and resources supporting

© Springer Nature Switzerland AG 2020
V. Golenkov et al. (Eds.): OSTIS 2020, CCIS 1282, pp. 198–211, 2020.
https://doi.org/10.1007/978-3-030-60447-9_12

the various aspects of human activities. One of important problem deals with interoperability of knowledge created and used by intelligent systems of different developers.

Open intelligent systems contain adaptive information retrieval tools for user-oriented search into the Web. Various approaches to retrieval procedure require formalized models that represent knowledge of the search domain and description of user needs and competences represented as elements of user profile structure. We consider this challenge in [1].

Ontologies are now widely used by the Web applications to represent consensual knowledge in the domain of discourse.

Standards of the Semantic Web [2] provides the universal ontology-based means of knowledge representation for common understanding and reuse of obtained knowledge. Increasingly, the kinds of information structures being standardized today are much more complex than they were even a decade ago. Now various domains are provided by ontology-based specifications of their typical information objects, tasks and services that differ by principles to user modelling, goals, scale and volume etc. However every practical task needs in specific methods of their choice, processing and integration.

In this work we analyse semantic similarity estimations of domain concepts based on ontological model as retrieval component of open intelligent systems that can be used for semantic search adopted for user tasks. The effectiveness of such estimations depends on pertinence of domain ontology to current user problem therefore we consider information sources and methods that can provide development of ontologies oriented on selected task and relevant to user profile elements. Ontologies are widely used by AI applications to describe domain knowledge, but in practice their processing causes a number of problems.

- Creating of ontologies is a slow and complex process that requires the involvement of a knowledge engineer and domain expert. The result depends on their individual conceptions and current task therefore task changes require the improvement of ontology.
- Complex ontology of domain contains usually a lot of unnecessary information for the specific task pertinent to user query.
- Processing of ontology and its matching with other information resources (such as unstructured natural-language texts) is a complicated process that requires the use of other background knowledge (e.g. linguistic knowledge bases). Therefore, it is advisable to use simpler information structures to formalize domain knowledge in information retrieval tasks.

We consider in this work the use of task thesauri as special cases of ontologies.

2   Problem Definition

An analysis of research works in the sphere of distributed information technologies shows that many intelligent tasks need in external sources of background knowledge from the Web, corporative and local networks, data warehouses etc. However, the problem of knowledge extracting in the general case is extremely complex, and one of its components is semantic search that applies knowledge about user and her/his current task for selection of pertinent information resources.

To ensure the effective use of ontologies for semantic search by the various intelligent applications and to simplify the knowledge processing process we propose to use such simplified ontology-based information structures as thesauri. Task thesaurus T is based on domain ontology O and consists of the ontological concepts (classes and individuals) joined by the semantic similarity to the user task in domain described by this ontology O. Every task thesaurus contains only such part of the domain knowledge that is applied to search for information pertinent to the user's current task. We propose to include task thesauri into user profile and process them with knowledge from domain ontologies selected in this profile.

This approach requires to justify the ways of ontology knowledge representation by means of thesaurus, to develop an algorithm for generating of such thesaurus based on the domain ontology and the description of the task. In addition, we need in development of methods for processing of this task thesaurus in applied retrieval systems and justification of their effectiveness of the received results for various types of such systems. It is also important to determine what information resources are used for creation of domain ontologies and what restrictions are imposed on them. In particular, Wiki-ontologies that are generated by semantically marked Wiki resources often contain enough knowledge to carry out semantic search, but their processing is much simpler due to restrictions on their structure.

3   Ontology-Based User Profiles

An important aspect of information systems (IS) development is their adaptation to special features and goals of individual user. The ultimate goal of IS adaptation is to modify behaviour of system according to the needs of individual user. Such adaptation is widely used by recommender systems, e-commerce, distance learning, information retrieval etc.

The term "user profile" defines traditionally various knowledge structures with information about users, such as demography, background, cognitive style, etc. Information about user represented by user profile depends on IS specifics and can contain demographic characteristics (age, gender, native language etc.), environment, information about a user's location and sphere of interests and competences, etc. Researchers usually differ concept "user model" that represents dynamic aspects of user activities (such as current task or request, learning item, etc.) from "user profile" with more permanent elements (such as domain of specialization, interests and preferences in data processing).

Knowledge about domain of user interests represented by formal and interoperable ontological means can be applied in various ISs. User models on base of ontologies can support "personal ontology view" (POV) – ontological representation of individual beliefs about domain conceptualisation [3].

Two basic variations of POVs are implemented into applied ISs: 1. sub-ontology of domain ontology; 2. an unique conceptualisation with structure deviated from the underlying domain ontology. POV built as a sub-graph of the domain ontology contains only a subset of domain ontology concepts linked by subset of domain relations. If POV consists only from concepts of domain ontology then relations from this ontology can be used for generation of this subset according to some rules. An example of this approach is adaptive recommender system Quickstep [4] oriented on retrieval of scientific articles. The user interest value to some concept is computed with use of information about user explicit and implicit feedback and inference by topic ontology (value of parent concept is computed by its children's values).

Implementations of POV as individual domain conceptualisation that differs from the original domain ontology in its structure and concept names are much more uncommon. For example, OWL-OLM [5] models student knowledge (true or faulty) about learning domain by information received from interactive dialogues to recognize various types of mistakes.

Many ISs collect data about their users and models various user aspects of their behaviour. The situation, when the same user works with multiple ISs is very common. Unfortunately, such systems often cannot get an access to each other's user model collections, but even the most typical characteristics of users can be modelled by user profiles with various terms and categories, and therefore ISs have to extract user interests on their own.

4   Task Thesauri and Their Features

Thesaurus is a representation of semantically similar (in the local sense of current task) domain concepts related to this task. Their similarity can be obtained by analysis of task definition, directly from user or with the help of knowledge from domain ontology. Wikipedia defines a thesaurus as a reference work that lists words grouped together according to similarity of meaning (containing synonyms and sometimes antonyms), in contrast to a dictionary, which provides word definitions [6].

Thesaurus in information retrieval is considered as a form of controlled vocabulary used for indexing of content objects. It is important that thesaurus as opposed to dictionary does not contain all word synonyms and their definitions and therefore is significantly simpler. In this meaning thesaurus has to contain at least three elements: - list of words that correspond to domain terms, – the hierarchical relations between these words (e.g. parent/broader term; synonym, etc.), - a set of rules for thesaurus usage. Such definition does not use ontological approach but reflects the main characteristic of thesauri deal with orientation on some particular task.

Thesaurus can be used for domain modelling. It contains only necessary ontological terms (classes and instances) but does not describe all semantics of relations between them. If thesaurus contains concepts of domain ontology as terms and uses relations of domain ontology to link these concepts then we can consider such thesaurus as a special case of domain ontology oriented on analyses of natural language texts.

Task thesaurus can be generated automatically by appropriate methods on base of the domain ontology selected by user and the natural language (NL) description of particular task that is interesting for this user [7]. A simple task thesaurus is a special case of task thesaurus based on the terms of a single domain ontology. A composite task thesaurus is a task thesaurus that is based on the terms of two or more domain ontologies by operations on simple task thesauri of these ontologies.

Generation of the simple task thesaurus uses two parameters as input data:

- domain ontology selected by user;
- task description – the NL text defines the current problem.

The text of task description contains NL elements related to the ontology concepts.

The process of simple thesaurus constructing contains two main steps:

Step 1. Automated generation of the subset of ontology concepts correlates with fragments of task description:

Substep 1.1. User explicitly and manually selects task-pertinent terms from the automatically generated list of classes and instance X. In the simplest cases, the construction of the thesaurus may be completed in this step, but it requires a lot of efforts from the user.

Substep 1.2. Thesaurus is expanded with the help of various methods for processing of natural-language applied to task description (linguistic analysis, statistical processing, semantic markup analysis) that allow to detect NL fragments related to terms from O.

Step 2. Expansion of the simple thesaurus by other ontology concepts according to the set of conditions that can use all elements of the O ontology.

Linguistic knowledge bases (KBs) are widely used for thesaurus construction. For example, specific domain-oriented linguistic KBs that accumulate a large amount of lexical information can propose domain-specific synonyms of terms. Such information is not universal and depends on domain and natural language used in task definition. Therefore we cannot use Text Mining systems oriented on processing of English texts for analysis of tasks represented by other languages.

In some cases, information about properties of ontological classes and individuals, their values and relations with other terms can be used in constructing of thesaurus. This information helps in refining the initial thesaurus formed in accordance with conditions explicitly formulated by user. For example, this thesaurus can be complemented by subclasses of ontological concepts or by individuals with object properties from selected class. These additional conditions depend on specific nature of user task, but are not derived from task description and can be considered as meta-rules of retrieved information.

If user can define the criteria of semantic similarity then task thesaurus can be complemented by concepts of domain ontology that are similar to earlier selected ones. User can find similar concepts for all elements of thesaurus or only for some of them.

Complex task thesauri are generated from the built earlier task thesauri (simple or complex) with the help of set theory operations such as sum, intersection etc.

5   Semantic Similarity Evaluations

Many researchers analyze the principles and measures of semantic similarity of domain concepts [8]. Various proposals for similarity measures are heuristic in nature and tied to a particular domain or form of knowledge representation [9]. In the cognitive domain, similarity is treated as a property characterized by human perception but use of this property in information systems requires the quantitative evaluations.

The most general definitions of similarity are based on three intuitive assumptions:

- the similarity between A and B depends directly on their commonality;
- the similarity between A and B depends inversely on the differences between them;
- the maximum similarity between A and B is reached if A and B are identical, no matter how much commonality they share.

The similarity of two objects is related to their commonality that depends directly on number of their common features and depends inversely on number of their differences. Concept similarity can be defines by similarity of strings and words. Feature vectors are widely used for knowledge representation, especially in case-based reasoning and machine learning. They can be applied for representation of words. Weights of features is used to account the importance of various features for word similarity. Some special features are applicative for natural language words and non-applicative for arbitrary strings of characters.

Now many ISs use various similarity estimations based on information content, mutual information, Dice coefficient [10], distance-based measurements [11] etc. In [12] similarity defined in terms of information theory is applicable if domain has a probabilistic model. The similarity estimations are derived from a set of assumptions about similarity and usually are not defined directly by some formula.

The similarity of concepts is also related to their content. One of the key factors in the similarity of two concepts is the degree of information sharing in the taxonomy. The edge-counting method takes this into account indirectly.

The information content of concept can be quantified by the logarithmic function of probability of concept use. Thus, the level of concept abstraction (i.e., its place in taxonomy) causes the less informational content. Information content of unique upper concept in taxonomy is 0. This quantitative characterization of information provides a new way of measuring semantic similarity based on the extension of concepts. The more information is shared by two concepts, the more similar they are, and the information co-shared by the two concepts is determined by the information content of the concepts included in them into taxonomy.

Some measures of similarity take into account only the depth of the concept nodes. Although the similarity is calculated taking into account all the upper bounds for the two concepts, the information measure allows to identify the minimum upper bound, but no class is less informative than its superclasses.

Measures to determine the semantic similar concepts (SSC) on the basis of ontologies use various semantic features of these concepts – their properties (attributes and relations with other concepts), the relative position in ontological hierarchies. The SSC set is a fuzzy set of concepts with the semantic distance less than the selected threshold.

The similarity measures suppose that words derived from the same root as some initial word have the better similarity rankings. Other similarity measures are based on the number of different trigrams in the matching strings and on proposed by user definition of similarity under the assumption that the probability of a trigram occurring in a word is independent of other trigrams in the word. Similarity measures between words correspond to their distribution in a text corpus.

Semantic similarity can be based on similarity between concepts in domain taxonomy (such as the WordNet or CYC). The semantic similarity between two classes characterize not the set of their individuals or subclasses classes. Instead, generic individuals of these classes are compared.

A problem with similarity measures is that each of them is tied to a particular application or assumes a particular domain model. For example, distance-based measures of concept similarity assume that the domain is represented in a network. Another problem with the similarity measures is that their underlying assumptions are often not explicitly stated. Without knowing those assumptions, it is impossible to make theoretical arguments for or against any particular measure.

Methods aimed at SSC finding in different ontologies can be used to analyze the semantic similarity between the domain concepts. The assessment of similarity of concepts may be based on their positions in the hierarchy of classes with defined similarity: if the subclasses and superclass of these concepts are similar, then the same concepts are also similar.

The following parameters (features) can be considered into quantified similarity assessment of the two ontological classes:

- similarity assessing of their direct superclasses;
- similarity assessing of all their superclasses;
- similarity assessing of subclasses of concepts;
- similarity assessing of instances of classes.

Semantic similarity is a special case of semantic affinity. For the individual case of ontology, where the only relation between concepts is applied - the hierarchical relation of type IS-A, - taxonomy - the similarity of the two terms can be estimated by the distance between the concepts into the taxonomy.

The semantic distance between the concepts depends on the length of the shortest path between the nodes and the overall specificity of the two nodes. The shorter the path from one node to another, the more similar they are. If there are several paths between elements then the length of the shortest path is used. This length is determined by the number of nodes (or edges) in the shortest path between two corresponding nodes of the taxonomy, taking into account the depth of the taxonomic hierarchy.

However, this approach is compounded by the notion that all taxonomy edges correspond to homogeneous distances. Unfortunately, in practice the homogeneity of distance in taxonomy is not supported.

Semantic similarity represents a special case of semantic relation between concepts. In [13] the assessment of similarity in semantic networks is defines with the help of taxonomic links. Although other types of links such as "part-of" can also be used for assessment of similarity.

In real taxonomies, there is great variability of distances covered by a single taxonomic relation, especially if some subsets of taxonomies (such as biological categories) are much denser than other ones. For example, WordNet [14] contains direct links between either fairly similar concepts or relatively distant ones. Therefore, it is advisable to take into account the semantics of relations between concepts for different taxonomic relationships and to consider the number of instances in subclasses [15].

All these researches use only some aspects of ontological representation of knowledge limited by:

- hierarchical relations – taxonomic relations between classes and relations between classes and their individuals;
- other types of relations which semantics influence on their weight for the similarity but does not used in logical inference;
- properties of class individuals and their properties that matched in process of similarity estimation but do not analyzed at the level of expressive possibilities.

However all these ontological features can be represented by semantic Wiki resources. Therefore we propose to use such Wiki resources as a source of semantic similar concepts for other intelligent systems.

Now a lot of software supports Wiki technologies. One of the most widely used is MediaWiki. The basic functionality allows to create pages connected by hyperlinks, set their categories and publish their content with some structure elements etc. Semantic MediaWiki (SMW) extends semantically this Wiki engine by use of semantic properties of pages [16]. SMW definitely displays content with these annotations in the formal description using the OWL DL ontology language [17].

6   Semantic Similarity of Concepts into the Wiki Resources

We approve the proposed above approach in development of semantic search and navigation means implemented into e-VUE – the portal version of the Great Ukrainian Encyclopedia (vue.gov.ua). This resource is based on ontological representation of knowledge base. To use a semantic Wiki resource as a distributed knowledge base we develop knowledge model of this resource represented by Wiki ontology [18]. This model provides semantic markup of typical information objects (IOs) by domain concepts. Application of semantic similarity estimation for this IR provides the functional extension of Encyclopedia by new ways of content access and analysis on the semantic level.

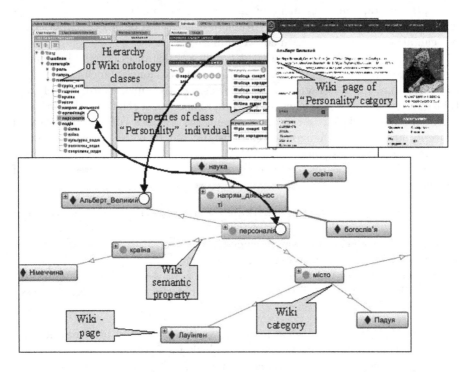

Fig. 1. Wiki ontology of e-VUE typical information objects (fragment).

One of the significant advantages of e-VUE as a semantic portal is the ability to find SSCs. Wiki ontology is a basis for research of similarity between concepts of Wiki resource because the estimates of similarity are based on such elements of semantic markup as categories and properties of these concepts. We can process in these estimates only those characteristics of IOs that are explicitly represented by ontology elements (Fig. 1).

Criteria of e-VUE concept similarity is based on the following assumptions:

- concepts that correspond to Wiki pages of the same set of categories are semantically closer than other e-VUE concepts;
- concepts corresponded to Wiki pages with the same or similar meanings of semantic properties are semantically closer than concepts corresponded to Wiki pages with different values of semantic properties or those ones with not defined values;
- concepts defined as semantically similar by the both preceding criteria are more semantically similar than concepts similar by one of criteria.

e-VUE users can apply SSC search if they are unable to select correctly the concept category or if they enter concept name with errors. Similar concepts help to find the desired Wiki page. We propose to user retrieval of globally similar (by the full set of categories and values of semantic properties) and locally similar (by some subset of these features) IOs. Therefore we realize the following examples of local SSPs retrived by:

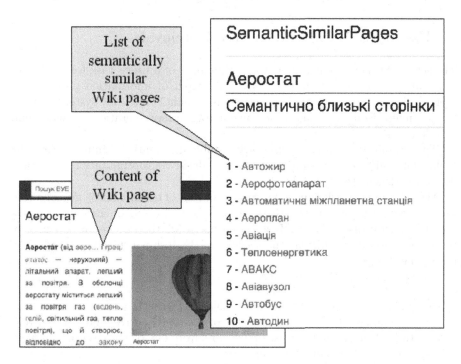

Fig. 2. Semantic similar concepts of e-VUE for concept "Aerostat".

- the used-defined subset of current page categories (Fig. 2 shows SSPs retrieved for page "aerostat" by categories "Technical sciences" and "Avuation");
- the used-defined values of the fixed subset of semantic properties of current page;

– the combination of categories and values of semantic properties of current page.

Therefore the development of Wiki ontology defines the expressiveness of search procedure on base of Wiki resource marked by this ontology. Similarity can be defined by any subset of ontological classes and values of their properties but all other content of Wiki pages is not available for this analysis (these characteristics can be received by statistic analyses of from NL processing systems but they are over the consideration of this work).

According to the specifics of encyclopedic IR, it is impractical to search for pages that match all available parameters because some parameter groups are unique (for example, last name and year of birth) and some other ones dependent functionally on other parameters (although they have independent importance e.g. the name in the original language).

It should be noted that built-in tools of Semantic MediaWiki don't support search for SSCs (local and global) and all of these requests are realized by special API queries that analyze code of the Wiki pages.

7   Use of SSCs for Information Retrieval

The set of SSCs can be considered as a thesaurus of a user's task for intelligent retrieval systems that support personified search of information pertinent to user needs. An example of such system is semantic retrieval system MAIPS (http://maips.isofts.kiev.ua/) based on ontological representation of background knowledge [19].

This system is oriented on users with stable informational interests into the Web. Ontologies and thesauri provide formalized conceptualization of subject domain pertinent to user tasks.

MAIPS uses OWL language for representation of domain ontologies and thesauri, it supports automated thesauri generation by NL documents and set-theoretic operations on them. Task thesaurus in MAIPS is constructed directly by the user in order to display the specifics of the task which causes these information needs.

User profile in MAIPS contains:

– the non-empty set of POV domain ontologies O(user);
– the non-empty set of thesauri (simple or complex) corresponded to current user tasks T(user) that consist of concepts from one or more ontologies from O(user) and weights of thees concepts;
– the non-empty set of search requests R(user) that consist of the non-empty set of user-defined keywords and one of thesauri from T(user);
– results of user requests with ratings of their pertinence Res(user);
– user-defined estimations for appropriate level of NL readability L(user) for retrieved documents defined for every ontology POV from O(user).

The search procedure in MAIPS is personified by individual indexes of NL text readability that consider terms from user profiles as understadeble.

We propose the possibility to import POVs from external Wiki resources where the set of thesaurus terms is generated as a group of SSCs. The most pertinent results user receives in situation if Wiki resource is pertinent to user task.

Fig. 3. Visualization of domain thesaurus in MAIPS.

User can improve this thesaurus on base the selected domain ontology by weights of concept importance for task. MAIPS visualise thesaurus by the cloud of tags (Fig. 3). Users can also manually edit any previously created thesaurus by adding or deleting some terms. In addition, MAIPS realizes such set-theoretic operations on thesauri as union, intersection and complement.

8   Conclusion

The main idea for the study is to ensure the integration of various intelligent systems that use domain knowledge represented by ontologies. In order to simplify the processing of such knowledge we propose to pass from ontologies to their special case – thesauri. Actuality of this problem is caused by development of intelligent ontology-oriented applications based on the Semantic Web technologies [20]. Thesaurus of task contains only limited subset of domain concepts and their relations.

Such knowledge structures as thesauri are more understandable for users, their creation and processing take less time and qualification. We demonstrate some methods of automatic generation of thesauri by appropriate ontologies and semantic Wikis. Portal version of the Great Ukrainian Encyclopedia (e-VUE) based on Semantic MediaWiki is used as a source of semantically similar concepts generated by user-defined conditions that provide the set of terms for task thesauri. Elements of e-VUE knowledge base structure define possible parameters for these conditions that depend on properties of information objects typical for e-VUE.

On example of MAIPS retrieval system we show the usage of such thesauri as a source of user task knowledge that provides adaptation of search results for individual information needs.

Acknowledgments. This work has been supported by the Institute of Software Systems of National Academy of Sciences of Ukraine.

References

1. Rogushina, J.: Use of similarity of wiki pages as an instrument of domain representation for semantic retrieval. In: Open Semantic Technologies for Intelligent Systems (OSTIS-2020), Minsk, vol. 4, pp. 111–116 (2020). https://libeldoc.bsuir.by/handle/123456789/38680. Accessed 29 May 2020
2. Ray, S.R.: Interoperability standards in the semantic web. J. Comput. Inf. Sci. Eng. **2**(1), 65–69 (2002)
3. Kalfoglou, Y., Domingue, J., Motta, E., Vargas-Vera, M., Buckingham Shum, S.: myPlanet: an ontology driven Web based personalised news service. In: International Joint Conference on Artificial Intelligence, Seatlle, WA, USA, vol. 2001, pp. 44–52 (2001). http://oro.open.ac.uk/23339/1/ontoIS01final.pdf. Accessed 10 May 2020
4. Middleton, S.E., Shadbolt, N.R., De Roure, D.C.: Ontological user profiling in recommender systems. ACM Trans. Inf. Syst. (TOIS) **22**(1), 54–88 (2004). https://dl.acm.org/doi/pdf/10.1145/963770.963773
5. Denaux, Ronald., Dimitrova, Vania, Aroyo, Lora: Integrating open user modeling and learning content management for the semantic web. In: Ardissono, Liliana, Brna, Paul, Mitrovic, Antonija (eds.) UM 2005. LNCS (LNAI), vol. 3538, pp. 9–18. Springer, Heidelberg (2005). https://doi.org/10.1007/11527886_4
6. Thesaurus. https://en.wikipedia.org/wiki/Thesaurus. Accessed 11 Nov 2019
7. Gladun, A., Rogushina, J.: Use of semantic web technologies and multilinguistic thesauri for knowledge-based access to biomedical resources. Int. J. Intell. Syst. Appl. **1**, 11–20 (2012)
8. Resnik, P.: Semantic similarity in a taxonomy: an information-based measure and its application to problems of ambiguity in natural language. J. Artif. Intell. Res. **11**, 95–130 (1999)
9. Rada, R., Mili, H., Bicknel, E., Blettner, M.: Development and application of a metric on semantic nets. IEEE Trans. Syst. Man Cybern. **19**(1), 17–30 (1989)

10. Hindle, D. Noun classification from predicate-argument structures. In: 28th Annual meeting of the Association for Computational Linguistics ACL-1990, pp. 68–275 (1990). https://www.aclweb.org/anthology/P90-1034.pdf. Accessed 21 May 2020

11. Lee, J.H., Kim, M.H., Lee, Y.J.: Information retrieval based on conceptual distance in IS-A hierarchies. J. Doc. **49**(2), 188–207 (1989)

12. Lin, D.: An information-theoretic definition of similarity. In: ICML, vol. 98, pp. 296–304 (1998)

13. Wu Z., Palmer M.: Verb semantics and lexical selection. In: 32nd Annual Meeting of the Association for Computational Linguistics, Las Cruces, pp. 133–138 (1994)

14. Fellbaum C.: WordNet. In: The encyclopedia of applied linguistics, pp. 231–243 (2012). https://www.overleaf.com/project/5ee08db98116780001133416

15. Richardson R., Smeaton A.F., Murphy J.: Using WordNet as a knowledge base for measuring semantic similarity between words, In: Working paper CA-1294, Dublin City University, School of Computer AppUcations, (1994)

16. Semantic mediawiki. https://www.semantic-mediawiki.org. Accessed 11 Apr 2020

17. OWL 2 Web Ontology Language Document Overview (Second Edition). W3C Recommendation (2012). https://www.w3.org/TR/owl2-overview/. Accessed 12 Apr 2020

18. Rogushina J.: Semantic Wiki-resources and their use for the construction of personalized ontologies. Problems Program. (2–3), 188–195 (2016). http://ceur-ws.org/Vol-1631. Accessed 16 May 2020

19. Rogushina J.: Use of semantic similarity estimates for unstructured data analysis. Inf. Technol. Secur. 246–258 (2019). http://ceur-ws.org/Vol-2577/paper20.pdf. Accessed 25 May 2020

20. Semantic Web. https://www.w3.org/standards/semanticweb/. Accessed 10 May 2020

Decision Making and Control of a Cognitive Agent's Knowledge Process Under Time Constraints

Igor Fominykh[1], Alexander Eremeev[1], Nikolay Alekseev[1(✉)],
and Natalia Gulyakina[2]

[1] National Research University "MPEI", 111250 Moscow, Russia
igborfomin@mail.ru, eremeev@appmat.ru, alekseevnp@list.ru
[2] Belarusian State University of Informatics and Radioelectronics,
220013 Minsk, Belarus
guliakina@bsuir.by

Abstract. Considered are the questions of designing a system for modeling the reasoning of a cognitive agent, capable of making conclusions based on its knowledge and observations of the external environment, solving problems in a hard enough real-time mode. To work in this mode, the existence of a critical time threshold is established, which is set to solve the problem facing the agent. Exceeding the threshold is fraught with grave, sometimes catastrophic consequences and for the agent is unacceptable. The formal basis of the modeling system (cognitive process control) is a logical system - extended step theory, that combines the concepts of active temporal logic and logical programming. Among the original methods proposed by the authors in the work, an approach to combining the concepts of active logic and logical programming in one logical system should be noted; an approach to constructing a consistent declarative semantics for extended step theory of active logic; a method of formalizing temporal, nonmonotonic reasoning of an agent using extended step theory of active temporal logic; a method of granulating time in a logical system to formalize meta-reasoning. A subclass of temporal logic is considered, oriented to application in real-time systems. Additionally, the issues of managing the agent's cognitive process in hard real-time, eliminating anomalies (unforeseen situations), and applying the temporal logic of branching time are investigated in more detail.

Keywords: Cognitive agent · Hard time constraints · Cognitive process · Active logic · Step theory · Temporal reasoning · Logical programming · Anomalies · Branching temporal logic

This work was supported by the Russian Foundation for Fundamental Research (RFFR) (projects 18-29-03088, 18-07-00213, 19-07-00123, 20-07-00498)) and Belarusian Republican Foundation for Fundamental Research (BRFR) (project 20-57-00015 Bel_a.

V. Golenkov et al. (Eds.): OSTIS 2020, CCIS 1282, pp. 212–221, 2020.
https://doi.org/10.1007/978-3-030-60447-9_13

1   Introduction

This work is a continuation and development of research reflected in[13]. In recent decades, one of the most significant areas of artificial intelligence in both theoretical and applied aspects has been the study and design of dynamic intelligent real-time systems. Specialists distinguish mainly two classes of such systems: soft (SRT IS) and hard real-time intelligent systems (HRT IS). For SRT IS [7,11] a gradual deterioration of functioning is characteristic when the delay in response to changes in the external environment is not critical and can even be neglected. Such an idealization, as a rule, is unacceptable in the HRT IS, because in this case, delaying the reaction after a certain time threshold may lead to an irreversible development of events. For such systems, the concept of a time threshold is introduced, the excess of which is unacceptable. HRT IS is not only, and not so much, a "fast" system, but, mainly, it is a system that "knows" about time thresholds and is able to plan its work in accordance with them.

The specificity of the HRT IS is that the lack of time in such systems is the main factor determining the incompleteness and dynamism of the knowledge and data used. Under these conditions, it turns out to be unacceptable one of the fundamental properties adopted in existing temporal nonmonotonic logic systems, which consists in the fact that the time necessary for conducting reasoning is not limited.

Various versions of active logic (AL) have been proposed for modeling reasoning HRT IS [2,6,12,17], which make it possible to observe the agent's reasoning process during its implementation.

The creators of AL emphasize its fundamental difference from traditional non-monotonic systems, such as default logic, auto-epistemic logic, etc. At present, there are dozens of different temporal logics, the purpose of which is to formalize the reasoning about time. The process of reasoning thus occurs as if out of time: the world as if stops while the system "thinks".

For HRT IS, when solving problems, it is important to be able to estimate the amount of time available to them "to think" until it is too late to think. To do this, it is necessary to be able to correlate the steps and results of the conducted reasoning with the events occurring in the external environment (real object). This type of reasoning is called reasoning situated in time.

The General concept of AL is described in [2]. As a deduction system, AL is characterized by language, many deductive rules, and many "observations". Reasoning situated in time is characterized by performing cycles of deduction called steps. Since the AL is based on a discrete model of time, these steps play the role of a time standard – time is measured in steps. Agent knowledge is associated with the index of the step at which it was first obtained. The principal difference between AL and other temporal epistemic logics is that temporal arguments are introduced into the language of agents own theories.

A common drawback of most AL systems is the interpretation of time, in a sense, as the internal essence of these systems, the course of which is determined by the structure of the rules of inference used to obtain new formulas from existing ones. In all cases, the measure of time (standard) implicitly refers to the duration of the deductive cycle (=output step). Each execution of the deductive cycle corresponds to one "tick" of the virtual internal clock. It is also implicitly assumed that the duration of execution does not change from cycle to cycle, or that the changes are so small that they can be ignored. In reality, the duration of the deductive cycle is influenced by changes in the composition and structure of knowledge as a result of ongoing reasoning and observations of the external environment. In addition, the duration of deductive cycles can be influenced by random factors, such as power failures, in the operation of other technical systems, etc. in fact, the assumption of a constant duration of deductive cycles is akin to logical omniscience [15] and, like the latter, it often conflicts with reality. In the work we presents an approach in which time is treated as an external entity that is not related to the structure of knowledge and the speed of deductive cycles. Moreover, we propose a logical system (extended step theory [10,16]) that integrates the AL concepts and logical programming, which allows us to optimize the relationship between the expressive capabilities of a cognitive agent and the complexity of calculations.

2   Main Results

Further, the main results in the field of generating methods for finding solutions and cognitive process management of a cognitive agent in HRT IS, obtained by the authors to date, are considered.

An analytical review of studies has been carried out, including studies on the capabilities of existing logical systems for formalizing reasoning (meta-reasoning) of a cognitive agent in HRT IS.

In the field of formalizing reasoning with limited time resources, there are several different directions, each of which is to one degree or another connected with solving the problem of logical omniscience, without which the conduct of reasoning (meta-reasoning), strictly limited in time, is not correct. Moreover, within the framework of existing epistemic logics, various restrictions on the ability of cognitive agents to logical inference (rational behavior) were proposed. This allowed us to solve the problem of logical omniscience, but at the same time there was a significant decrease in the capabilities of the cognitive agent, whose behavior was modeled. Today, only a few approaches to the creation of logical systems are known in which the problem of logical omniscience is solved without a serious limitation of the "mental abilities" of agents. One such example is the epistemic logic proposed by D. Ho [8]. It is based on the idea of introducing into the logical language special modal operators interpreted as "mental efforts" necessary to obtain any knowledge expressed in the form of logical formulas. This system overcomes the problem of logical omniscience, but it does not allow to model the reasoning of a cognitive agent when it is necessary to determine whether it is able to solve a problem without going beyond certain time boundaries. Another example is AL, created by a team of specialists from Active Logic Grupp, and the like [2,6,12,17]. It is a fairly general concept, which meets the logic presented in this work, a system based on the interpretation of reasoning as a process that proceeds in time. For this purpose, a temporal parameter is introduced into the metalanguage of logical systems that meet this concept. However, today there are a number of problems associated with AL and other similar systems that hinder its actual practical application. Among the most important, it is necessary to highlight the absence of logical systems that meet the concept of AL and have paraconsistent semantics, which makes it difficult to use AL systems if there are contradictions in the information available; the lack of estimates of the computational complexity of reasoning and meta-reasoning, which are formalized by systems that meet the concept of AL; lack of research results regarding the completeness and semantic consistency of systems that meet the concept of AL. The logical system proposed in this report is largely free from these shortcomings due to the integration of formalisms of AL and logical programming implemented in it.

The concept of time granulation as a special case of information granulation is developed, and like information granules, this representation of time in the form of granules - indistinguishable objects (a neighborhood of points, intervals, fuzzy sets, etc.). In the AL formalism, time granulation is introduced by analogy with TLC (Temporal Logic with Clocks) and reduces to the fact that the duration of deductive cycles, assumed constant in classical AL, is not performed for HRT IS.

In reality, the duration of the deductive cycle is influenced by changes in the composition and structure of the agent's knowledge as a result of his reasoning and observations of the external environment. In addition, random factors, such as power outages, other technical systems, etc., may affect the duration of deductive cycles. Also, "thinking abilities", in this case, the duration of the computational cycles of different agents, ceteris paribus, can be different. To simulate the possibility of changing the duration, we propose a modification of the classical AL - Step Logic [9] (see below for more details), which provides these capabilities by assigning the so-called "hours of model run", simulating the behavior of the system in various conditions (runs). A model run clock is a finite or infinite strictly increasing subsequence of a global clock whose elements are interpreted as time instants (on a global clock) of the completion of deductive cycles, for example, (3, 5, 7, 10, ...). By changing the model's running hours, it is possible to simulate various operating conditions of the system and better reflect, for example, features such as an increase in the duration of deductive agent cycles as the amount of information known to him increases or in connection with the failure of part of his computing resources.

The concepts of metacognition and counting the time spent on conducting reasoning.

The term metacognition was proposed in the works of J. Flavell [4] and is defined by him as the individual's awareness of his cognitive processes and related strategies, or, in other words, as reasoning about reasoning, meaning "cognition second order". The difference between cognitive and metacognitive strategies should be noted. The former helps the individual to achieve a specific cognitive goal (for example, to understand the text), and the latter are used to monitor the achievement of this goal (for example, self-inquiry for understanding this text). Metacognitive components are usually activated when cognition fails (in this case, it may be a misunderstanding of the text from the first reading). Such failure activates metacognitive processes that allow the individual to correct the situation. Thus, metacognition is responsible for the active control and sequential regulation of cognitive processes. In [1] M. Anderson proposed the concept of "metacognitive cycle" in the context of using the principles of metacognition to improve resistance to anomalies of a cognitive agent with a limited time resource. It is defined as the cyclical implementation of the following three stages: self-observation (monitoring); self-esteem (analysis of the revealed anomaly), self-improvement (regulation of the cognitive process). At the self-observation stage, meta-reasoning comes down to checking for the presence in the argument of an agent that solves a certain problem, formal signs of the presence of anomalies. These formal features are often direct contradictions in the agent's knowledge (the presence of a counter pair of formulas expressing the agent's current knowledge). At the self-assessment stage, the degree of threat to the quality of the agent's functioning that the identified anomaly bears is established, and at the self-improvement stage, if the threat is real, a new strategy for solving the problem faced by the agent is selected.

The countdown is achieved using the special predicate now(.), introduced in the rules. Moreover, now(t) takes the value "true" if and only if t is the time moment of completion of the last of the deductive cycles already completed, that is, in other words, when t is the current time. At the same time, the time counting principle used in this project is free from the unrealistic assumption of a constant duration of deductive cycles inherent in other existing approaches to solving the problem of modeling metareasoning.

To further improve cognitive process control, formalisms of step theories [9] and extended step theories [10,16] are proposed. The latter differ from standard step theories by the introduction of subjective negation along with a strong negation, which allows the agent to be aware and express in an explicit form not only what he knows, but also what he does not know at the moment.

The step theories semantics are described in terms of sets of literals, and not more complex structures in the Kripke style, than better characteristics of computational complexity are achieved in comparison with other AL systems and that determines their similarity to logical programming systems in "ordinary" logic. In addition, step theories have the property of paraconsistency and they implement the principle of granulation of time, interpreted as an external entity, independent of the internal structure of the logical program.

A step theory is a set of rules, sometimes with a binary preference relation given on it. The sets of rules can be divided into two subsets - strict and believable rules. In what follows, without sacrificing generality, we restrict ourselves only to cases where the preference relation is empty, and in theory there are only plausible rules of the form:

$$N : a_1 \wedge a_2... \wedge a_m \tag{1}$$

Where N is a string of characters denoting the name of the rule, b is a propositional literal, $a_1....a_m$ are propositional literals or literals of the first-order logic language of the form $later(j)$ or $\neg later(j)$, where j is a natural number.

A *step theory* is a pair $T = (R, Ck)$, where R is a finite set of rules of the form (1), Ck is a clock of step theory, which is a finite subsequence of a sequence of natural numbers. The members of this subsequence characterize the duration of sequentially performed deductive cycles that determine the process of reasoning in all AL systems. Without losing the generality of the results, we will set $Ck = (0, 1, 2, 3, 4, ...]$.

For any step theory $T = (R, Ck)$ we denote by $R[q]$ the set of all the rules whose consequent is q. The set of literals that form the antecedent of rule r is denoted by $A(r)$. Let Lit_T be the set of all literals found in the rules of step theory T. *The set of convictions* of the step theory T is the set of the form $now(t) \cup L_T^t$, where t is a natural number or 0, the time on the clock Ck of this step theory, $L_T^t \subset Lit_T$. Consider the operator ϑ_T, which transforms sets of beliefs into sets of beliefs in such a way that if B is a set of beliefs such that $now(t) \in B$, then $now(t + 1) \in \vartheta_T(B)$. Let B be the set of convictions of the theory T such that the literal $now(t) \in B$. *History* in the step theory T is called a finite sequence B of sets of beliefs. Moreover, $B(i)$ denotes the i-th term in history, $B(0) = \{now(0)\}$, for any t $B(t+1) = \vartheta_T(B(t))$. The last element of the story is a multitude of beliefs, denoted by B_{fin}, (final). *The output step* of the step theory T is called any pair of the form $(B(i), B(i+1))$, while the number of the output step is the number equal to $(i+1)$. A *consequence* (t-consequence) of the step theory T is a literal belonging to the set of beliefs $B_{fin}(B(t), t \in Ck)$.

The extended step theory is the pair $T = < R, Ck >$, where R is a finite set of rules, Ck is the clock of the step theory, for example, $Ck = (0, 1, 2, 4, 7, 11)$. Rules look like:

$$N : a_1 \wedge a_2... \wedge a_m \wedge not^t c_1 \wedge not^t c_2... \wedge not^t c_n \Rightarrow b \qquad (2)$$

Where N is a string of characters denoting the name of the rule, b is a propositional literal, $a_1....a_m$ are propositional literals or literals of the first-order logic language of the form $later(j)$ or $\neg later(j)$, where j is a natural number. $c_1....c_m$ are propositional literals, not^t is the operator of subjective negation introduced by analogy with formalisms of extended logical programs [5].

An expression of the form $not^t c$, where c is a propositional literal, is interpreted as "the literal c has not been derived by the current moment in time". Note that the introduction of subjective negation is directly related to the implementation of the principle of self-knowledge, which allows the agent to realize and express explicitly not only what he knows, but also what he does not know at the moment, which improves the expressive capabilities of the theory and, in particular, the temporal sensitivity property of extended step theories.

Based on the proposed formalisms, methods have been developed for controlling the cognitive process (reasoning process) of a cognitive agent under significant time constraints. A cognitive agent should have the following interrelated capabilities: evaluate its temporary resource, control time points for obtaining intermediate results, adjust the reasoning process and, as necessary, changing its strategy.

Evaluation. For agents with a strictly limited time resource, it is impossible to control this resource without correlating the results of the reasoning process with the times when these results were obtained. In accordance with the extended step theory, each set of beliefs contains exactly one literal of the form $now(t)$, where t is the moment in time on the internal clock Ck, indicating when this set of beliefs was formed (the time when the next deductive cycle was completed).

This information is sufficient to control the decrease of the temporary resource as the cognitive process develops. So, using a literal of the form $later(t)$ allows us to estimate the current time resource from above, while a literal of the form $\neg later(t)$ allows us to estimate the lower bound of the current time resource.

Example 1. Consider the theory $T_1 = (R_1, Ck_1)$, where $R_1 = \{N1 :\Rightarrow \alpha, N2 : \alpha \Rightarrow \beta, N3 : \beta \Rightarrow \gamma, N4 : \neg later(5) \wedge \gamma \Rightarrow subgoal\_A, N5 : later(5) \wedge not^t subgoal\_A \Rightarrow subgoal\_B\}$, $Ck1 = (1, 3, 6, 10, ...)$.

The history of this T_1 theory looks like this:

$B(0) = \{now(0)\}, B(1) = \{now(1), \alpha\}, B(2) = \{now(3), \alpha, \beta, \}, B(3) = \{now(6), \alpha, \beta, \gamma\}, B(4) = B_{fin} = \{now(10), \alpha, \beta, \gamma, subgoal\_B\}$.

At the substantive level, the withdrawal process can be commented as follows. during the cognitive process, formalized using the T_1 theory, at step $B(3)$, the time resource was evaluated for the possibility of establishing a local subgoal A using rule $N4$. The resource was insufficient and a local sub-goal B was established. Note that if we consider the theory $T_2 = (R_1, Ck_2)$, which differs from T_1 only in hours $Ck_2 = (1, 3, 4, 6, ...)$, then $B(4) = B_{fin} = \{now(6), \alpha, \beta, \gamma, subgoal\_A\}$. Here, step 3 was shorter than in the previous case, and the available resource at the time of step 3 was enough to set subgoal A.

Control. In the context of HRT it is extremely important to control the course of the process of reasoning, identifying emerging anomalies. Under these conditions, the manifestation of anomalies is primarily associated with a delay in obtaining the expected results. To do this, it is necessary for the agent to be able to realize not only what he knows at a given moment in time, but also what he does not know at that moment. In the formalism of extended step theories, this ability (self-knowledge) is realized through the use of the operator of subjective negation not^t. Note that in other existing formalisms of step theories, where the operator of subjective negation is absent, the ability to self-knowledge is also absent.

Example 2. Consider the theory $T_3 = (R_3, Ck_3)$, where $R_3 = \{N1 :\Rightarrow \alpha, N2 : \alpha \Rightarrow \beta, N3 : \beta \Rightarrow \gamma, N4 : later(3) \wedge not^t\gamma \Rightarrow anomaly\}$, $Ck_3 = (1, 5, 9, ...)$. The history of the T3 theory looks like this: $B(0) = \{now(0)\}, B(1) = \{now(1), \alpha\}, B(2) = \{now(5), \alpha, \beta\}, B(3) = B_{fin} = \{now(9), \alpha, \beta, \gamma, anomaly\}$. In this case, at step 2, when the control time line was reached, but the literal, contrary to expectations, did not appear in the set of beliefs $B(2)$, rule $N4$ worked, fixing the presence of an anomaly.

Correction. The main tasks of the analysis of identified anomalies under hard time constraints are to assess the degree of threat of crossing the deadline (time threshold) associated with the identified anomaly, as well as the size of the available temporary resource that can be used to avoid this threat. It seems that in such cases special "emergency" strategies should be provided (based, in particular, on the use of flexible algorithms for finding a solution), when the quality of the solution is sacrificed to the speed of its finding. The following is an example when, when an anomaly is detected, the rules specially provided for such a case are activated. Of course, in practice, situations associated with anomalies of various types are possible and then for each such type its own rules are provided, but this does not change the essence of what is considered in this example.

Example 3. Consider the theory $T_4 = (R_4, Ck_4)$, where $R_4 = \{N1 :\Rightarrow \alpha, N2 : not^t anomaly \wedge \alpha \Rightarrow \beta, N3 : not^t anomaly \wedge \beta \Rightarrow \gamma, N4 : not^t anomaly \wedge \gamma \Rightarrow \delta, N5 : later(3) \wedge not^t \gamma \Rightarrow anomaly, N6 : anomaly \wedge \alpha \Rightarrow \epsilon, N7 : anomaly \wedge \epsilon \Rightarrow \zeta\}$, $Ck_4 = (1, 4, 7, 12, 13, ...)$. The history of the T_4 theory will be as follows: $B(0) = \{now(0)\}$, $B(1) = \{now(1), \alpha\}$, $B(2) = \{now(4), \alpha, \beta\}$, $B(3) = \{now(7), \alpha, anomaly\}$, $B(4) = \{now(12), \alpha, anomaly, \epsilon\}$, $B(5) = B_{fin} = \{now(13), \alpha, anomaly, \zeta\}$. In this case, rule N5 in step 3, due to the lack of the literal deduced by that time, deduced the objective literal anomaly, after which the cognitive process passed under the "crisis control": now only the rules that have the anomaly literal in the antecedent have become applicable, while rules that have in the antecedent a subjective literal $not^t anomaly$ have become inapplicable.

The syntax and declarative semantics of the language of Extended Step Theory are developed, combining the concepts of AL and logical programming (LP). The theory got its name by analogy with the extended logical programs introduced by A. Lifshitz and M. Gelfond [5] as applied to the LP paradigm. The language of this logical system includes two types of negation. One of them corresponds to the usual ("strong") logical negation, while the second, called "subjective", in a sense is similar to the default negation (negation as failure) in the LP, but has the following important difference. While in LP the meaning of negation by default lies in the fact that the negated formula (in the LP is always a literal) could not be deduced using the given logical program, the subjective negation in the considered logical system means that the negated literal could not be deduced by the current moment in time. Thus, in the system under consideration, the principle of self-knowledge is implemented, which consists in the fact that an agent whose behavior is modeled by a logical system is able to recognize and express explicitly not only what he knows, but also what he does not know at the moment. Note that such an opportunity is especially in demand when managing the cognitive process in the conditions of severe time constraints. This allows you to make managing the process of solving the problem more efficient compared to using other existing meta-reasoning formalisms in which this principle is not implemented.

The temporal logic of branching time (branching temporal logic) was further developed. This logic can be used to solve the problems of training, forecasting and modeling in intelligent systems, when it is necessary to consider time branching into the future. The application of this logic allows us to simulate, as noted earlier, the possible consequences of the solution (or solutions) found by the agent under rather tight time constraints. In work [3], various temporal logics were considered in terms of their application in intelligent real-time systems (RT IS) including HRT IS. As a basis for use in the RT IS, the recommended BPTL (Branching-Time Propositional Temporal logic), proposed in [14] and is an extension of propositional temporal logic (PTL). PTL is a modal temporal logic built on the basis of classical logic with added modal operators for discrete linear time.

BPTL is proved to be complete with respect to all branching time structures. Inference algorithms for BPTLs with a focus on RT IS were proposed in [3].

3   Conclusion

The principal differences of AL from traditional nonmonotonic logics such as default logic, auto-epistemic logic, etc. are formulated. (rejection of logical omniscience, the presence of temporal sensitivity and self-knowledge). The advantages of the step theory are formulated in comparison with other AL systems (improved characteristics of computational complexity, paraconsistency, implementation of the principle of time granulation). The consistency of the step logic allows one to avoid the destruction of the entire system of reasoning, despite the presence of conflicting information. To further improve the management of the process of reasoning, formalisms of extended step theories are used, which differ from standard step theories by the introduction, along with a strong negation of subjective negation, which allows the cognitive agent to recognize and express explicitly not only what he knows, but also what he does not knows at the moment. This improves the expressive capabilities of the theory and, in particular, the property of temporal sensitivity. Based on the proposed formalisms, methods have been developed for controlling the cognitive process (reasoning process) of a cognitive agent under significant time constraints.

The use of temporal logic of branching time is proposed, which allows modeling (deriving) various consequences of a solution found by an plaingent. A subclass of such logic, oriented to application in HRT IS, is considered. The possibilities of integrating branching time logic and flexible decision search algorithms are currently being considered.

On the whole, the obtained results create the necessary conceptual basis for constructing promising systems for modeling the reasoning of a cognitive agent operating under conditions of HRT IS based on a combination of the concepts of active logic, temporal logic, and logical programming.

References

1. Anderson, M.L., Oates, T., Chong, W., Perlis, D.: The metacognitive loop I: enhancing reinforcement learning with metacognitive monitoring and control for improved perturbation tolerance. J. Exp. Theoret. Artif. Intell. **18**, 387–411 (2006). https://doi.org/10.1080/09528130600926066
2. Elgot-Drapkin, J.: Step logic: reasoning situated in time. Ph.D. thesis (1988)
3. Eremeev, A.P., Kurilenko, I.E.: An implementation of inference in temporal branching time models. J. Comput. Syst. Sci. Int. **56**, 105–124 (2017). https://doi.org/10.1134/s1064230716060046
4. Flavell, J.H.: Metacognition and cognitive monitoring: a new area of cognitive-developmental inquiry. Am. Psychol. **34**, 906–911 (1979). https://doi.org/10.1037/0003-066x.34.10.906
5. Gelfond, M., Lifschitz, V.: Classical negation in logic programs and disjunctive databases. New Gener. Comput. **9**, 365–385 (1991). https://doi.org/10.1007/bf03037169
6. Hovold, J.: On a semantics for active logic. Ph.D. thesis (2011)
7. Liu, C., Orgun, M.A.: Verification of reactive systems using temporal logic with clocks. Theoret. Comput. Sci. **220**, 377–408 (1999). https://doi.org/10.1016/s0304-3975(99)00008-0
8. Duc, H.N.: Logical omniscience vs. logical ignorance on a dilemma of epistemic logic. In: Pinto-Ferreira, C., Mamede, N.J. (eds.) EPIA 1995. LNCS, vol. 990, pp. 237–248. Springer, Heidelberg (1995). https://doi.org/10.1007/3-540-60428-6_20
9. Proceedings of the 10th National Conference with International Participation "KII": argumentation semantics for active logic step theories, vol. 1 (2006)
10. Vinkov, M., Fominykh, I.: Extended stepping theories of active logic: paraconsistent semantics. In: Kuznetsov, S.O., Osipov, G.S., Stefanuk, V.L. (eds.) RCAI 2018. CCIS, vol. 934, pp. 70–78. Springer, Cham (2018). https://doi.org/10.1007/978-3-030-00617-4_7
11. Proceedings of the 7th Russian Conference RCAI 2000 Moscow: Formalization of reasoning with defaults in intelligent real-time systems based on time logic (2000)
12. Proceedings of the IJCAI 1999 Workshop on Practical Reasoning and Rationality: Practical Reasoning and Plan Executing with Active Logic (1999)
13. Proceedings of the X International Scientific Conference "Open Semantic Technologies for Intelligent Systems": Modeling of Reasoning a Cognitive Agent with Significant Time Restrictions (2020)
14. Torsun, I.S.: Foundations of Intelligent Knowledge-based Systems. Academic Press, Cop, Cambridge (1995)
15. Vinkov, M., Fominykh, I.: Discussions about knowledge and the problem of logical omniscience. Part 1. Modal approach. Artif. Intell. Decis. Mak. **4**, 4–12 (2011)
16. Vinkov, M.M., Fominykh, I.B.: Stepping theories of active logic with two kinds of negation. In: Advances in Electrical and Electronic Engineering, vol. 15 (2017). https://doi.org/10.15598/aeee.v15i1.1990
17. Working Notes of AAAI Fall Symposium on Psychological Models of Communication: Modeling Time and Metareasoning in Dialog via Active Logic (2005)

Interactive Adaptation of Digital Fields in the System GeoBazaDannych

Valery B. Taranchuk[(✉)] [iD]

Belarusian State University, 4, Nezavisimosti Avenue,
220030 Minsk, Republic of Belarus
taranchuk@bsu.by

Abstract. The interactive computer system GeoBazaDannych is a complex of intelligent computer subsystems, mathematical, algorithmic and software tools for filling, maintaining and visualizing input and output data, creating continuously updated computer models. The purpose and functionality of the main components of the system GeoBazaDannych are briefly described. Examples of interactive formation of digital models of geological objects in computational experiments that meet the intuitive requirements of the expert are discussed. Methodological and algorithmic solutions, corresponding special tools of the system GeoBazaDannych for the formation of digital distributions that meet the requirements set by the expert are noted. The results of comparison with standard solutions in the complex "Generator of the geological model of the deposit" are presented. Examples of approximation and reconstruction of the digital field and its interactive adaptation by means of the system GeoBazaDannych are given and discussed; the obtained solutions and their accuracy are illustrated by maps of isolines.

Keywords: Digital geological model · System GeoBazaDannych · Interactive graphical visualization · Intelligent adaptation of digital fields · "Smart" methods of computer model adaptation

1 Introduction

Geological modeling is an independent direction that includes the improvement of mathematical methods and algorithms; development of computer programs that provide a cycle of model construction, forming, filling and maintenance of databases [1,2]. The corresponding software includes the loading from different sources and data preprocessing, correlation, creation of digital cubes of reservoir properties, interactive data analysis, visualization with the help of any type graphics, mapping. The task of developing and implementing various computer-based geological models with self-tuning tools is one of the priorities. Herewith, an important component is the task of evaluating the adequacy and accuracy of the proposed digital models. The key issues are automation, adaptation of models

Supported by BSU Research Institute for Applied Mathematics and Informatics.

ⓒ Springer Nature Switzerland AG 2020
V. Golenkov et al. (Eds.): OSTIS 2020, CCIS 1282, pp. 222–233, 2020.
https://doi.org/10.1007/978-3-030-60447-9_14

taking into account continuously incoming additional data, as well as a revision of the results of processing the initial information using new interpretation methods [2,3].

The data used in geological and geoecological models are a representative part of the geodata, which classify, summarize information about processes and phenomena on the earth's surface. This information becomes really useful when integrated into a single system. Geodata, as a generalization of accumulated information, include information not only from the field of Earth sciences, but also from others, such as transport, economics, ecology, management, education, analysis, artificial intelligence. Technological, system, and information features of geodata are noted in [4].

Geodata volumes are growing at a very high rate. Accordingly, it is natural to use "big data" technologies (the specifics for geodata are described in [5]), including automated data mining. One of the main aims of data mining is to find previously unknown, non-trivial, practically useful and understandable interpretations of knowledge in "raw" (primary) data sets [6,7]. At the same time, following [6], "data mining does not exclude human participation in processing and analysis, but significantly simplifies the process of finding the necessary data from raw data, making it available to a wide range of analysts who are not specialists in statistics, mathematics or programming. Human participation is expressed in the cognitive aspects of participation and the application of informational cognitive models".

Geodata mining tools are the same as for usual data; the basis is the theory, methods, and algorithms of applied statistics, databases, artificial intelligence, and image recognition. There are many different active and applied software tools for data mining, for example, 8 classes of data mining systems are identified in [6]. The variety of proposed methods and software tools make it necessary to assess the quality of geodata and determine their main characteristics. Criteria for evaluating the quality of geodata are discussed in [8].

A number of issues related to the analysis and evaluation of spatial data quality can be solved using the computer system GeoBazaDannych [9–11]. Possible options, methodological solutions, and software tools that allow you to confirm the validity of interpretations, visualize and obtain numerical values of errors calculated by different methods of intellectual data processing results included and used in computer geological models are discussed below. For illustrations, the key task of forming and processing digital fields used in computer models is selected. In particular, we discuss the proposed methods that have been tested for solving different applied problems, as well as implemented in the interactive computer system GeoBazaDannych specialized algorithms for calculating approximating digital fields.

The interactive computer system GeoBazaDannych is the complex of intelligent computer subsystems, mathematical, algorithmic and software for filling, maintaining and visualizing databases, input data for simulation and mathematical models, tools for conducting computational experiments, algorithmic tools and software for creating continuously updated computer models. By means of the system GeoBazaDannych, it is possible to generate and visualize digital descriptions of spatial distributions of data on sources of contamination, on the geological structure of the studied objects; graphically illustrate solutions to problems describing the dynamic processes of multiphase filtration, fluid migration, heat transfer, moisture, and mineral water-soluble compounds in rock strata; design and implement interactive scenarios for visualization and processing the results of computational experiments. GeoBazaDannych's subsystems allow you to calculate and perform expert assessments of local and integral characteristics of ecosystems in different approximations, calculate distributions of concentrations and mass balances of pollutants; create permanent models of oil production facilities; generate and display thematic maps on hard copies. The main components of the system GeoBazaDannych [9–13]:

- the data generator Gen_DATv;
- the generator and editor of thematic maps and digital fields Gen_MAPw;
- modules for organizing the operation of geographic information systems in interactive or batch modes;
- the software package Geo_mdl – mathematical, algorithmic and software tools for building geological models of soil layers, multi-layer reservoirs; modules for three-dimensional visualization of dynamic processes of distribution of water-soluble pollutants in active soil layers;
- software and algorithmic support for the formation and maintenance of permanent hydrodynamic models of multiphase filtration in porous, fractured media;
- the integrated software complex of the composer of digital geological and geoecological models (GGMD).

2   Examples of Interactive Adaptation of Digital Fields

Integration of the capabilities of various geographic information systems (GIS) and the GeoBazaDannych is provided by a wide range of tools of the system for importing and exporting data, images, and functions. This article discusses several non-standard solutions that are recognized as difficult for all geodata processing packages. The examples of approximation and reconstruction of the digital field, its interactive adaptation by means of the system GeoBazaDannych and evaluation of the accuracy of results using the tools of the GGMD complex illustrate the unique capabilities of the developed methods and software.

The task of reconstruction of the grid function involves calculating the values of the approximating function at regular grid points from the values of randomly located experimental data points (observations), i.e. creating a regular array of Z values of node points from an irregular array of (X,Y,Z) values. The term "irregular array of values" means that the X, Y coordinates of data points are distributed irregularly across the function definition area. The procedure for constructing a regular network of level values and restoring the grid function is an interpolation or extrapolation of values from a collection of scattered sets of source points and values of surface levels in them to uniformly distributed nodes in the study area.

Methods for restoring grid functions and the corresponding algorithms are implemented in several specialized computer graphics and GIS packages. They can be divided into two classes: exact and smoothing interpolators [14,15]. In fact, the method falls into a particular class depending on the user-defined settings when performing value calculations. Most methods for restoring the function and constructing a digital field are based on calculating weighted coefficients that are used to weigh the values of the measurement data at the nearest points. This means that, all other things being equal, the closer the data point is to a network node, the more weight it has in determining the value of the function being restored at that node.

It should be understood that restoring a grid function does not imply finding a single solution to a certain mathematical problem. Subjective opinion and expert qualifications are factors that are always present in such activities [16]. To create computer models, you need to have tools for interactive data processing and implementation of possible situations of receiving and correcting input information, modules for mathematical processing, interpretation and statistical analysis [14,17]. For the compiler of any computer model, it is important to be able to perform data analysis using different methods and algorithms in several software environments, to have tools that allow him to "play" with the source data and compare the results with the prepared reference models. This assumes that there are tools for exchanging data between modules that use different formats. How these requirements are implemented in the system GeoBazaDannych is described below.

The examples of approximation and reconstruction of the digital field, its interactive adaptation by means of the system GeoBazaDannych and evaluation of the accuracy of results using the GGMD complex illustrate the unique capabilities of the developed methods and software. Using the tools of the GGMD complex [12,13,18], estimates of the accuracy of digital field reconstruction are obtained and illustrated with graphics.

The capabilities of the algorithms implemented in the system GeoBazaDannych for interactive preparation and adaptation of digital parameter distributions in relation to the tasks of composing computer models of geological objects are illustrated by examples using the results of [13,18]. At the same time, we will not consider typical graphic objects (pyramids, parallelepipeds, cylinders, cones). The reason is that three-dimensional geometric patterns can be processed separately in the system GeoBazaDannych. A special module of the system can be used to "restore surfaces when the digital field is not calculated using the approximation method on the selected sections, but is filled in with the calculated values of functions from the template library (by the generator of defining functions)" [11]. Also, to demonstrate the special capabilities of the system GeoBazaDannych, in addition to the perturbations of the type (2) considered in [13], perturbations simulating a plateau and a split are introduced. They are set by expressions (1)–(3):

$$fH(x,y) = cos(\pi x/2) + cos(\pi y/2),$$

$$fHill3(x,y) = \begin{cases} fH(x,y), -1 \le x \le 1 \cap -1 \le y \le 1 \cap fH(x,y) \le 1/4, \\ 1/4, -1 \le x \le 1 \cap -1 \le y \le 1 \cap fH(x,y) > 1/4, \end{cases} \quad (1)$$

$$fHill5(x,y) = \begin{cases} fH(x,y), -1 \le x \le 1 \cap -1 \le y \le 0, \\ 0, \end{cases} \quad (2)$$

$$fHill6(x,y) = \begin{cases} fH(x,y), -1 \le x \le 1 \cap -1 \le y \le 0 \cap -1 \le x+y \cap x+y > 0, \\ 0. \end{cases}$$

$$(3)$$

The reference surface in the following examples is objects described by the expression (4)

$$fOriginF(x,y) = zBasicF(x),$$
$$zSurfF(x,y) = fOriginF(x,y)+$$
$$+400 \cdot fHill6(0.005 \cdot (x - 250), 0.007 \cdot (y - 400))+$$
$$+500 \cdot fHill3(0.01 \cdot (x - 200), 0.01 \cdot (y - 150))- \quad (4)$$
$$-150 \cdot fHill(0.01 \cdot (x - 880), 0.015 \cdot (y - 100))-$$
$$-150 \cdot fHill(0.02 \cdot (x - 920), 0.004 \cdot (y - 500))+$$
$$+200 \cdot fHill5(0.008 \cdot (x - 550), 0.01 \cdot (y - 150)).$$

Its important that in the resulting expression (4) coefficients in the formulas of perturbation elements are chosen by the user while visual construction. An example of creating a model of the reference surface, which is obtained from the base surface by adding elements of the listed types, is shown in Fig. 1, Fig. 2.

We emphasize attention on fragments of the zSurfF surface, namely, perturbations fHill3, fHill5, fHill6. The element $fHill3(200,150)$ simulates the presence of a plateau (clipping with a horizontal plane), $fHill5(550,150)$ and $fHill6(250,400)$ simulate splits (in geology shift-overshoot), and is mathematically described by clipping a smooth hill-type shape with a vertical plane. Such fragments of fHill5 and fHill6 cannot be reproduced using standard methods for restoring digital fields. Also note that in the following illustrations, the isolines corresponding to the plateau level (for zSurfF level 225) are not displayed. In the zSurfF illustration, level 210 is shown to further emphasize the boundaries of disturbances placed on the plateau section.

The images zSurfF in Fig. 1 give an aggregate vision of the reference surface. Individual, details can be studied on the contour map Fig. 2. It displays the isolines and density distribution (color filling of intervals) of the digital field of the function $zSurfF(x,y)$. In addition, color intervals are explained by the legend and value labels that match the levels of the isolines.

The illustrations below (Fig. 3–Fig. 7) show examples of reconstruction of the grid function using standard algorithms and application of possible solutions and methods for "adjustment" distributions in the system GeoBazaDannych. Typical steps for simulating observations and preparing initial data for the subsequent reconstruction of the digital field from a scattered set of points with measurements were performed beforehand. It is assumed that the measurement points

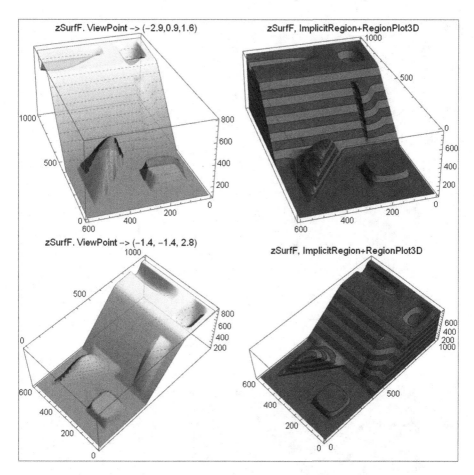

Fig. 1. ZsurfF surface and volume graphs.

are placed on profiles; they are shown for different observation profiles by different primitives (112 dots). The centers of form perturbations are marked with red circles, which are 6 points (Fig. 3). Two pairs of red diamond markers show split segments. There was no goal to choose a good system of profiles, they are formed sketchily, and about how often designers do this.

Figure 3 shows the results obtained in the complex GMMD of digital field reconstruction, when the simplest variant is implemented using the standard interpolation function of the 1st order in Wolfram Mathematica. Note that when working with irregularly placed data points in the system Mathematica, interpolation can only be performed using this method. But this is enough, since in other specialized packages, the most common, this problem is solved by the method of triangulation, which also corresponds to linear interpolation. The corresponding results obtained in the GMMD are shown on the contour map in Fig. 3, where the isolines of the reference field are given as solid purple lines, and in the restored field – as dashed black lines.

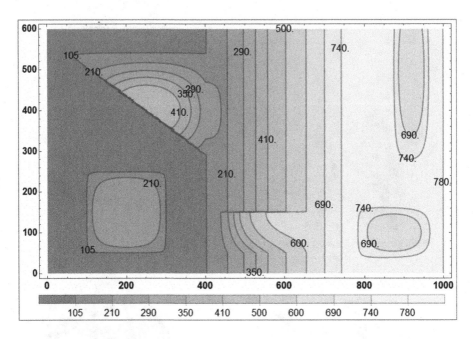

Fig. 2. Isolines and density maps of *zSurfF*(x,y) function.

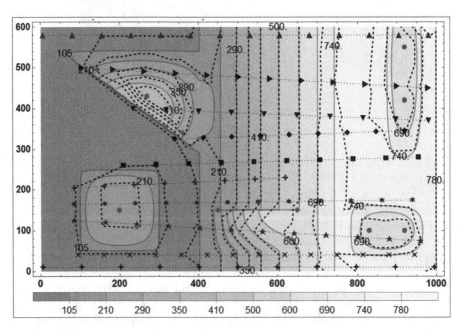

Fig. 3. Isolines of the digital fields of the reference (purple lines) and restored in the GMMD (dashed black lines) distributions. (Color figure online)

To get results in the system GeoBazaDannych, the data of measurements on profiles and control points in GGMD are exported to an XLS file that is imported into Gen_MAPw. The corresponding illustration is given in Fig. 4, where the profiles, points of observation are shown; the values of measurements are displayed near their primitives. In the database, values are stored with machine precision, for brevity, the output of the map is made in the format of the integer numbers.

Figure 5–Fig. 7 show the results of restoring the digital field obtained in the system GeoBazaDannych. At the initial stage (to compare the results of restoring the digital field), calculations of the field reconstruction using the GeoBazaDannych's spline approximation method were performed in Gen_MAPw without any additions. The calculated grid was formed in the Gen_MAPw automatically taking into account the coverage of the entire area edged by the Granica G border, its step was set to 10. In this case, the GeoBazaDannych "subdomain" element (Granica G) "works". The results are shown on the contour map Fig. 5, the corresponding isolines are displayed as dash-dotted green polygons. The dashed isolines of the graphic layer from Fig. 4 is also added to the illustration. There is an understandable difference, because the results are calculated using different interpolation methods. Basically, both methods provide visualization of fHill perturbation forms, but with significant reproduction errors for fHill5 and fHill6.

How to understand the results shown in Fig. 6, Fig. 7? In these cases, the task is to correct the digital fields obtained by the approximation algorithm via using such GeoBazaDannych's elements as "selected", "split", and "boundary conditions" [11]. In fact, it is an interactive intellectual adaptation.

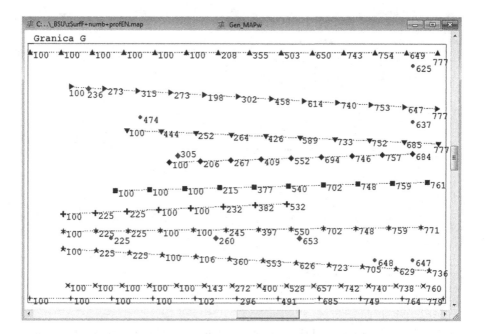

Fig. 4. Results of exporting points with measurements from GGMD to Gen_MAPw.

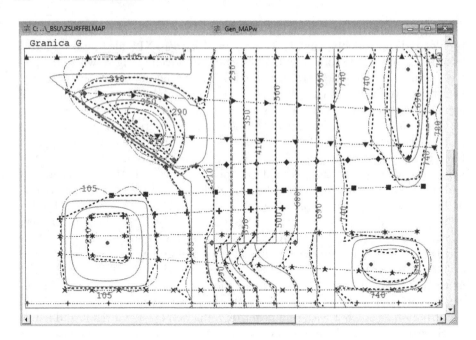

Fig. 5. Isolines of reference and restored fields in GGMD (dashed black lines) and in Gen_MAPw (spline approximation algorithm, dash-dotted green lines). (Color figure online)

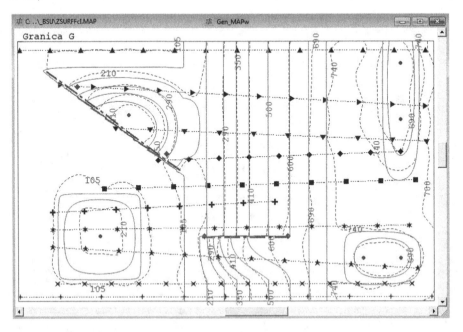

Fig. 6. Effects of correction of the reconstructed digital field using the "split" method. (Color figure online)

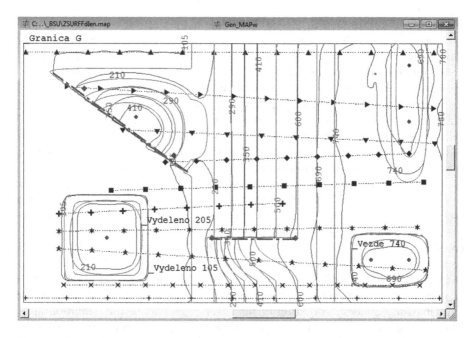

Fig. 7. Effects of correction of the reconstructed digital field using the "selected", and "boundary conditions" methods. (Color figure online)

An example of adapting digital fields in Gen_MAPw using the "split" element of the GeoBazaDannych is illustrated in Fig. 6. When executing the approximation (forming a digital field on the grid), in addition to the Granica G, 2 contours were added to the input map – bold dash-dotted red lines. In [11] it is explained that the system GeoBazaDannych "recognizes" special contours (in particular, subdomains, inclusions, boundary conditions, splits) by line attributes, which include: color, thickness, line type, closed or not. The isolines in this version (with the addition of "split" category contours to the input data) are shown as dotted green lines. The illustration Fig. 6 expressively demonstrates the effect of the of "split" element in the lower central part, in particular, the levels 290, 350, 410, 500, 600.

Figure 7 illustrates the possibilities of additional refinements of the digital field that should correspond to the user's a priori opinion using the "Selected" and "Boundary conditions" GeoBazaDannych's tools. The "Selected" method allows you to perform a separate (autonomous) calculation of grid values within a user-defined subdomain, taking into account only the points with measurements that are included in the subdomain. When approximating outside the subdomain, measurements that fall within the subdomain are not taken into account. Such a subdomain is enough to sketch a closed non-self-intersecting polyline on the area of the function definition, and set the appropriate attribute for this contour. In addition, in the Gen_MAPw, the user can "assign" a numeric value to the polyline nodes, which will be taken into account when calculating the grid function. In fact, in this case, the original set of values is supplemented with measurements. The grid function (digital field) adopted by the approximation algorithm will be gradually independently calculated in the subdomain and outside it separately, in each only by "their" reference points with values. The "Boundary conditions" method should be used in the part where it is necessary to "correct" the digital field obtained during approximation. The user draws a polyline with the corresponding attributes in the definition area and "assigns" values, one or more (the interpolation algorithm for setting multiple values is described in [11]). The reference nodes of this contour "go" as an addition to the set of values with measurements.

In the calculation variant illustrated in Fig. 7, the "Selected" and "Boundary conditions" methods are used. In the illustration in this version, the isolines are shown as green solid lines, unlike the dot dashed and dashed lines in the previous versions. In the lower-left part of the grid function definition area, the conditions "Vydeleno_105" and "Vydeleno_205" are used. The corresponding contour borders are drawn on the input map with red solid thin lines. Comparing the isolines of Fig. 6 and Fig. 7, the effect of the applied method of digital field adaptation is clearly positive. You can also clearly see the positive effect of applying the boundary condition in the lower-right part of the definition area. The effect is provided by the introduction of a contour border with a value of 740 (a dash-dotted bold line of magenta color).

It should be noted that the capabilities of the system GeoBazaDannych have been significantly expanded in recent years. This was achieved by integrating and addition the system with the tools of the GGMD complex and the functions of the computer algebra system. In the current state, the GeoBazaDannych provides users not only with the means to solve specific industrial tasks, but also with the possibility of scientific research on new methods of analysis and processing of initial data and used computer models. In particular, for the above problem, error estimates are obtained using the method described in [13]. We do not give particular error digits here, because in the model problem under consideration, the eliminated errors on the adapted field are comparable to the accuracy of obtaining grid functions, although these errors are noticeably lower than in the unadapted field.

3   Conclusion

The article discusses the questions of instrumental filling and use of the interactive computer system GeoBazaDannych. The results of intellectual processing of data included and used in computer geological models are presented and discussed.

References

1. Bedrikovetsky, P.: Mathematical Theory of Oil and Gas Recovery: With Applications to ex-USSR Oil and Gas. Springer, Heidelberg (2013)
2. Dmitrievskii, A.N., Eremin, N.A.: Bolshie geodannye v cifrovoi neftegazovoi ekosisteme. Energeticheskaya politika **2**, 31–39 (2018). (in Russian)
3. 13th International Symposium on Software Engineering for Adaptive and Self-Managing Systems. Gothenburg, Sweden, 28–29 May 2018. https://conf.researchr.org/track/seams-2018/seams-2018-papers. Accessed 29 Jun 2020
4. Savinyh, V.P., Cvetkov, V.Ya.: Geodannye kak sistemnyi informacionnyi resurs. Vestnik Rossiiskoi akademii nauk **84**(9), 826–829 (2014). (in Russian)
5. Tsvetkov, V.Ya., Lobanov, A.A.: Big Data as Information Barrier. Eur. Res. **78**(7-1), 1237–1242 (2014)
6. Shaitura, S.V.: Intellektual'nyi analiz geodannyh. Perspektivy nauki i obrazovaniya **18**(6), 24–30 (2015). (in Russian)
7. Golenkov, V.V.: Ontology-based design of intelligent system. In: Golenkov, V.V. (ed.) Conference 2017, OSTIIS, pp. 37–56. BSUIR, Minsk (2017)
8. Dyshlenko, S.G.: Analiz i razrabotka harakteristik kachestva geodannyh. Perspektivy nauki i (2016)
9. Taranchuk, V.B.: Chislennoe modelirovanie processov dvuhfaznoi mnogokomponentnoi fil'tracii v neodnorodnoi poristoi srede. Doktorskaya dissertaciya, Kazan' State University (1992). (in Russian)
10. Barvenov, S.A., Kibash, M.F., Taranchuk, V.B.: Metodika, instrumentarii adaptacii matematicheskih modelei processov podzemnoi gidrodinamiki. Vybranyya navukovyya pracy BDU, Matematika, 34–65 (2001). (in Russian)
11. Taranchuk, V.B.: Postroenie cifrovyh geologo-ekologicheskih modelei v sisteme GBD-e. Geoekologiya Belarusi, Pravo i ekonomika, 72–96 (2006). (in Russian)
12. Taranchuk, V.: The integrated computer complex of an estimation and adapting of digital geological models. Studia i Materialy **14**(2), 73–86 (2017)
13. Taranchuk, V.B.: Metody i instrumentarii ocenki tochnosti komp'yuternyh geologicheskih modelei Vestnik BrGTU (2), 64–69 (2018). (in Russian)
14. Davis, J.C.: Statistics and Data Analysis in Geology. Wiley, New York (1986)
15. Sacks, J., Welch, W.J., Mitchell, T.J., Wynn, H.P.: Design and analysis of computer experiments. Stat. Sci. **4**, 409–435 (1989)
16. Halimov, E.M.: Detal'nye geologicheskie modeli i trehmernoe modelirovanie. Neftegazovaya geologiya. Teoriya i praktika **7**(3), 1–10 (2012)
17. Wolfram Mathematica. http://www.wolfram.com/mathematica/. Accessed 29 Jun 2020
18. Taranchuk, V.B.: New computer technologies, analysis and interpretation of geodata. In: MATEC Web of Conferences IPICSE-2018, vol. 251, pp. 1–8 (2018). https://doi.org/10.1051/matecconf/201825104059

Neural Network Data Processing Technology Based on Deep Belief Networks

Viktor V. Krasnoproshin(ID) and Vadim V. Matskevich(✉)(ID)

Faculty of Applied Mathematics and Computer Science, Belarusian State University,
4 Nezavisimost av., 220030 Minsk, Belarus
krasnoproshin@bsu.by, matskevich1997@gmail.com

Abstract. The paper provides approach for building neural network data processing technology based on deep belief networks. A neural network architecture, focused on parallel data processing and an original training algorithm implementing the annealing method, is proposed. The approach effectiveness is demonstrated by solving the image compression problem as an example.

Keywords: Framework · Annealing method · Deep belief network · Parallel computations

1 Introduction

Recently, neural network data processing technologies have been very popular among researchers of various specializations. In particular, they are widely used in solving urgent problems of machine learning and intellectual information processing.

By now, large number of frameworks have been developed, which are based on various types of neural network architectures. Despite the variety of these architectures and their orientation towards various classes of applied problems, many of the frameworks have common properties. Most technologies are typically implemented using the CUDA libraries, and the training is based on the gradient descent methodology. Gradient descent methods are widespread due to fast convergence, and CUDA libraries due to their orientation on previously popular NVIDIA graphics cards and multi-core processors.

At the same time, gradient descent methods are not without drawbacks [5]. In particular, they, as a rule, converge to local minima, which reduces the training quality [7]. Moreover, they require differentiability of the objective function [6], which significantly narrows the class of problems being solved.

Orienting frameworks to NVIDIA graphics cards also significantly limits their application scope. To speed up data processing, an increasing number of practical tasks are reduced to the problems of mass parallelism. This has led to the rapid growth in popularity of FPGA devices and graphics cards. Compared to processors, they have one or two orders of magnitude higher performance and energy

© Springer Nature Switzerland AG 2020
V. Golenkov et al. (Eds.): OSTIS 2020, CCIS 1282, pp. 234–244, 2020.
https://doi.org/10.1007/978-3-030-60447-9_15

efficiency. In addition, the share of NVIDIA graphics cards today has dropped from 85% to 68%. It should also be noted that Intel Corp. has begun production of its own graphics cards. Thus, the share of NVIDIA graphics cards has a tendency to decrease, and, therefore, the application scope of CUDA frameworks is also narrowing. At the same time, OpenCL libraries (unlike CUDA libraries) are supported by computing devices of almost any manufacturer. Thus, these libraries are rapidly gaining popularity.

The paper considers neural network data processing technology construction approach based on the deep belief networks architecture and the use of OpenCL libraries. It is proposed to use an algorithm that implements a random search methodology as a training method.

2   Problem Analysis

Currently, deep belief networks are widely used to solve many application problems. These are the tasks of medical diagnostics, pattern recognition and image processing, highlighting semantically significant features, etc. [9].

It is well known that deep belief networks are based on a restricted Boltzmann machine. Therefore, before moving on to the consideration of the indicated network, first we give brief information about the architecture of the restricted Boltzmann machine.

Any restricted Boltzmann machine is based on the concept of a stochastic neuron.

Formally, a restricted Boltzmann machine can be represented as a fully connected bipartite graph $G = (X, U)$,

$$\begin{cases} X = X_1 \cup X_2, X_1 \cap X_2 = \emptyset \\ U = \{u = (x_1, x_2) | \forall x_1 \in X_1, \forall x_2 \in X_2\}, \end{cases} \tag{1}$$

where X - vertex set - stochastic neurons, U - edges set - synaptic connections, while vertices of subset X_1 – set the neurons of the input layer, X_2 – output layer neurons.

The number of neurons in the input layer is determined by the size of the input image, and the number of neurons in the output layer is determined based on requirements, for example, to the data compress ratio.

The output signals of the layers implement the corresponding laws of the probability distribution. Different types of machines are built depending on the laws used. This paper investigates the most common machines of the Gauss-Bernoulli and Bernoulli-Bernoulli types.

Let us describe the restricted Boltzmann machine of the Gauss-Bernoulli type, which we use in what follows. To each vertex of the input layer of such a machine, we associate a set of parameters $VB = \{b\}$ - bias and $\sigma = \{\sigma\}$ - variance of the vertices. And the vertices of the output layer - a set of parameters $HB = \{g\}$ - the offset of the vertices. The sizes of the sets are equal respectively

$$|VB| = |\sigma| = |X_1|, |HB| = |X_2| \tag{2}$$

Each edge connecting a pair of vertices of the input and output layers will be assigned a set of parameters $W = \{w\}$ - the weights of the edges. In this case, the size of the set is equal to the following value

$$|W| = |X_1||X_2| \tag{3}$$

As a result, the family of neural networks described above can be specified by four types of parameters:

$$RBM = (W, VB, \sigma, HB) \tag{4}$$

It should be noted that in the case of consideration of a restricted Boltzmann machine of the Bernoulli-Bernoulli type, it will lack set of parameters σ.

Any deep belief network, as a rule, contains several layers consisting of restricted Boltzmann machines. And to generate the output signal (depending on the problem being solved), it may additionally contain a multilayer perceptron.

A deep belief network in layers consisting of restricted Boltzmann machines solves the problem of data compression, which can be formally described as follows.

Let X be the space of input images of some fixed dimension, Y - the space of compressed images of much smaller dimension than the space X. I.e:

$$\begin{cases} dimX = fix \\ dimY \ll dimX \end{cases} \tag{5}$$

Then the problem of data compression is to build compression functions f and recovery g, such that:

$$\begin{cases} f : X \to Y, g : Y \to X \\ d : X \times X \to \Re \\ d(x, g(f(x))) \to min, \forall x \in X, \end{cases} \tag{6}$$

where d is a function that evaluates the differences between two given vectors.

Note. In practice, data compression is carried out for a specific subject area. This, in turn, imposes certain restrictions on the input data and, therefore, reduces the dimension of the space X.

The most time-consuming step in the use of neural networks is the training process [8, 13, 15]. Since a deep belief network always contains layers of restricted Boltzmann machines, the effectiveness of solving the problem depends on the effectiveness of training the entire network as a whole.

Network training can be written as an optimization problem for each of the layers.

Let a training dataset x and a functional for evaluating the quality of data compression d (6) be given. It is needed to find the values of the parameters $(w^*, b^*, g^*, \sigma^*)$, giving a minimum of functional F, i.e.

$$F(x, d, w^*, b^*, g^*, \sigma^*) = \min_{w,b,g,\sigma} F(x, d, w, b, g, \sigma) \tag{7}$$

Note. A restricted Boltzmann machine of Bernoulli-Bernoulli type does not contain the parameter σ and the quality functional F, therefore, does not depend on σ.

To solve optimization problems, you can use either the gradient descent method or random search.

The gradient descent method has fast convergence, but at the same time has several disadvantages:

1) converges to local minimum points [20], which significantly reduces the quality of the solution;

2) requires differentiability of the objective function [6], which significantly reduces the class of problems to be solved.

The random search method is not widespread [14], but it has some noteworthy advantages, in particular:

1) does not require objective function differentiability, which significantly expands the class of applied problems;

2) under certain conditions [10] and from any initial approximation [16] it has convergence to the global minimum.

In view of the foregoing, we formulate the following training task.

Let a training dataset of N input images of dimension dimX be given and requirements for data compression be fixed, i.e. dimY = fix.

It is necessary to develop a deep belief network architecture and build a training algorithm (based on the annealing method) so that the following conditions are met:

1) training time should be acceptable (no more than a day);

2) the quality of training should be as high as possible, while the algorithm should require as little data as possible for training.

We now turn to a description of the structure and composition of software technology, designed in the form of a standard framework.

3   Framework Description

To solve this problem, software was developed in the form of a framework that includes all the necessary algorithms that implement the functioning of deep belief networks.

The framework control unit consists of three main modules (see Fig. 1): training, quality control and functioning.

The compressImages function makes color images compression. The decompressImages function - restoration of the original images from their compressed representation. And finally, the functions loadFromFileDeepNN, loadFromFileImages loads from the hard drive network and images respectively.

The buildDeepNN module builds a deep belief network with the following architecture (see Fig. 2).

Since the input data are usually images, the first layer of a deep belief network is formed as an ensemble of M_1 restricted Boltzmann machines of Gauss-Bernoulli type. This made it possible to "cover" the entire numerical range of

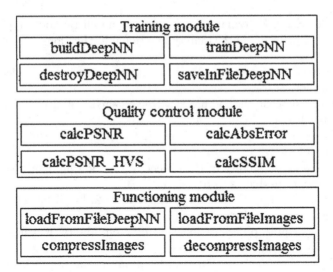

Fig. 1. Framework control unit.

input data. All machines forming one layer have the same architecture within the layer, so dimX must be a multiple of M_1. All subsequent ones are represented by ensembles of restricted Boltzmann machines of Bernoulli-Bernoulli type. Therefore, for each network layer, the following restriction must be satisfied. The product of the number of machines in the layer by the size of the input layer of each should be equal to the product of the number of machines in the previous layer and the size of the hidden layer of each. The output layer of the network is represented by an ensemble of M_s restricted Boltzmann machines of Bernoulli-Bernoulli type. To complete the data compression requirement, the total number of neurons in the hidden layers of machines must be strictly equal to dimY. The number of adjustable parameters in each of the machines must be strictly less than N. This is necessary to ensure the generalizing ability of the network.

The proposed architecture has several advantages:

1) decomposition of network layers ensures complete independence of the trained machines-components within the network layer, which allows to parallelize the training process;

2) the architecture can significantly reduce the number of configurable network parameters, which reduces the training dataset size and significantly reduces the computational complexity of the training process;

3) the architecture fully meets the constraints of the problem for an effective solution using heterogeneous computing devices [11, 12].

Function destroyDeepNN - removes a deep belief network. The saveIn-FileDeepNN function saves a deep belief network to the hard drive.

The quality control module calculates the numerical values of various quality functionals for given data and a deep belief network.

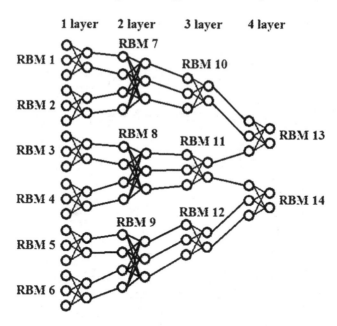

Fig. 2. Original deep belief network architecture.

The trainDeepNN module implements the main function of the framework. It provides training of received deep belief network. The internal composition of this block is presented in the form of the following scheme (see Fig. 3). At the beginning of the module execution, OpenCL is configured on computing devices. Then, a deep belief network training cycle by layers begins. When moving to the next layer, data is preliminarily converted to the architecture of the current layer. After this, cyclic training of the restricted Boltzmann machines that form the current layer is started. The cycle includes initialization of the initial state of the machines, data transfer to computing devices and a training cycle using the original annealing method algorithm.

The general scheme of the training algorithm includes two main stages.

At the preliminary stage, initialization (setting the initial values) of the parameters (W, VB, HB, σ), initial temperature T_0 is performed.

At the second main stage, the procedure for sequentially updating the values of the specified parameters using the specified quality functional is implemented.

Describe the process to update parameters in more detail. For simplicity, we consider it using the example of the set of parameters W. For other sets, this procedure is completely the same.

To the set of parameters W, we associate a segment L_w of length l. After that, each element of the set W is sequentially placed in the center of the given segment. To determine the direction of change of parameter values, we generate a random variable from 0 to 1. If it is more than 0.5, then the value of the parameter increases, otherwise it decreases.

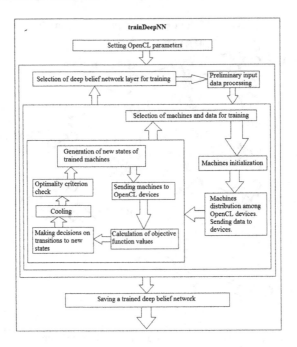

Fig. 3. Function trainDeepNN.

New parameter values are defined as follows. A random permutation is generated, the number of elements of which is equal to the number of elements of the set W. We order the elements of the set W in accordance with the permutation and change the values of the first W_p elements of the set. The new value of the parameter is determined as a result of the implementation of a uniformly distributed random variable on the segment, the ends of which are the current value of the parameter, and the end of the segment towards which the change is made.

Similarly, actions are sequentially performed for the sets VB, HB, σ.

For newly obtained parameter values, the quality functional is calculated. As the latter, it is proposed to use the following function:

$$F(W, VB, HB, \sigma) = \frac{1}{NR} \sum_{i=1,N} \sum_{j=1,R} |x_{ij} - f^{-1}(y_{ij})|, \tag{8}$$

where y_{ij} - reconstituted input signal of restricted Boltzmann machine, f^{-1} - inverse function of the preliminary transformation of input data.

Then a decision is made to move to a new state with probability:

$$P(y|x) = \min\{1, \exp(-(F(y) - F(x))/T_i)\}, \tag{9}$$

where x - current state, y - state selected for transition, F - minimized objective function, T_i - temperature of i-th iteration.

- in case of change of state cooling takes place by the rule:

$$T_{i+1} = T_0/\ln(k+1), \tag{10}$$

where k is the number of completed transitions to a new state.
- otherwise the temperature does not change.
After cooling, the received solution is checked for optimality:
- the solution is optimal if the time allocated for training has expired.
If the received solution is optimal then:
- algorithm stop,
- otherwise move to the next iteration.
We will check the effectiveness of using the proposed architecture using the example of solving the compressing color images problem.

4   Results and Discussion

As the input data, we used the STL-10 dataset from the Stanford University repository [3] and CIFAR-10 [1] from the University of Toronto repository.

The STL-10 dataset contains one hundred thousand unmarked color images measuring 96×96 pixels. Each image is described by 27648 integer numbers (in the range from 0 to 255) specifying the content of red, green and blue colors [4].

The CIFAR-10 dataset contains sixty thousand color images 32×32 in size and each image describes one of ten classes of objects: an airplane, a car, a bird, a cat, a deer, a dog, a frog, a horse, a ship, a truck. Each image is described in the same way as in STL-10, but adjusted for 32×32 resolution.

Based on the fact that the STL-10 dataset contains images of arbitrary objects, and the images from CIFAR-10 have a low resolution, we can conclude that the compressing images process of these datasets with low losses is a rather complicated computational problem.

For neural network data processing, a standard computer with an 4-core processor and a video card was used: video card: nvidia 1060 3 Gb; processor: intel i7 4770k 3.5 GHz; RAM: 2×8 Gb 1600 MHz; hard disk: samsung 850 pro 256 Gb; operating system: Lubuntu 16.04.

The compiler gcc was used as software (libraries OpenMP and CUDA version 9.1 [2]) with options:
"gcc superOpenCLFramework.cpp -lstdc++ -D_FORCE_INLINES -O2 -l OpenCL -lgomp -lm -fopenmp". Measurement of operations time was performed using function "gettimeofday".

In the experiments for the STL-10 dataset, the following deep belief network architecture was used.

The first layer consisted of a combination of 432 restricted Boltzmann machines of Gauss-Bernoulli type. The number of neurons in the input layer and hidden was 64 and 16, respectively, for all machines in the layer. The second layer consisted of a combination of 108 restricted Boltzmann machines of Bernoulli-Bernoulli type. The number of neurons in the input layer and hidden was 64 and 16, respectively, for all machines in the layer. The third layer consisted of a combination of 27 restricted Boltzmann machines of Bernoulli-Bernoulli type. The number of neurons in the input layer and hidden was 64 and 16, respectively, for all machines in the layer.

For the CIFAR-10 dataset, a similar architecture of a deep belief network was used. Due to the lower resolution of the images, the number of machines in each network layer was reduced by 9 times.

Images compression ratio was tuned by disabling the last layers of the deep belief network. So 3 layers of the network provided 512-fold compression, 2 layers - 128-fold, and the first layer of the network - 32-fold. For the training of the first layer of the network, 2000 images were used, for the second and third - 4000.

In experiments, an indicator of the number of bits for encoding one pixel of the image was used as the compression ratio. For encoding without compression of one pixel of a color image, 24 bits are required. Reducing the number of bits for encoding a pixel leads to image compression, for example, with 24-fold compression, the number of bits per image pixel will be equal to one.

As a quality functional, the most common PSNR [18] (peak signal-to-noise ratio) functionality was used to estimate image compression loss. It does not require fixing parameters and a large amount of computations.

This functionality calculates the ratio of the maximum possible signal to the mean square error for color raster images.

$$PSNR(X,Y) = 10\log_{10}\frac{3N * 255^2}{\sum_i (x_i - y_i)^2}, \qquad (11)$$

where X, Y - comparable images, N - the number of pixels in the image X.

The higher the value of the functional, the less compression loss and higher quality. For lossless compression, this quality function is equal to plus infinity. For a high compression ratio (approximately 0.05 bits per pixel or less), values in the range of 8 and higher are considered adequate. For medium compression (1 bit per pixel), normal values are considered to be from 20 and above.

Based on the results of the experiments, the following results were obtained (see Table 1, Table 2):

Table 1. Deep belief network training (STL-10)

Framework efficiency	Compress ratio (bit/pixel)		
	0,75	0,1875	0,046875
Quality function (PSNR)	19,183	17,391	14,875
Training time (h)	6	10	10,5

The results show the high efficiency of the deep belief neural network architecture and the training algorithm. To configure a separate machine consisting of 1168 parameters in the first layer of the network, only 2000 images were needed. While for machines of subsequent layers consisting of 1104 parameters, only

Table 2. Deep belief network training (CIFAR-10)

Framework efficiency	Compress ratio (bit/pixel)		
	0,75	*0,1875*	*0,046875*
Quality function (PSNR)	19,315	16,633	14,394
Training time (h)	6	10	10,5

4000 images were needed. This indicates a very high efficiency of the annealing method in training neural networks.

The time spent on training the network shows that, with the proper selection of parameters, the annealing method has a high convergence rate.

The results confirm the assumption that the annealing method can be used to train deep belief networks [17]. Given the complexity of the STL-10 dataset (in comparison with other results [19,21]), it can be argued that the presented algorithm that implements the annealing method is quite effective.

5   Conclusion

The report describes the structure and composition of a framework built on the basis of a deep belief network. An original network architecture and a set of algorithms implementing training processes and problem solving are proposed. The effectiveness of the framework is demonstrated by the example of the compressing color images problem. The problem was solved on a computer with a multi-core processor and video card.

It is shown that the developed learning algorithm for deep belief networks lacks many of the disadvantages of gradient methods. Based on the results of experiments, we can make an assumption that the developed framework, with the corresponding revision for a wider class of applied problems, has good prospects.

References

1. Cifar-10 dataset. https://www.cs.toronto.edu/~kriz/cifar.html. Accessed 4 Mar 2020
2. Cuda toolkit. http://www.developer.nvidia.com/cuda-downloads. Accessed 23 Feb 2018
3. Stl-10 dataset. http://www.academictorrents.com/details/a799a2845ac29a66c07c f74e2a2838b6c5698a6a. Accessed 25 Feb 2018
4. Stl-10 dataset description. http://www.stanford.edu/acoates//stl10/. Accessed 24 Feb 2018
5. Aicher, C., Foti, N.J., Fox, E.B.: Adaptively truncating backpropagation through time to control gradient bias. http://www.arxiv.org/abs/1905.07473
6. Brakel, P., Dieleman, S., Schrauwen, B.: Training restricted Boltzmann machines with multi-tempering: harnessing parallelization. In: Villa, A.E.P., Duch, W., Érdi, P., Masulli, F., Palm, G. (eds.) ICANN 2012. LNCS, vol. 7553, pp. 92–99. Springer, Heidelberg (2012). https://doi.org/10.1007/978-3-642-33266-1_12

7. Desjardins, G., Luo, H.G., Courville, A., Bengio, Y.: Deep tempering. https://arxiv.org/abs/1410.0123
8. Glorot, X., Bengio, Y.: Understanding the difficulty of training deep feedforward neural networks. In: Proceedings of the Thirteenth International Conference on Artificial Intelligence and Statistics, PMLR, vol. 9, pp. 249–256 (2010)
9. Golovko, V., Kroshenko, A.: Using deep belief neural networks to highlight semantically significant attributes. In: Proceedings of the 5-th International Conference - OSTIS 2015, pp. 481–486 (2015)
10. Hajek, B.: Cooling schedules for optimal annealing. Math. Oper. Res. **13**(2), 311–329 (1988)
11. Krasnoproshin, V., Matskevich, V.: Effective data processing on heterogeneous computing devices. Bull. Brest State Tech. Univ. Ser. Phys. Math Comput. Sci. 113(5), 15–18 (2018)
12. Krasnoproshin, V., Matskevich, V.: Algorithm for fast image compression on heterogeneous computing devices. In: Research Papers Collection Open Semantic Technologies for Intelligent Systems - OSTIS 2019, pp. 265–268 (2019)
13. Krasnoproshin, V., Matskevich, V.: Statistical approach to image compression based on a restricted Boltzmann machine. In: Proceedings of the 12-th International Conference Computer Data Analysis and Modeling- CDAM 2019, pp. 207–213 (2019)
14. Locatelli, M.: Convergence properties of simulated annealing for continuous global optimization. J. Appl. Probab. **33**(4), 1127–1140 (1996)
15. Matskevich, V., Krasnoproshin, V.: Annealing method in training restricted Boltzmann machine. In: Proceedings of the 14-th International Conference Pattern Recognition and Information Processing - PRIP 2019, pp. 264–268 (2019)
16. Rajasekaran, S.: On the convergence time of simulated annealing. http://www.repository.upenn.edu/cis_reports/356
17. Rere, L.R., Fanany, M.I., Arymurthy, A.M.: Simulated annealing algorithm for deep learning. Procedia Comput. Sci. **72**, 137–144 (2015)
18. Temel, D., AlRegib, G.: Perceptual image quality assessment through spectral analysis of error representations. Sign. Process. Image Commun. **70**, 37–46 (2019)
19. Toderici, G., et al.: Full resolution image compression with recurrent neural networks. http://www.arxiv.org/abs/1608.05148. Accessed 4 Jan 2020
20. Treadgold, N., Gedeon, T.: Simulated annealing and weight decay in adaptive learning: the SARPROP algorithm. IEEE Trans. Neural Netw. **9**(4), 662–668 (1998)
21. Zhou, X., Xu, L., Liu, S., Lin, Y., Zhang, L., Zhuo, C.: An efficient compressive convolutional network for unified object detection and image compression. In: Proceedings of the AAAI Conference on Artificial Intelligence, vol. 33, pp. 5949–5956 (2019)

Hybrid Intelligent Multi-agent System for Power Restoration

Sergey Listopad[(✉)] [iD]

Kaliningrad Branch of the Federal Research Center
"Computer Science and Control" of the Russian Academy of Sciences,
Kaliningrad 236022, Russian Federation
ser-list-post@yandex.ru

Abstract. The problem of restoration of the power grid after shut-downs requires extensive heterogeneous knowledge, has high combina-torial complexity, many limitations and conditions, including limita-tion on the decision-making time. Under such conditions, traditional abstract-mathematical methods are irrelevant to the complexity of the control object, and solving the problem by expert team is irrelevant to its dynamism. In this regard, hybrid intelligent multi-agent system that model collective heterogeneous thinking processes during the decision-making under the guidance of a facilitator are proposed to solve prob-lems in dynamic environments, in particular distribution grid restoration-planning problem. The paper discusses the model, the functional struc-ture, and the collective heterogeneous thinking protocol of such systems.

Keywords: Heterogeneous thinking · Hybrid intelligent multi-agent system · Agent interaction protocol · Distribution power grid restoration

1 Introduction

In the case of an accident in the distribution power grid, despite the size and complexity of the event, a methodical, balanced decision is necessary in the conditions of time pressure. It is important for network operators to quickly rec-ognize the magnitude, significance of the event and restore energy supply. Then, a wider range of experts is involved, who evaluate the operation of the distribu-tion grid, identify the root causes, draw lessons and develop recommendations for the operational and dispatching personnel to eliminate future emergencies [42]. The disadvantage of this approach is that the state of the power grid at the time of the accident can seriously differ from the one assumed while developing the recommendations. As a result, the operating and dispatching personnel have to rely only on their knowledge and experience, which can lead to ineffective solutions, violation of the grid operating conditions, and triggering of protection

The reported study was funded by RFBR according to the research project No. 18-07-00448A.

V. Golenkov et al. (Eds.): OSTIS 2020, CCIS 1282, pp. 245–260, 2020.
https://doi.org/10.1007/978-3-030-60447-9_16

systems [2]. Thus, it is important to develop intelligent automated systems that can simulate the work of expert team with members, having diverse knowledge and experience, considering the problem from different points of view, taking into account various restrictions. In this paper, the hybrid intelligent multi-agent systems of heterogeneous thinking (HIMSHT) are proposed for this purpose [23]. They combine the methods of the hybrid intelligent systems (HIS) [14], multi-agent systems [39], and heterogeneous thinking [6,7,13].

2 The Problem of the Power Grid Restoration After Large-Scale Accidents

Planning of the power grid restoration (PPGR) is a problem with high computational complexity, many restrictions and conditions, which have to be evaluated by the operator of the grid [42]. It is especially exciting because of its insufficient observability, high dimension of the state space, making impossible complete enumeration of the control object's states, and the interdependence of the recovery actions that are difficult to model [41].

There are different formulations of PPGR, as well as algorithms of its solution, for example, based on integer programming [1], knowledge bases [4,24,30], binary search tree [27], analytic hierarchical process [3], heuristic algorithms [37], fuzzy logic [21], neural networks [20], genetic algorithms [5,8,11,36], simulated annealing [36], multi-agent approach [28], tabu search [40,42], combined tabu search and node depth coding [26].

Most of these papers address the problem in a simplified, "game" form. In such "game" problem of power grid restoration (GPPGR), the initial data is the graph, nodes of which represent power centers, consumers, and buses [18]. The edges of this graph denote power transition lines with switches, turning it on or off. Cycles of energized lines are prohibited. The power center has the only property that is the nominal generated power. The consumer has two characteristics: the nominal power consumption and the state (powered/disconnected). The power line is described by the following properties: carrying capacity, the state (switched on/off) and operability (good/accident). The problem is to develop a sequence of the switching events to maximize the power consumption. The following restrictions must not be violated: absence of cycles of energized lines; limitation on the total power transmitted through a power line; initially powered consumers should not be disconnected because of switching.

In such formulation, PPGR can only be considered as a "testing ground" for optimization methods. Due to the small number of types of objects and their properties considered during planning, as well as the lack of non-factors [29], which are typical for practical situation of the power grid restoration, methods designed to solve GPPGR are irrelevant to the practical planning of power grid restoration. In this regard, problem formulations appear that expand the number of simulated non-factors and types of objects.

In paper [19], the method based on the genetic algorithm for PPGR after a long shutdown (a minute or more), i.e. in cold start state, was proposed. In this case, when power is restored, transients occur and additional power is consumed, which limits the simultaneous recovery of all network loads due to excessive load on the power grid elements and violation of restrictions. In [12], an approach based on fuzzy reasoning was proposed in accordance with the experience and heuristic rules of operators expressed in linguistic terms. In [10], an agent-based greedy routing algorithm is proposed, based on the power grid usage heuristic, taking into account not only the technical parameters of the grid, but also the issues of delivery of materials and specialists for recovery. The methodology for restoring power supply, taking into account the irregular and stochastic nature of the operation of distributed generation sources, which can lead to an increase in failure rates and a deterioration in network protection, is presented in [45]. In [41], PPGR is considered, which assumes that information from fault detectors only is not enough to identify faulty lines, because they can send false signals. The authors of [44] note, that when planning the restoration of power supply, the use of the nominal load value to obtain knowledge of the current or load power is not relevant to the practical situation, since the actual load usually varies with time and can significantly differ from the nominal value.

Based on the analysis of the above papers, the practical problem of the power grid restoration (PPPGR) is designed [23]. It is in the building of the switching sequence and the sequence of the mobile crews' trips to make switching and rehabilitation of the power grid's elements. Baseline data for PPPGR are elements of the power grid and following sets:

- incidence relations between elements of the power grid;
- locations;
- routes between locations;
- repair crews;
- vehicles;
- resources for restoration of the power grid;
- actions for restoration of the power grid.

The optimality criteria of the PPPGR are following:

- minimizing the time of disconnection of the priority load;
- maximizing the recovered power;
- maximizing the reliability of the grid (resistance to shutdowns).

The PPPGR has following restrictions:

- absence of cycles of energized lines;
- the total power transmitted through a power line is limited by its carrying capacity;
- compliance of the active and reactive power balances;
- limits of frequency and voltage in the power grid;
- initially powered consumers should not be disconnected after executing the recovery plan;

- restoration and switching must be carried out by repair crews with appropriate admission;
- mobile crew needs to have necessary resources in its vehicle to begin restoration;
- capacity of the vehicles could not be exceeded;
- working time of crews;
- mobile crews have to return base;
- if, in order to restore the power grid, it is necessary to divide it into "islands" temporarily, the power lines, connecting them, must have equipment for their subsequent synchronization and merging.

The modelling complexity, i.e. the complexity of constructing a method, of the above problems was analyzed using the measure proposed in [15]. It reduces the diversity and heterogeneity of the problem, i.e. fundamental reasons of the modeling complexity of the problem solving process, to the diversity and heterogeneity of two fundamental concepts: variable and relationship. To assess the problem in accordance with this measure, it is necessary to build problem's conceptual model [14], in which each variable and relation refers to a particular class from the limited set of classes. The following classes of variables are distinguished: deterministic, stochastic, logical (propositional), linguistic, symbolic, and unknown to science. The class of a relationship is determined by the classes of variables that it binds, for example, "deterministic variable - linguistic variable" class of the relationship. If relations bind variables of the same class, they are called homogeneous, otherwise they are heterogeneous. Thus, the complexity measure is the tuple, consisting of two components: the number of classes of variables in the problem model, and the number of classes of heterogeneous relations between them.

Conceptual models of the following problems were built: GPPGR [23], PPGR in cold start state (PPGRCSS) [19], PPGR with operator's fuzzy rules (PPGROFR) [12], PPGR with delivery of materials and specialists (PPGRDMS) [10], PPGR with stochastic power generation and supply (PPGRSPGS) [45], PPGR with defective fault detectors (PPGRDFD) [41], PPGR with actual load (PPGRAL) [44], PPPGR [23]. The results of the assessment of problems of power grid restoration in accordance with the measure of modeling complexity [15], taking into account the non-factors [29] of practical problems, and also their classification on the "simple – complex" scale [15] are summarized in Table 1.

As can be seen from Table 1, the most simple in modeling are GPPGR, PPGRCSS. To solve them, it is sufficient to use the methods developed within the framework of one intelligent technology [15]. PPGROFR, PPGRDMS, PPGRSPGS, PPGRDFD, and PPGRAL are more complex and require hybrid methods to solve them. As practice has shown, di- and trihybrids successfully cope with such problems. PPPGR has the highest complexity of constructing method among all the problems considered. For such problems, it is already difficult to build hybrid intelligent solution method with fixed connections between its elements. In this regard, the HIMSHT are relevant to the PPPGR, because it is able to synthesize dynamically an intelligent method for solving problems during the interaction of autonomous intelligent agents.

Table 1. Comparative analysis of the modeling complexity of the problems of the power grid restoration

Problem	Non-factors	Modeling complexity score	Class of the problem
GPPGR	Absent	(1,0)	Simple
PPGRCSS	Absent	(1,0)	Simple
PPGROFR	Fuzziness	(2,1)	Complex
PPGRDMS	Absent	(2,1)	Complex
PPGRSPGS	Uncertainty	(2,1)	Complex
PPGRDFD	Uncertainty	(2,1)	Complex
PPGRAL	Uncertainty	(2,1)	Complex
PPPGR	Uncertainty, fuzziness	(5,8)	Complex

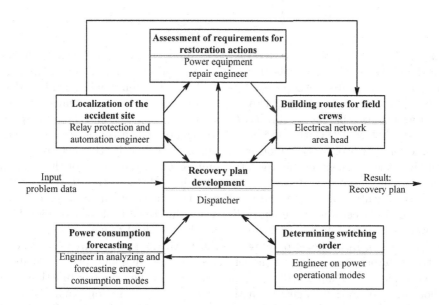

Fig. 1. Decomposition of the practical problem of the power grid restoration.

The PPPGR was reduced into the decomposition of several tasks to develop the HIMSHT in accordance with the approach proposed in [14]: localization of the accident site, which takes into account the possibility of erroneous data from sensors; operational and short-term forecasting of active and reactive power consumed by customers after connecting to the grid; assessment of requirements for restoration actions of the power grid elements; building routes for field crews to perform switching and restoration; determining the switching order; recovery plan development ensuring the coordination and integration of solutions to other tasks [22]. Figure 1 shows the relationships between the tasks from the PPPGR decomposition, as well as the correspondence between the task and the specialty of the expert, whose knowledge is required to solve it. Thus, in order to model the work of expert team on solving of the PPPGR, the HIMSHT should include agents with the knowledge and experience of experts in the corresponding specialties.

3   The Model of the Hybrid Intelligent Multi-agent System of Heterogeneous Thinking

The model of the HIMSHT is defined by the following expressions [18]:

$$himsht = <AG^*, env, INT^*, ORG, \{ht\}>,\qquad(1)$$

$$act_{himsht} = \left(\bigcup_{ag \in AG^*} act_{ag} \right) \cup act_{dmsa} \cup act_{htmc} \cup act_{col},\qquad(2)$$

$$act_{ag} = (MET_{ag}, IT_{ag}), \left| \bigcup_{ag \in AG^*} IT_{ag} \right| \geqslant 2,\qquad(3)$$

where $AG^* = AG^{ex} \cup AG^{it} \cup AG^{sc} \cup \{ag^{dm}, ag^{fc}\}$ is the set of agents, including the subset of expert agents (EA) AG^{ex}, the subset of intelligent technology agents AG^{it}, the subset of service agents AG^{sc}, the decision-making agent (DMA) ag^{dm}, and the facilitator agent (FA) ag^{fc}; env represents the system's environment as a conceptual model [14]; $INT^* = \{prot_{ht}, lang, ont, dmscl\}$ is the set of elements that structure the interactions of agents, which consists of the agent interaction protocol $prot_{ht}$, allowing to organize their collective heterogeneous thinking, the language of messages transmitted $lang$, the model of the domain ont, and the classifier of situations arising during solving of the PPPGR by the HIMSHT agents $dmscl$, intended to identify the stages of this process; ORG is the set of architectures of the HIMSHT, describing the established relationships between the agents during problem solving; $\{ht\}$ is used to specify the conceptual models of macro-level processes in the HIMSHT such as ht, which is collective heterogeneous thinking model based on the "diamond of participatory decision-making" (Fig. 2) [13]; act_{himsht} represents the system's function as a whole; act_{ag} denotes the agent's function; act_{dmsa} is the function "analysis of the collective problem solving situation" of the FA, which provides identification of the heterogeneous thinking process stage based on the private solutions offered by the EA, the conflict intensity between them and the previous stage; act_{htmc} is the function "choice of heterogeneous thinking method" of the FA that uses the FA's fuzzy knowledge base about the relevance of methods to the problem, the stage, and the situation in the system; $act_{col} = <met_{ma}, it_{ma}>$ is the collective dynamically constructed function of the HIMSHT with the multi-agent method met_{ma} and the intelligent technology it_{ma}; $met_{ag} \in MET_{ag}$ is the problem solving method; $it_{ag} \in IT_{ag}$ denotes the intelligent technology, implementing the method met_{ag}.

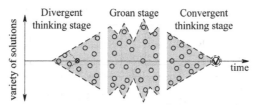

Denotations: o - alternative; ⊗ - early uncoordinated solution; ⊘ - negotiated solution

Fig. 2. The "diamond of participatory decision-making" model by S. Kaner et al.

According to the "diamond of participatory decision-making" model, there could be distinguished three stages in the process of problem solving: divergent thinking, groan and convergent thinking. During the divergent thinking stage, EAs generate as much as possible alternative solutions to the PPPGR, and the FA forces this process with various methods, for example brainstorming with leading questions, brain-writing pool, challenging restrictions and lateral thinking [16]. If the PPPGR has obvious solution and contradictions between EAs do not arise or they are insignificant, the process is completed. Otherwise, the HIMSHT goes to the groan stage of the problem solving process, because many cognitive conflicts [16,38] between the agents arise over knowledge, beliefs, and opinions. Thus the high intensity of the conflicts in the HIMSHT is intrinsic to the groan stage, at which the FA is responsible for bringing together agents' opinions using such methods as looking from other's point of view, returning from decisions to needs and parallel thinking [16]. During the convergent thinking stage, the EAs have to refine the solutions proposed at the previous stages until they receive agreed one using such methods of collective convergent thinking as consensus, voting and choice by DMA after discussion with EAs [16].

4   The Functional Structure of the System

In accordance with the proposed formalized model of the HIMSHT, its functional structure, presented in Fig. 3, was developed to solve the PPPGR [17]. As shown in Fig. 3, it inherits the decomposition of the PPPGR. In particular, its problem solving subsystem contains EAs (the equipment repair agent, the agent of grid area, the agent of consumption prediction, the agent of operational modes, the relay protection agent, and the agent-dispatcher) that model knowledge and experience of the specialists to generate solutions to corresponding tasks (Fig. 1) of the PPPGR. In addition, the proposed functional structure of the HIMSHT contains a sufficient number of various intelligent technologies for constructing a hybrid method that provides a solution to the problem with modeling complexity of PPPGR. The hybrid component of the HIMSHT is represented by five agents of intelligent technology, presented at the top of Fig. 3, and the agent-converter. Various intelligent methods realized by these agents are used by agents of the problem solving subsystem to dynamically build integrated method relevant to the modelling complexity of the PPPGR. The agent-converter contains methods for transforming variables of one class of intelligent technologies into

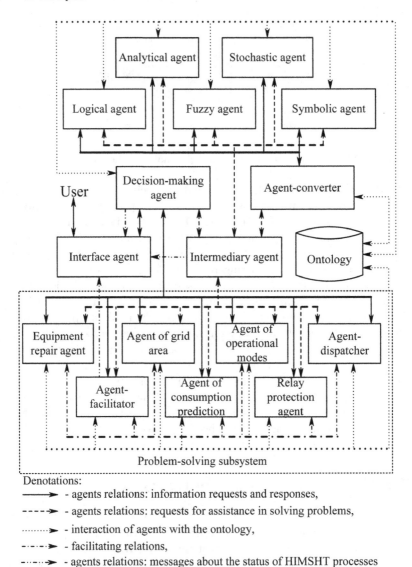

Denotations:

⟶ - agents relations: information requests and responses,

----▶ - agents relations: requests for assistance in solving problems,

·········▶ - interaction of agents with the ontology,

-·--·▶ - facilitating relations,

-··-··▶ - agents relations: messages about the status of HIMSHT processes
for their visualization by the interface agent

Fig. 3. The functional structure of the system.

another within the framework of a hybrid intelligent method developed by agents dynamically during the operation of the HIMSHT.

Other agents presented in Fig. 3 are typical for hybrid intelligent multi-agent systems (HIMAS), so consider them briefly [15]. To provide the interaction of the user and the HIMSHT the interface agent is used. It requests PPPGR's conditions, displays the solutions, and visualizes processes in the system, including collective heterogeneous thinking. The DMA sends tasks to the EAs, gathers the problem solutions, chooses the final agreed problem solution, according to the heterogeneous thinking method assigned by the FA, and sends it to the interface agent. The intermediary agent maintains the database of the agents registered in the HIMSHT, which contains their names, models, addresses and capabilities. The ontology is the semantic network based on the PPPGR model common for all agents, used as the basis for interaction of agents and understanding the messages' semantics by them. It describes distribution grid resources (consumers, buses, switches, power lines, repair crews, vehicles and others), their properties and methods for working with them, types of transmitted messages, HIMSHT's architecture models etc.

Interaction of agents in the HIMSHT is described by protocols [32]. Agent relations, such as the information requests and responses, as well as requests for assistance in solving problems (Fig. 3), are described by the standard protocol of speech acts [43]. The interaction of agents with the ontology is provided by the software platform, implementing the HIMSHT, by processing requests for creating the objects represented in it and executing the methods defined in these objects. Facilitation relationships are described by the heterogeneous thinking protocol described in the following section.

5   Collective Heterogeneous Thinking Protocol

The main purpose of the development of the agent interaction protocol of the HIMSHT is to encapsulate allowed interactions. It defines the schemes (distributed algorithm) of information and knowledge exchange, coordination of agents during problem solving [9]. On the one hand, the protocol serves to combine agents through the conceptual interface and organize their joint work, on the other hand, it defines clear boundaries of system components [32]. When describing the protocol, the following should be specified: agent roles; message types between role pairs; the semantics of each message type declaratively; any additional restrictions on messages, such as the order in which they follow or the rules for transferring information from one message to another. Such protocol specification unambiguously determines whether a specific implementation of agent interaction satisfies the specified protocol and whether specific agent is compatible with the HIMSHT [32].

To date, a lot of protocols have been developed for multi-agent systems both for general purposes and for solving specific problems. The most well-known classes of protocols are [9,33]:

- based on the contract network [34,35]. They are intended for automatic planning of agent interactions and minimization of costs by means of the metaphor of negotiating agents at market auctions;
- based on the theory of speech acts [43]. In this type of protocols, negotiations are built using a small number of primitives, through exchange of which agents discuss a certain topic, update their knowledge bases, exchange "opinions" and come to a common solution [9];

- negotiation [25, 46], which offer conflict resolution mechanisms to increase the total utility achieved by agents;
- based on a bulletin board, when a common memory area is allocated for agent interaction.

The proposed protocol for organizing the collective heterogeneous thinking of agents is designed to simulate the work of a small team of experts at the round table, where there is no need to bring down the price of services or select experts, therefore it is based on the theory of speech acts. It has several additional types of messages, which are used for interaction of the FA, the DMA and the EAs: "request-ch-tt", "commit-ch-tt", "request-start-ps", "request-stop-ps", "request-task", "report-decision". The interaction between other agents is based on the speech act protocol [43]. The scheme of the agent's interaction by the collective heterogeneous thinking protocol is presented in Fig. 4 [23].

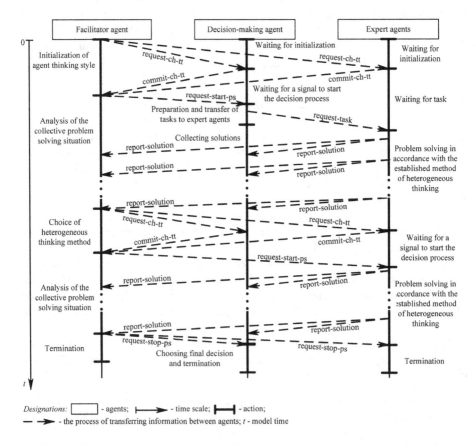

Fig. 4. The schematic view of the collective heterogeneous thinking protocol.

As shown in Fig. 4, at the beginning of the system's operation the FA sends "request-ch-tt" messages, which contain the name and characteristics of the heterogeneous thinking method, to the DMA and all EAs, setting up the initial method of heterogeneous thinking. After that, the FA awaits for messages from the DMA and EAs, confirming their initialization. When an agent (the DMA or any of EAs) receives the initialization message from the FA, it selects the assigned thinking method, sends to the FA message of the "commit-ch-tt" type to confirm the readiness for solving the PPPGR according to the assigned algorithm, and suspends its work, awaiting for the signal from the FA. When the FA received confirmation-commit messages from the DMA and all EAs, it generates the message of the "request-start-ps" type and transmits it to the DMA, indicating that the most relevant to the current situation method of the collective thinking is set in the HIMSHT, and waits for messages containing problem solutions generated by EAs.

The DMA, having received the FA's message of the "request-start-ps" type, initiates the problem solving process by generating for each EA the task as well as the initial data for its solution and sending them within the body of the "request-task" message. After that, the DMA waits for messages of the "report-solution" type, containing solutions generated by EAs, and processes them using the algorithm of the collective heterogeneous thinking assigned by the FA at the current stage of the problem solving process. EA, having received message of the "request-start-ps" type from the DMA, solves its task using the heterogeneous thinking algorithm assigned to it by the FA. Each EA develops one or more task's solutions, forwarding the to the DMA and the FA simultaneously with the "report-solution" type message.

The FA, having received the "report-solution" message from EA, analyses the situation in the HIMSHT with its function act_{dmsa} (2) determining the value of the conflict intensity pairwise between EAs and overall in the system [18]. After that, the FA launches fuzzy inference with its function act_{htmc} (2), leaving the current or choosing another collective thinking method relevant to the problem solving situation. If the FA decides to change the collective heterogeneous thinking method to more relevant one, it generates messages of the type "request-ch-tt", containing the name as well as characteristics of this method, and forwards them to the DMA and all EAs. After that, the FA awaits messages of type "commit-ch-tt" from them, confirming the readiness for solving the PPPGR, according to the new method of heterogeneous thinking. When all confirmations are received, FA forwards to all EAs messages of the "request-start-ps" type. This mechanism is necessary to synchronize EAs and prevent the situation, when they solve problem with different thinking methods. Then the FA waits for "report-solution" messages from EAs, provides the analysis of the problem solving situation in HIMSHT, and ensures that the system uses the most relevant method of the collective heterogeneous thinking, while the stopping criterion of the convergent thinking stage (Fig. 2) is reached, which means the end of the problem solving process. When it happens, the FA sends the "request-stop-ps" signal to the DMA as well as all EAs and terminates. After receiving this message from the FA, the EA shuts down. The DMA, having receive the "request-stop-ps" signal from the FA, starts the procedure of the final solution producing using the established heterogeneous thinking method. Depending on the algorithm, the final solution could be the consensus alternative or the alternative chosen by the most EAs. The DMA sends this solution using speech act protocol to the interface agent and shuts down.

6   Estimation of the Expected Performance of the System

For evaluation of performance of the HIMSHT, its implementation have to be accomplished and computational experiments for solving various restoration problems of power grids have to be conducted. At present, only an estimate of the expected efficiency of the system based on the comparison of its characteristics with systems having similar architecture and principles of operation is possible. For comparison, two intelligent systems developed by various teams of Kaliningrad school of artificial intelligence led by A.V. Kolesnikov was chosen: HIS "AGRO" [14], which is designed for planning of agricultural activities; HIMAS "TRANSMAR" [15], for solving practical problems of delivery goods. "AGRO" provided a four-fold acceleration of the process of building a plan of agricultural activities with an increase in its quality by 7–14%. "TRANSMAR" allowed to speed up the planning of delivery routes by an average of 23% compared to the methods used at the time of creation of the system, increasing the quality of routes by an average of 7%.

Table 2. Comparative analysis of the features of intelligent systems for solving heterogeneous problems

Features	AGRO	TRANSMAR	HIMSHT
Handling problem heterogeneity	+	+	+
Handling tool heterogeneity	+	+	+
Modelling expert reasoning	+	−	+
Autonomy of elements/agents	−	+	+
Ontology-based reasoning	−	+	+
Modelling collective heterogeneous thinking	−	−	+
Self-organization type	−	Weak	Strong

Designations: + - feature present; − no feature

As the comparative analysis of systems shows (Table 2) [22], HIMSHT, by analogy with AGRO, ensures that the functional heterogeneity of the problem is taken into account by modeling the knowledge and experience of experts in various specialties. Implementation of computer models of experts as autonomous agents, by analogy with TRANSMAR, makes it possible to simulate collective processes that provide a synergistic effect, when the result of the system's work is better than those of its agents working separately. The use of ontology as a basis for the reasoning of EAs makes it possible to reconfigure HIMSHT, when the problem model changes and there is need to take into account new objects, dependencies or constraints. The use of methods of collective heterogeneous thinking provides a variety of generated solutions of the problem, their finalization, coordination and selection in the same way as it happens in the most effective expert teams. In total, taking into account functional and tool heterogeneity, applying the multi-agent approach, ontology-based reasoning, and modeling collective heterogeneous thinking create prerequisites for the emergence of self-organization in a strong sense [31] in HIMSHT. The concept of strong self-organization implies that a hybrid intelligent method for solving posed problem is developed during agent interactions without strict control of this process by one of them, for example, by specifying relations between agents or their goal functions. Such self-organization is characteristic of expert teams, solving problems at "round table", mediated by a facilitator. Thus, HIMSHT is more relevant to real expert teams and has significant advantages over AGRO and TRMS-MAR, so it could be expected that after software implementation, the system performance will be no worse than that of the compared systems.

7   Conclusion

The features of restoration of power supply in the power grid after shutdowns are considered, a comparative analysis of the problem statements by their modeling complexity is performed. The necessity of constructing hybrid methods is shown and the HIMSHT is proposed for solving the problem in practice. A formalized description of HIMSHT, its main components, as well as its functional structure is presented. The protocol of the organization of collective heterogeneous thinking of agents based on the theory of speech acts is described. Its use in hybrid intelligent multi-agent systems, containing heterogeneous intelligent self-organizing agents, makes it possible to reliably model effective practices for collective problem solving. The use of HIMSHT will allow the operational and dispatching personnel of power supply organizations to make relevant decisions to restore the power grid in a time-constrained environment.

References

1. Aoki, K., Nara, K., Itoh, M., Satoh, T., Kuwabara, H.: A new algorithm for service restoration in distribution systems. IEEE Trans. Power Delivery 4(3), 1832–1839 (1989)
2. Barabashi, A.L., Bonabo, E.: Bezmasshtabnyye seti [Non-scale networks]. V mire nauki [In the world of science] 8, 54–63 (2003). (in Russian)
3. Bernardon, D., Sperandio, M., Garcia, V., Pfitscher, L., Reck, W.: Automatic restoration of power supply in distribution systems by computer-aided technologies. In: Kongoli, F. (ed.) Automation. InTech, Rijeka (2012)
4. Chen, C.S., Lin, C.H., Tsai, H.Y.: A rule-based expert system with colored Petri net models for distribution system service restoration. IEEE Trans. Power Syst. 17(4), 1073–1080 (2002)

5. Dahalan, W.M., Zarina, M.K.P., Othman, A.G., Salih, N.M.: Service restoration based on simultaneous network reconfiguration and distributed generation sizing for loss minimization using a modified genetic algorithm. Adv. Struct. Mater. **85**, 239–258 (2018)

6. De Bono, E.: Parallel Thinking: From Socratic to De Bono Thinking. Penguin-Books, Melbourne (1994)

7. Gardner, H.: Multiple Intelligences - The Theory in Practice. Basic Books, New York (1993)

8. Gois, M.M., Sanches, D.S., Martins, J., Junior, J.B.A.L., Delbem, A.C.B.: Multi-objective evolutionary algorithm with node-depth encoding and strength pareto for service restoration in large-scale distribution systems. In: Purshouse, R.C., Fleming, P.J., Fonseca, C.M., Greco, S., Shaw, J. (eds.) EMO 2013. LNCS, vol. 7811, pp. 771–786. Springer, Heidelberg (2013). https://doi.org/10.1007/978-3-642-37140-0_57

9. Gorodetskiy, V.I., Grushinskiy, M.S., Khabalov, A.V.: Mnogoagentnyye sistemy (obzor) [Multiagent systems (review)]. Novosti iskusstvennogo intellekta [Artif. Intell. News] **2**, 64–116 (1998). (in Russian)

10. Van Hentenryck, P., Coffrin, C.: Transmission system repair and restoration. Math. Program. **151**(1), 347–373 (2015). https://doi.org/10.1007/s10107-015-0887-0

11. Hsiao, Y.T., Chien, C.Y.: Enhancement of restoration service in distribution systems using a combination fuzzy-GA method. IEEE Trans. Power Syst. **15**(4), 1394–1400 (2000)

12. Hsu, Y.Y., Kuo, H.C.: A heuristic based fuzzy reasoning approach for distribution system service restoration. IEEE Trans. Power Delivery **9**(2), 948–953 (1994)

13. Kaner, S., Lind, L., Toldi, C., Fisk, S., Beger, D.: The Facilitator's Guideto Participatory Decision-Making. Jossey-Bass, San Francisco (2011)

14. Kolesnikov, A.V.: Gibridnye intellektual'nye sistemy. Teoriya i tekhnologiya razrabotki [Hybrid intelligent systems: theory and technology of development]. SPbGTU, Saint Petersburg (2001). (in Russian)

15. Kolesnikov, A.V., Kirikov, I.A., Listopad, S.V., Rumovskaya, S.B., Domanitskiy,A.A.: Reshenie slozhnykh zadach kommivoyazhera metodami funktsional'nykhgibridnykh intellektual'nykh system [Complex travelling salesman problems solving by the methods of the functional hybrid intelligent systems]. IPIRAN, Moscow (2011). (in Russian)

16. Kolesnikov, A.V., Listopad, S.V.: Model' gibridnoy intellektual'noy mnogoagentnoy sistemy geterogennogo myshleniya dlya informatsionnoy podgotovki operativnykh resheniy v regional'nykh elektricheskikh setyakh [Model of hybrid intelligent multi-agent system of heterogeneous thinking for the information preparation of operational decisions in regional power system]. Sistemy i sredstva informatiki [Syst. Means Inform.] **28**(4), 31–41 (2018). (in Russian)

17. Kolesnikov, A.V., Listopad, S.V.: Funktsional'naya struktura gibridnoy intellektual'noy mnogoagentnoy sistemy geterogennogo myshleniya dlya resheniya problemy vosstanovleniya raspredelitel'noy elektroseti [Functional structure of the hybrid intelligent multiagent system of heterogeneous thinking for solving the problem of restoring the distribution power grid]. Sistemy i sredstva informatiki [Syst. Means Inform.] **29**(1), 41–52 (2019). (in Russian)

18. Kolesnikov, A.V., Listopad, S.V.: Hybrid intelligent multiagent system of heterogeneous thinking for solving the problem of restoring the distribution power grid after failures. In: Open Semantic Technologies for Intelligent Systems (OSTIS-2019): Research Papers Collection, pp. 133–138. BGUIR, Minsk (2019)

19. Kumar, V., Kumar, H.C.R., Gupta, I., Gupta, H.O.: DG integrated approach for service restoration under cold load pickup. IEEE Trans. Power Delivery **25**(1), 398–406 (2010)

20. Kyzrodev, I.V., Uspensky, M.I.: Avtomatizatsiya vosstanovleniya elektrosnabzheniya v raspredelitel'nykh setyakh [Automating the restoration of power supply in distribution networks]. Izvestiya Komi nauchnogo tsentra UrO RAN [Izvestiya Komi Scientific Center, Ural Branch of the Russian Academy of Sciences] **2**, 84–91 (2010). (in Russian)

21. Lim, S.I., Lee, S.J., Choi, M.S., Lim, D.J., Ha, B.N.: Service restoration methodology for multiple fault case in distribution systems. IEEE Trans. Power Syst. **21**(4), 1638–1643 (2006)

22. Listopad, S.: Distribution grid restoration planning using methods of hybrid intelligent multi-agent systems of heterogeneous thinking. In: 2019 1st International Conference on Control Systems, Mathematical Modelling, Automation and Energy Efficiency (SUMMA), pp. 159–165. IEEE (2019)

23. Listopad, S.V.: Agent interaction protocol of hybrid intelligent multi-agent system of heterogeneous thinking. In: Open Semantic Technologies for Intelligent Systems (OSTIS-2020): Research Papers Collection, pp. 51–56. BGUIR, Minsk (2020)

24. Liu, C.C., Lee, S.J., Venkata, S.S.: An expert system operational aid for restoration and loss reduction of distribution systems. IEEE Trans. Power Syst. **3**(2), 619–626 (1988)

25. Marzougui, B., Barkaoui, K.: Interaction protocols in multi-agent systems based on agent Petri nets model. Int. J. Adv. Comput. Sci. Appl. **4**(7), 166–173 (2013)

26. Mathias-Neto, W.P., Mantovani, J.R.S.: A node-depth encoding-based tabu search algorithm for power distribution system restoration. J. Control Autom. Electr. Syst. **27**, 317–327 (2016). https://doi.org/10.1007/s40313-016-0234-6

27. Morelato, A.L., Monticelli, A.J.: Heuristic search approach to distribution system restoration. IEEE Trans. Power Delivery **4**(4), 2235–2241 (1989)

28. Nagata, T., Sasaki, H.: A multi-agent approach to power system restoration. IEEE Trans. Power Systems **17**(2), 457–462 (2002)

29. Narinyani, A.S.: Inzheneriya znaniy i ne-faktory: kratkiy obzor-08 [Knowledge engineering and non-factors: a brief overview-08]. Voprosy iskusstvennogo intellekta [Artif. Intell. Issues] **1**, 61–77 (2008). (in Russian)

30. Sakaguchi, T., Matsumoto, K.: Development of a knowledge based system for power system restoration. IEEE Trans. Power Apparatus Syst. **102**, 320–329 (1983)

31. Serugendo, G.D.M., Gleizes, M.P., Karageorgos, A.: Self-organization in multiagent systems. Knowl. Eng. Rev. **20**(2), 165–189 (2005)

32. Singh, M.P., Chopra, A.K.: Programming multiagent systems without programming agents. In: Braubach, L., Briot, J.-P., Thangarajah, J. (eds.) ProMAS 2009. LNCS (LNAI), vol. 5919, pp. 1–14. Springer, Heidelberg (2010). https://doi.org/10.1007/978-3-642-14843-9_1

33. Singh, R., Singh, A., Mukherjee, S.: A critical investigation of agent interaction protocols in multiagent systems. Int. J. Adv. Technol. **5**(2), 72–81 (2014)

34. Smith, G.: The contract net protocol: high level communication and control in a distributed problem solve. IEEE Trans. Comput. **29**(12), 1104–1113 (1980)

35. Smith, R.G.: A Framework for Distributed Problem Solving. UMI Research Press, Ann Arbor (1981)

36. Susheela Devi, V., Narasimha Murty, M.: Stochastic search techniques for postfault restoration of electrical distribution systems. Sadhana **25**(1), 45–56 (2000). https://doi.org/10.1007/BF02703806

37. Susheela Devi, V., Sen Gupta, D.P., Anandalingam, G.: Optimal restoration of power supply in large distribution systems in developing countries. IEEE Trans. Power Delivery **10**(1), 430–438 (1995)

38. Tang, A.Y.C., Basheer, G.S.: A conflict resolution strategy selection method (ConfRSSM) in multi-agent systems. Int. J. Adv. Comput. Sci. Appl. **8**(5), 398–404 (2017)

39. Tarasov, V.B.: Ot mnogoagentnykh sistem k intellektualnym organizatsiyam:filosofiya, psikhologiya, informatika [From multiagent systems to intelligentorganizations: philosophy, psychology, and informatics]. Editorial URSS, Moscow (2002). (in Russian)

40. Thakur, T., Jaswanti, J.: Tabu search based algorithm for multi-objective network reconfiguration problem. Energy Sci. Technol. **1**(2), 1–10 (2011)

41. Thiebaux, S., Cordier, M.O.: Supply restoration in power distribution systems - a benchmark for planning under uncertainty. In: Proceedings of the 6th European Conference on Planning (ECP-01), pp. 85–96. AAAI Press, Palo Alto (2001)

42. Uspenskiy, M.I., Kyzrodev, I.V.: Metody vosstanovleniya elektrosnabzheniya vraspredelitel'nykh setyakh [Methods for restoring electrical supply indistribution networks]. Komi Scientific Center Ural Branch of RAS, Syktyvkar(2010). (in Russian)

43. Weerasooriya, D., Rao, A., Ramamohanarao, K.: Design of a concurrent agent-oriented language. In: Wooldridge, M.J., Jennings, N.R. (eds.) ATAL 1994. LNCS, vol. 890, pp. 386–401. Springer, Heidelberg (1995). https://doi.org/10.1007/3-540-58855-8_25

44. Yang, F., Donde, V., Li, Z., Wang, Z.: Advances in power distribution system management technology. In: Wang, L. (eds.) Modeling and Control of Sustainable Power Systems. Green Energy and Technology. Springer, Heidelberg (2012). https://doi.org/10.1007/978-3-642-22904-6_6

45. Yang, Q., Jiang, L., Ehsan, A., Gao, Y., Guo, S.: Robust power supply restoration for self-healing active distribution networks considering the availability of distributed generation. Energies **11**(1), 210 (2018)

46. Zlotkin, G., Rosenschtein, J.: Mechanisms for automated negotiation in state oriented domain. J. Artif. Intell. Res. **5**, 163–238 (1996)

Author Index

Printed in the United States
By Bookmasters